FISKE

Real College Essays *That* Work

EDWARD B. FISKE
BRUCE G. HAMMOND

SOURCEBOOKS, INC.®
NAPERVILLE, ILLINOIS

Published by Sourcebooks, Inc.
P.O. Box 4410, Naperville, Illinois 60567–4410
(630) 961–3900
Fax: (630) 961–2168
www.sourcebooks.com

Library of Congress Cataloging-in-Publication Data

Fiske, Edward B.
  Fiske real college essays that work / Edward Fiske, Bruce Hammond.
    p. cm.
  ISBN-13: 978-1-4022-0164-6
  ISBN-10: 1-4022-0164-8
  1. College applications—United States—Handbooks, manuals, etc. 2. Universities and colleges—United States—Admissions—Handbooks, manuals, etc. I. Hammond, Bruce. II. Title.

LB2351.52.U6F56 2006
378.1'616—dc22

2006012429

Printed and bound in the United States of America.
DR 10 9 8 7 6 5 4 3 2 1

Contents

Also by Edward B. Fiske
The Fiske Guide to Colleges

Also by Edward B. Fiske and Bruce G. Hammond
The Fiske Guide to Getting Into the Right College
Fiske Nailing the New SAT
Fiske What to Do When for College

Why Couldn't I Just Write about Things That Make Me Happy?

When it was time to tackle my essay topic, I assumed that I needed to take the most emotionally gut-wrenching story from my life and work my way into a school by breaking the hearts of the admissions committee. If I couldn't pull that off, I figured that I should write the most intellectual five hundred words that I could get on paper. It would probably be a good idea to use lots of really big words and make allusions to really obscure works of literature, all the while analyzing why my (nonexistent) groundbreaking lab work was going to save the world. It took me a week-long essay writing seminar, an entire summer vacation, and several subsequent trips to the college counseling office to realize something that should have occurred to me in the first place: why couldn't I just write about things that make me happy?

—*Laura Cobb*
Class of 2009
Washington University in St. Louis

On the list of life's most unpleasant experiences, writing a college essay ranks somewhere between getting a root canal and passing a kidney stone. Every fall, thousands of aspiring essayists spend hour upon hour staring into a computer screen. They wrack their brains for a clever opening line—always seemingly just out of reach—or a life-changing experience that they can presumably dust off and insert on cue. No wonder the process is such an ordeal.

We wrote this book to try to take some of the stress out of writing the essay. Not all of it, but enough to make writing the essay more bearable, and maybe even a little fun. As students like Laura Cobb eventually realize, a good essay does not necessarily need to be a Hemingwayesque literary masterpiece, or a scholarly treatise worthy of Albert Einstein. The best essays come from high school students being themselves, with all the depth, wit, charm, and quirkiness that they bring to their daily lives. A good essay reflects the best qualities of its author—nothing more, and nothing less.

That said, getting your best self down on paper is not easy. To help with the process, we have gone to a logical source—students who have written a successful college essay and lived to tell about it. With the help of a network of high school counselors, we received hundreds of submissions from all corners of the country and chose 109 of the best for inclusion in this book. Many of the students also offered commentary about the writing process, and we think you will find their insights to be a valuable tool.

We should add that these are not the 109 best essays in the history of the civilized world. If you're a typical student, you'll have enough trouble psyching yourself up to write an essay without being demoralized by 109 of them that could have been written by Virginia Woolf. In compiling the essays, we tried to choose a variety that exhibit outstanding qualities but also represent an attainable standard for significant numbers of students.

We hope you will find this book to be browsable, and your first move may be to flip through it and sample some of the essays that catch your eye. Eventually, we hope you will find your way to Part 1, which includes three chapters that take you step-by-step through the writing process. Chapter 1, "What Is a Good Essay?" gives a concise overview of do's and don'ts. Chapter 2, "Rescue from Writer's Block," offers thoughts on choosing a topic and strategies for getting started. Chapter 3, "Crafting a Narrative," provides ideas on how to hook your admissions-officer reader at the beginning and keep him or her interested throughout your entire essay. We also give some pointers on how to avoid embarrassing mistakes.

The rumor mill aside, there is no single stroke that will get you into a selective college—not sky-high test scores, not great recommendations, not a truckload of extracurricular activities, not even a killer essay. Colleges weigh each application as a unified whole. But if you're a junior or senior in high school, your essay is the most important part of your application that is not set in stone. Among students with similar grades and test scores, essays are often decisive in determining who gets in, and who does not. No less than the director of admissions at Duke University has told us, "The better we get to know the students as people, the more likely that they will be admitted."

Laura Cobb figured as much when she wondered to herself, "Why couldn't I just write about things that make me happy?" She could, and she did.

> It all just hit me really quickly one Saturday…I was being lazy and my mind was wandering, and it suddenly wandered right into the first line of my essay. A lightbulb went off in my head, I repeated the line a few times, and then I sprinted as fast as I could to my computer. I liked it! As I typed it in, something clicked in my mind and the floodgates opened. The vast majority of my essay was produced within an hour.

Laura's essay, which begins with the fact that she won her school's pickleball tournament in tenth grade, is # 70. Most essays take more than an hour to come together, but we hope that with a few helpful hints from this book, you can arrive at the same kind of realization as Laura did without the week-long essay seminar.

The key to a successful essay lies inside you, dear reader. Let's begin the process of finding it.

Part One:
Writing a Great Essay

What Makes a Great Essay?

Mention that you're writing a college essay and you'll probably get an earful of advice:

- "Write about your trip to Mexico," offers your mom. "You can show that you've broadened your horizons."
- "Community service always looks good," says Dad. "Talk about your work with Habitat for Humanity."
- "Write something funny," advises your best friend. "They love essays that make them laugh."
- "Make yourself stand out," says your guidance counselor. "In a pile of one thousand essays, yours should be the one they remember."

If you're lucky, you won't hear all of the above—at least not all at once. But the odds are good that you'll get some of it, particularly the one about making yourself stand out. How, exactly, do you accomplish that one? Have you scaled Mount Everest? Overcome a terminal disease? Saved a toddler from a burning building?

Of course not. Neither have 99.9 percent of the rest of us. The best essays are seldom about a dramatic event or "significant experience" that changes the author's life. Real people don't get hit by lightning and suddenly realize that they should live their lives differently. Human development is a step-by-step, day-by-day process that happens almost imperceptibly.

Stand Out by Being Yourself

Instead of trying to be dramatic, be interesting. That's all a good essay needs to be—interesting to the admissions officers who read it. Forget the idea that your essay needs to be the one in a thousand that jumps out of the pile. That's too much pressure. Go for writing one that is among the 25 percent, more or less, that are reasonably interesting. It isn't as easy as it sounds. Among your first thoughts might be to tell about a trip, describe a community service project, analyze a political issue, or talk about the significance of your sport. Are any of these topics likely to be interesting? In the hands of a professional writer, they might have a fighting chance. In a college essay—even one written by gifted student—these topics are likely to be painfully boring.

Fortunately, there is a solution that does not involve phony dramatics. Any of the topics above can be extremely interesting provided that you use them to talk about yourself. Hear that? *You* are by far the most interesting possible topic. If this sounds crazy, think of the most popular magazine in the United States. It has a one-word name: *People*. The magazine sells so well because people are interesting: their hopes and fears, their relationships, what they believe, and how their minds work. Call it gossip, the inside dirt—whatever. People are fascinating and you are a person. By happy coincidence, there is no topic in the world about which you are better prepared to write. If all the applicants in the country suddenly wised up and wrote about themselves, most would have good essays. Everyone is different, and people are endlessly interesting.

If you're still in doubt, think about the essay from the point of view of the admissions officers. They don't wade through all those essays to learn about the importance of self-discipline, or that persistence pays off. They want to learn about the applicants as people: their hopes and fears, their relationships, what they believe, and how their minds work.

In one way or another, every good essay is about the person who wrote it.

Details, Details

Your English teacher has told you one hundred times: if you want to write a good essay, you need concrete evidence to back up whatever you say. We'll take it a step further: you can't write a good college essay without details, by which we mean anecdotes, thoughts, and observations that are unique to you. Look at the 109 essays in this book. Every one of them crackles with specific references. In Essay 26, the author is an actor gazing out into the audience before a performance. He doesn't just see faces in the crowd. Nor does he see anything so generic as "a sea of faces waiting expectantly." Instead, he sees "the homely older women looking around the crowd for a familiar face" and "the seven-year-old whose parents dragged him along to the theater." In Essay 79, the author remembers an exchange student who lived in her home by "the tights scented with French perfume in my sock drawer." The author of Essay 101 writes about her trip to London. She didn't merely see Westminster Abbey, or even "the ancient splendor of Westminster Abbey." Instead, she was "moved almost to tears while wandering through Westminster Abbey, seeing the stained glass windows that had been pieced back together with such courage and diligence after being smashed during the bombings of the Second World War."

When stories involve people, a great way to make them more concrete is to use dialogue. Among the dozens in this book that use dialogue are Essays 2, 40, and 42.

The author of Essay 65 gets concrete by building her entire essay around the "256 steps" that it takes to walk from her mother's house to her father's house. She writes, "Twelve steps up the road, I see the crack in the pavement and I remember the first time I rode a tricycle—a hot pink contraption with a white wicker basket." Concrete detail is also crucial if you want to make your imagination become real, as the author of Essay 74 demonstrates:

There are two kinds of Perrier drinkers. There are those who are snobby and sophisticated who take small snooty sips from a glass while at a swanky café, and there are the free-spirited drinkers. I am the latter. I am one of the c'est la vie, I-have-class-but-appreciate-chaos, fine art loving, passionate drinkers.

Even the most mundane paragraph is more engaging if it is concrete, such as this passage from Essay 21:

No matter how tired I am, every Sunday morning I wake up, brush my teeth, put on my blue sweatpants and red sweatshirt, grab the keys to the car and head out into the driveway. Not even my puppy follows me outside; he likes to sleep till eleven o'clock on Sundays. I pull the car out into the driveway and position it just right so that the morning sun is blocked by the thick leaves and branches of the tall maple, and so that I can easily walk around the back end.

Not the most exciting paragraph you've ever read, but we'll bet that it held your attention.

Telling a Story

To translate our talk about concrete detail into slightly different terms, good essays use nouns and verbs while weak ones use adjectives. Strong essays "show" and weak ones "tell." Or again, good essays describe action while weak ones are a series of static images.

Allow us to explain. The adjective is a perfectly good part of speech, but only when serving strong verbs and nouns. An adjective by itself is an abstract category. If you say that your friend is "crazy," "zany," or even "off-the-wall," you haven't said much. But if you describe the time when she got out of her car and locked it with the keys still in the ignition, you're beginning to make progress. Or the time she got the hiccups during an assembly, couldn't stop laughing, and had to run out the back of the auditorium. If you describe the basketball game when she grabbed a rebound, raced to the wrong basket, and sank a shot, then froze in her tracks and exclaimed "Oh s_ _ _" loud enough for everyone to hear.... Now we get the idea. After recounting a few anecdotes like these, you don't need to tell the reader that she is crazy because you have shown what she is like.

Strong verbs always drive interesting writing. But as essay writers grope and strain, too many of them reach instead for adjectives, as in the following:

> It was a chilly, grey twilight as the enormous stadium scoreboard announced the fourth quarter. I felt a damp, cool hint of dew under my aching feet. My muscles were tired but taut. The atmosphere was electric as the fans watched expectantly...

Though it is only a fragment, notice how this passage seems to move in slow motion. It is a series of images without much action (verbs) to link them. The over-worked adjectives are not necessarily weak words, but they weigh down the prose. A trying-too-hard quality creeps in. Nothing is happening, but the author attempts to convey significance by lingering on every detail of the scene. The passage sounds forced and self-important.

A good essay consists of anecdotes and concrete observations that illustrate a story or make a point.

Think Metaphorically

Is your life boring? Does it leave you with nothing to write about? With metaphors (and similes), anybody's life can be the subject of an engaging essay. Consider Essay 93, in which the author likens his middle school years to the Dark Ages in Europe. He had been an active learner in his elementary years—which he compares to Greek and Roman antiquity. After a middle-school slump, he experiences a renaissance in ninth grade which he likens to, well, the Renaissance. By twelfth grade, he has undergone an enlightenment worthy of the Enlightenment and written an essay with real substance about his relatively typical school career.

There are numerous other examples in this book. In Essay 19, the author uses sailing as a metaphor for life. In Essay 56, the author begins by writing that he "had sailed on the *Mayflower*"—not the real one, but his own "Mayflower," Continental Airlines Flight 011, which took him from his native Pakistan to a new home in America. In Essay 47, an author who grew up in the Caribbean imagines himself as a palm tree in conversation with a baobab tree that represents his African heritage.

Metaphors and similes show a student's ability to do big-picture thinking. If you're ever at a loss for what to write, think of analogies that apply to your life. Exploring such comparisons through simile or metaphor can transform mundane events into interesting ones.

WHEN PERSISTENCE PAYS OFF

I had a lot of difficulty picking a topic for my essay. I kept trying to find one aspect of my life that would represent me well, and eventually I realized that it was not going to happen for me like that. One day, after countless drafts of crappy essays, I finally sat down in front of my computer and did a stream-of-consciousness thing, typing down everything I saw that I felt represented me. I took this draft in to my history teacher, and we discussed what this meant. We came up with the idea of using my desk as a metaphor for my life, and showing my well-roundedness through the diversity of stuff on it. I rewrote this essay probably twenty or more times—an entire month's worth of second-period study halls was spent in my history teacher's office, discussing this essay and how to improve it! He was a great mentor because he understood me and was good at extracting what I was really trying to say out of failed attempts to do so.

—Christina Xu, Essay 22

How Long Should It Be?

We ask this question tongue-in-cheek—it drives teachers crazy. Students keep asking, of course, and the real answer is going to sound teacherly. An essay should be long enough to be good.

One of the best essays in this book, Essay 107, is also the shortest. It includes all of seventy-eight words on why the author wanted to attend Yale. (He got in—and the admissions office made a point of commending the essay to his school counselor.) The longest, Essay 78, tips the scale at 1,227 words. It was written for the University of Chicago, which asks famously off-beat questions that tend to promote long-winded answers.

There are times when it is possible to be more precise about a suggested length. For those who still apply on paper, colleges sometimes ask that students "use the space provided." In such cases, we recommend doing so. (Play with your margins if you need to shoehorn in a few extra lines.) Online, students may occasionally find that their cursors stop moving at the end of the allotted space. If you simply can't wedge your essay into the field, consider applying on paper, or contact the admissions office to get help with your dilemma.

A few colleges specify a word length. In recent years, Princeton has asked for essays on various topics of about 250 and 500 words, respectively. Two hundred forty or 520, respectively, would fill the bill, but not 700 or 1,227. When the question specifies neither a length nor an amount of space, a reasonable target for those in doubt is not more than four to five hundred words, which means about two-thirds of a page to a page, single-spaced. (Write less for a sidebar essay about your favorite activity or why you are interested in the college.)

There is an interesting footnote to the length issue that we must fess up about. In previous books, notably *The Fiske Guide to Getting into the Right College*, we have preached the virtues of brevity, or at least of not going on forever. Yet in sifting through the essay submissions for this book—all from successful applicants to highly selective colleges, all identified as excellent by college counselors—we were surprised by the number of nominations that were longer than five hundred words. (There were also plenty of short and sweet ones like our seventy-eight-word masterpiece.)

Our theory is that when an essay is outstanding—really outstanding—the reader doesn't mind if it goes on longer. Doing so gives the author more space to add the concrete details that make it memorable. You'll see a number of these longer essays in this book. (For examples, check out Essays 91 and 101.) We are at pains to add that the number of brilliant long essays is far outnumbered by the long ones that could be improved by cutting, sometimes ruthless cutting. If you're in doubt, consult a teacher who can give you feedback. We'll say more about that in chapter 3.

There are good essays and bad essays of all lengths. We recommend that your first concern be writing a good one.

What Do You Want to Show?

Many applicants don't begin with a theme for their essays. They just write what comes naturally. Others choose a theme before they write. Either method can work, but at some point in the process, think about whether your essay conveys the qualities that you most want to emphasize.

One applicant we know intended to write an essay about her love of reading. She talked about some of her favorite books, but the essay turned out to be about how she used reading as a retreat from the world. The girl had many other outstanding qualities—she was a campus leader and one of the most adventuresome students in the school—but her essay made her appear much more withdrawn than she really was. The essay was well-written and an accurate portrayal of part of her life, but it did not highlight her most appealing qualities.

There is, however, a balance to be struck. Some applicants are so worried about pandering to the admissions officers that they aren't true to themselves. Others are so packaged by college counselors or consultants that their voices are drowned out. Still others are so focused on their theme that they are heavy-handed and tell rather than show.

There are innumerable qualities that you might emphasize in an essay, including that you:

- have a sense of humor

- value diversity
- embrace learning
- notice the little things
- are deeply committed to an activity or idea
- can overcome adversity
- have initiative

Colleges want people who are passionate about life and learning, and who will add to their community with participation and leadership.

There are also qualities that can be real turn offs. They generally appear unbeknownst to the author and can undermine anything good in the essay. Avoid any suggestion that you:

- are cynical
- think you are a finished product
- are likely to turn inward in college
- are depressed
- are self-destructive
- lack integrity
- tend to blame others

Colleges don't want people who are complainers, or people who will withdraw from a community rather than embrace it. Many students do all the "right" things but lack real passion, a fact that can be revealed by a passionless essay. Feel free to talk about the challenges in your life, including some that may be ongoing, but avoid giving information that could raise red flags about your mental health or the potential for destructive behavior of any kind.

Your essay may be the only time that the admissions office gets to hear your voice. Think of it as *you* on the page.

Rescue from Writer's Block

Sooner or later, there comes a time when all your reasons to procrastinate have been exhausted, and you settle yourself in front of the computer to begin work on your essay. Again. The screen is just as blank as it was the last time you tried to get started. After ten minutes of vacant staring, your right leg begins to fidget uncontrollably. After ten more, you feel the muscles in your throat tighten. Your heart begins to race and your head jerks up to see a wild-eyed face in the mirror with teeth clenched in a silent scream. You grab the computer in a bear hug, and with one motion tear away the cables and lurch toward your bedroom window. As your arms feel the impact of shattering glass, you thrust the computer forward and watch it hurtle, cords and all, toward the pavement below. Just as you are about to dive headlong after it, the sound of your mother's voice gives you a start.

"This is the last time I'm going to tell you," she says in an exasperated voice. "Wake up now!" After several seconds of groggy confusion, you stagger out of bed and head for the shower.

We hope you manage to avoid nightmares about the essay, but if you do find yourself losing sleep over it, join the club. Getting started can be hard, even agonizing. To avoid a false start, give yourself thinking time before putting pressure on yourself to start writing. Chirps one of our student authors, "My personal statement was something that I had thought about for weeks, and when I finally sat down to write it, the words flowed straight out of my head onto the page. I finished in about thirty-five minutes." Some of the best ideas tend to come when you're in the shower, or after you've turned out the light to go to bed. Reason: you're more relaxed at times like these and can let your mind wander. To save the thoughts that occur at odd moments, keep a pen and paper handy and jot them down as they come to you.

Your first order of business is deciding what to write about. A few highly selective private institutions—places like Princeton and the University of Chicago—require students to wrestle with very specific (and slightly oddball) questions that will dictate your topic. Others, including those on the Common Application, give you much more room to be creative. Many applicants try too hard to manufacture a good topic and end up with an essay that sounds forced or phony. The best topic is often right under your nose. The key is knowing where to look.

The Best Essays Are about Nothing

Think we jest? Let's see if we can convince you.

The title of this section is an allusion to *Seinfeld*, the classic TV show known as "the show about nothing." Other shows have characters and situations that are reasonably predictable. When you watch *Friends*, you know that Joey and Phoebe are going to be the dopey ones, that Monica is obsessive, that Ross is the brainy one, etc. On *Seinfeld*, there is no telling what bizarre situations the characters will find themselves in, or what weirdo characteristics they will take on. Because it is "about nothing," *Seinfeld* is much more free-wheeling than other comedy shows and gives the writers more room to showcase their creativity.

The same is true for college essays. Let's say you scored the winning goal in the state championship soccer game. You could

TAPPING YOUR INNER DORKINESS

As for advice, I'd say write about something you really care about, even if others find it dorky or strange. My friends would always laugh at me for preferring old-fashioned snail mail to the phone. They rolled their eyes when I said I was writing a college essay about it. However, I knew that my true self would shine through if I wrote about something I was head-over-heels in love with, and writing letters is one of those things.

So if you tell someone else your idea for an essay and they think it's dumb, don't let that deter you. Sometimes the things that make us dorky or weird are the exact qualities that will make us stand out from a pile of fifteen thousand other application essays.

—Francie Neukom, Essay 17

narrate events—the ball coming your way, your charge down the field, teammates carrying you off the field, and so on. You could probably hold the reader's attention with a narrative like this, but what would he or she learn about you? Not much, other than that you are a good athlete, which would be obvious from your activity list.

With a big event such as this hogging the stage, there is less space available for self-disclosure. You could add it with flashbacks about earlier experiences or conversations, or with a description of your thoughts before and after the game, but making this clinker into a decent essay would not be easy.

THE COMMON APPLICATION TAKES OVER

Though acceptance rates are grim at the nation's most selective colleges, there is one silver lining in today's admission scene. The process is easier now than it was a generation ago because of the rise of the Common Application. Three hundred colleges and universities have joined up, most recently long-time hold-outs Penn and Northwestern. Even public universities are jumping on board. The Common App is cool because it gives maximum flexibility on the essay. A 250- to 500-word composition is required on one of six topics. The options are as follows:

1) Evaluate a significant experience, achievement, risk you have taken, or ethical dilemma you have faced and its impact on you.
2) Discuss some issue of personal, local, national, or international concern and its importance to you.
3) Indicate a person who has had a significant influence on you, and describe that influence.
4) Describe a character in fiction, an historical figure, or a creative work (as in art, music, science, etc.) that has had an influence on you, and explain that influence.
5) A range of academic interests, personal perspectives, and life experiences adds much to the educational mix. Given your personal background, describe an experience that illustrates what you would bring to the diversity in a college community, or an encounter that demonstrated the importance of diversity to you.
6) Topic of your choice.

So what do we mean by "writing about nothing"? Perhaps a better way to say it is: write about something small. Some examples from the essays in this book include: remembering a letter the author wrote to the president when she was six (Essay 90); buying a bottle of shampoo (Essay 72); the author looking at her own face in the mirror (Essay 52); the significance of AOL Instant Messenger (Essay 7); why the author loves drinking Perrier (Essay 74); a dinner with extended family (Essay 82); why the author bites her nails (Essay 75); why the author likes bowling (Essay 18); the author's various pairs of shoes (Essay 15); cleaning up vomit at summer camp (Essay 42); bringing underwear to college (Essay 76); and the home-spun wisdom of two pain-in-the-neck kids who were the author's counselees at summer camp (Essay 40).

In each of these essays, the insignificant surface topic is not the real point of the essay but merely an occasion for reflection. In Essay 52, the author is in a restroom looking at herself in the mirror. She reflects on herself and the fact that, as an international student, she is different from two classmates who enter the restroom. She ponders her immigrant status before the *whoosh* of the door brings her back to the present. In Essay 72, the author ponders buying a bottle of shampoo, which gives her a jumping off place for various whimsical reflections about herself. In Essay 40, the author quotes the excuses and rationalizations of misbehaving elementary schoolers at summer camp, and in the process finds wisdom for his own life in an unexpected place.

One of our contributors hit the nail on the head when she wrote, "Some of the best essays I have read are descriptions of mundane events: people-watching at the mall, overhearing pieces of conversations in a restaurant, working out Saturday mornings before anyone in the house awakes."

Many of the essays in this book are about larger issues, but even these essays typically begin small. Essay 65 is about the divorce of the author's parents, but its title, "256 Steps," shows her approach. Rather than tackling the issue head-on, she describes sights along the 256-step walk between the houses of her mother and father as a way of reflecting on what the divorce means. In Essay 53, the author writes about the meaty issue of racial stereotypes, but she begins with a low-key anecdote about her encounter with a prying sales clerk.

The best essays about nothing? Let's just say that the best ones are often about small incidents or experiences because these leave you more room to talk about yourself. *Seinfeld* isn't really about nothing; it is about the human condition, as revealed by the show's wacky send-ups of life's everyday details. Be they serious or funny, good college essays also tend to flow from the routine of daily living.

FIVE WAYS TO SHOOT YOURSELF IN THE FOOT

- **A Phony Life-Changing Experience**—Have you been a different person since the day you lost the big game while learning a valuable lesson? We doubt that you are, and so will the admissions officer reading your essay.
- **Making Everything Peachy Keen**—Avoid telling how you encountered a problem, found a solution, and lived happily ever after. Self-congratulation does not play well in an essay, and neither does the superficial sense that everything works out in the end.
- **Social Problem of the Year Bandwagon**—Remember Hurricane Katrina? Want to guess how many essays were written that year about responding to disasters and taking care of refugees? Don't touch global warming with a ten-foot pole and don't write about any issue that everybody else is talking about.
- **Melodrama**—Straining for the dramatic always ends badly. Do so, and you'll get something like, "the last gleaming rays of the sun bathed the field in a soft orange glow as we strode confidently from the huddle to begin the fourth quarter."
- **Quoting Pop Lyrics**—What sounds profound on your iPod may seem silly or trite in an essay. It's fine to quote Bob Dylan, Boxcar Willy, or something similarly out of the ordinary. But Green Day? No way.

Brainstorming for a Topic

For words of wisdom about choosing your subject, we turn to our contributors. A number of them cite the importance of staying as stress-free as possible. Says one, "Sitting down knowing that you're writing a big, scary college essay can make your writing start to sound really wooden and formulaic. Instead, have fun writing about yourself, or remembering something important to you, in whatever your most natural writing style is" (Essay 90). Another student author believes that picking a topic isn't such a big deal. "I don't think the topic is as important as the tone of the essay. It's like two people can say the same thing, but you'll be attracted to the person whose personality shines even when they say a simple 'hello'" (Essay 59).

Even if there are many topics that could work, you still must pick one, or at least a way to open your essay. One of our contributors made a list of fifteen possible essay topics, then gradually eliminated choices until she had her topic (Essay 17). Another writes that she "reflected on what was important to me, and what aspects of my personality I felt were those most worth knowing" (Essay 51). Yet another student suggests a stream of consciousness. "Write down things that make you happy, or random things that cross your mind, or that one weird thing that happened that one time," she says. "Get any and all ideas down on paper somewhere, and if one of them stirs your imagination, go with it" (Essay 70).

If you have plenty of time, consider beginning a journal to test out ideas. If you put down one hundred words a night, or at least every few days, the odds are good that you will hit on something interesting.

For those without a topic or any notion of where to begin, we offer the following five ideas to get you unstuck. Try writing about:

- **An article of clothing**—Many people have an item such as a favorite sweater, a beloved T-shirt, or a well-worn pair of shoes. One student author in this book writes about all the shoes in her closet, and how each pair reflects different facets of her personality (Essay 15). It is often possible to spin stories around an item that has been with you through many experiences, or that can be made to represent truths in your life.
- **The groups in your school and where you fit in**—Every school has groups of people who associate together based on common interests or traits—jocks, musicians, Goths, skaters, cheerleaders, grunges, "smart" kids, and everything in-

between. Not that you want to reduce anyone to a stereotype, but some perceptive comments about social life at your school can be very effective. Have you tried to bridge the groups? Ever gotten caught in a test of loyalty between them? One of our authors wrote a superb essay about how his mind was opened when some of the toughest football players in the school joined the choir (Essay 39). Another, a football player himself, writes about joining a drama group and expanding his circle of friends (Essay 38).

- **A family gathering or tradition**—You could pick anything from your family at the dinner table to an annual trip to the beach. You may decide to write about an extended family gathering, and thereby give yourself more characters and interactions to describe. One of our authors writes about the happy confusion when he has dinner with his extended family (Essay 82). Another writes about family vacations, and the lessons she draws are not the ones a reader—or her mother—might have predicted (Essay 98).

- **Your walk or ride to school**—Any trip that you take on familiar ground, day after day, is a good possibility. A walk through your neighborhood would allow you to reflect on experiences that you have had at each place you pass. Essay 65 is a classic in this genre. If you are a runner, another idea would be to describe a course that you have run many times, and your thoughts along the way. If you've lived in your house a long time, a look around the backyard could bring to mind good times with family or friends that might come together in an essay.

- **Your favorite things**—One of our authors writes about "Seven Wonders"—ranging from potter's clay to the dual-density mid-soles on his shoes—and tells how each is meaningful to him. Another student describes herself via twelve items on her desk, from a piece of cheesecake to a copy of Stephen Hawking's *A Brief History of Time* (Essay 22).

An advantage of the topics here is that they give you plenty of opportunity to drop out of factual description and probe your thoughts and feelings. Whether you choose one of these something else, make sure it is a topic about which you are passionate, enthusiastic, and/or otherwise entertained. In the words of one of our contributors, "If you can write about something you enjoy, the writing will be much easier and your voice will come through much better." No matter what direction you take, *you* are the real topic.

ANOTHER LOOK AT SHOW, DON'T TELL

If you really want to understand "Show, Don't Tell"—or if you simply need a hand in getting started—try the following exercise. Think of a friend and then an adjective to describe him or her. (Make the adjective as specific as possible.) Without using the word or any synonyms, write a paragraph that shows why the adjective describes the person. You'll be forced to use anecdotes to show why, which is exactly the sort of writing that you need for a college essay.

Crafting a Narrative

O nce you've picked a topic and gotten a reasonable amount on paper, the real work begins. If you're a one-draft writer who cranks out perfect prose on the first try, more power to you. For most people, polishing an essay takes time and several pairs of eyes. If at all possible, get your first draft done at least two weeks, and preferably two months, before you plan to submit the essay. You'll need plenty of time go over it—both for yourself and for any adults or friends that you recruit to help.

Your most important task is to make sure that the essay says what you want it to say with as much flair and pizzazz as you can muster. The second one, no less important, is to make sure that typos, spelling mistakes, and grammar errors are edited out.

The Opening Paragraph

We'll give you one guess as to the most important sentence in your essay. (The title of this section is a hint.) To understand why the first sentence, and the first paragraph, are so crucial, consider the plight of a typical admissions officer (AO). At the peak of application reading, she probably has a quota somewhere between thirty and fifty per day. Admissions officers spend as little as ten minutes per application, of which perhaps three minutes may be devoted to the essay. When the AO finally gets to your application, while munching on cold pizza at 1:47 a.m. having read forty-nine others that day, it is crucial that your opening paragraph grab her attention before she nods off. The way you begin will shape the admissions officer's perceptions of the whole essay and may even determine whether she reads or skims.

To get your juices going, turn to the appendix on page 327. There, you'll find the opening lines of every essay in this book. Each one is unique, but they fall into three basic categories:

- **An Anecdote**—The most tried and true way to begin is to describe an incident or event that relates to your main point.
- **A Zinger**—Some excellent writers don't need an anecdote. They may begin with humor, wordplay, or some other creative twist to grab the reader.
- **A Straightforward Statement**—Though good anecdotes and zingers are hard to beat, a simple beginning is preferable to a failed attempt at either of the former.

Many essays in this book begin with an anecdote. In Essay 48, the author describes volunteer work for an Indian cultural organization that often has her working late and neglecting homework: "I'm tired and a little bit desperate. My clock angrily glares at me through its neon green dial. It's 11:24. The biology exam tomorrow will be murder. I resolutely pass over my textbook, and instead return to the screen where Pandit Jasraj stares back at me."

Another of our contributors begins her essay standing at the blackboard in English class, drawing a figure to illustrate her reaction to a line in John Keats's "Ode to a Grecian Urn":

Now I was at the front of the classroom, using what little artistic coordination I had to draw a great big figure on the board: yes, those had to be eyes, an L-shaped nose, wrinkled eyebrows, a gaping O for a mouth. I added little stress lines on either corner of the cheeks, just to show how intent my hastily composed figure was on examining this

"Sylvan historian, who canst thus express a flowery tale more sweetly than our rhyme" (Essay 2).

Notice how deftly she relates a necessary fact—that she is writing at the board—without breaking the flow of her narrative. The essay continues with dialogue between her and the teacher.

It takes skillful writing to achieve a zinger opening, but a number of our authors were equal to the task. One student writes about the pitfalls of being known as a feminist. Her essay begins, "Sometime between waking up at the crack of dawn and fourth period I became a teenage werewolf. No, wait, I mean feminist." Another of our authors with an active funny bone turns his attention to the college search with this opening:

Do you ever have those dreams where you've arrived at school and suddenly realize you've forgotten to wear pants? Well, for most high school seniors that dream becomes a reality, at least figuratively. We must bare our souls, not to best friends, or family, but to complete strangers who may not even want to hear about it and may even flat out reject us. What twisted institution would ever subject young adults in the formative stages of emotional growth to this experience? Oh, right. College (Essay 71).

Don't feel bad if you can't pull off a stream of consciousness like this; most of us can't.

Straightforward openings can work well when you have a lot of information to convey. One of our student authors writes about a robot he designed, opening this way: "'E2V2' was my own creation and I would drive it in BattleBotsIQ 2003, a national robotics competition. I felt my body tense for the battle against the spinbot, Chromedome" (Essay 9). With most of the crucial information conveyed, the rest of the essay describes the battle between the two robots.

Another of our contributors writes about how his self-image changed when he decided to experiment with an acting class. The essay begins, "Before last year I had always thought of myself as a very shy, uncreative, introspective individual. And I was happy that way. I had found my little niche in the Kinkaid society. I was the jock who excelled in sports and also managed to make pretty good grades as well" (Essay 38). By outlining all of his preconceptions about himself upfront, he sets the stage for talking about his change in attitude after taking a drama class.

A LAST-MINUTE DO-OVER

My writing process was actually extremely long and painful. I wrote an essay about my passion (art and painting) and worked on it for almost a year. I think I overworked it because it never seemed quite right. Then basically the night before I had to send in my applications, I decided to rewrite the essay from a slightly different angle that better answered the question. My essay is the product of four hours work in one night. I was able to write it so quickly and well because I knew exactly what I wanted to say and even used many phrases and sentences from my original essay.

—Emily Stein, Essay 37

Managing the Flow

Once you've gotten the reader's attention with your opening, you should have a story to tell. But first, it is often necessary to pull back from the narrative to fill in background information. Beginning writers often struggle with how to manage the balance between describing an experience and reflecting on it, and how to create seamless transitions between the two. Below is one example of how it's done from Essay 43:

"Hey, Nickelback, I know that band. You like them?" I ask, leaning over Chipu's shoulder to look at the stickers and pictures she has all over the front matter of her binder.

"Yeah," she looks up at me with her big brown eyes and smiles, clearly as relieved as I am to find something in common. It's my first day tutoring at Webster Middle

School. I'm working with Team Prime Time, an organization that provides a place for children to go after school where their parents can pick them up after work....

"Oh that's cool," I say, "I listen to Nickelback all the time. What's your favorite song?" The conversation moves haltingly on from there as we both become more comfortable.

The beginning of this essay is also the beginning of a conversation between the author and a girl whom she is tutoring. In order for the scene to make sense, the author drops out of the anecdote in the second line of the second paragraph to explain that it is her first day tutoring at Webster Middle School and that she is working with Team Prime Time. Having conveyed the necessary information, she jumps back into the conversation about Nickelback.

The ability to pull back from a narrative also comes in handy when you want to interject your thoughts and feelings, or if you simply want to broaden your scope to include more general reflections. In Essay 34, the author explains the significance of a figure in a Renoir painting that hangs on her wall and then begins a broader examination of dance, art, and creativity:

The lady in the red hat represents a side of myself not often seen, one that dances in the street without a care in the world... Renoir's painting constantly reminds me not to completely let go of that spontaneity.

Dancing is an act of passion; it is an act of freedom. Sometimes I search for this type of freedom in life, but at times, it can only be found in the subtleties of artwork.

It is logical to jump from an analysis of a Renoir painting to a more general discussion of art, but many students fail to make similar transitions that are just as obvious.

One of the surest marks of a well-written essay is a concluding "kicker"—a final sentence that echoes the beginning or provides an unexpected twist. One of our student authors (Essay 7) writes about why AOL Instant Messenger "symbolizes many of my generation's positive attributes, but also symbolizes many of our negative ones, too." After analyzing the issue throughout the essay, he ends with a wink: "I would love to explain in more detail, but I just got IMed."

In response to a question about what she would do if given a year to spend any way she wished, another of our authors (Essay 5) responds that she would read books. Among them was Tolstoy's *Anna Karenina*, which, she writes, she has been "trying to finish for the last three years." After discussing other books, she concludes the essay with the thought that a year of reading would "not only expand my mind further—I could finally find out what happens to Anna and Count Vronsky!"

For more good examples of kickers, check out Essays 34, 71, and 88.

Dotting the I's and Crossing the T's

If you're looking for the simplest way to improve your essay, we can summarize it in three words: edit, edit, edit. Then proofread and edit some more. Too many students spend countless hours on their essays, then get an itchy trigger finger and submit them before correcting obvious spelling mistakes, grammatical inconsistencies, words that have been left out—and worse. Don't underestimate your ability to make silly mistakes when you've been staring at your essay for a week. When students are under pressure they just want to be done, but to do your best essay it may be necessary to prolong the agony a little longer.

We'll assume that you've followed our advice about doing your essay in time to edit it properly. Once you get a draft we think you need at least two weeks. Set it aside for the first week without looking at it. When you do pick it up again, you'll be able to look at it with fresh eyes. Material that seemed to flow logically after you had been staring at it for hours may now seem disjointed. Errors that had camouflaged themselves will jump out. After you have gone over the essay yourself, get an adult such as your English teacher, guidance counselor, or parent to read it. Hopefully, he or she can give you two kinds of advice:

- Big-picture feedback about your ideas and whether your essay says what you want it to say.
- Micro-level feedback on details like typos, word choice, and spelling.

If you don't agree with the advice, get a second adult and see what he or she says. Though we respect the fact that some students want the essay to be theirs alone, we cannot overemphasize the importance of having another pair of eyes go over it.

BUILDING A COLLAGE OR GOING TO COLLEGE?

Garden variety typos are one thing, but goofs like the ones here are downright embarrassing. And if you think the spell check will catch them, don't be so sure.

Common Blooper	Correct Form
calculas	calculus
collage	college
councilor	counselor
financial aide	financial aid
honor role	honor roll
perspective student	prospective student
prepatory	preparatory
psycology	psychology

The following is a laundry list of things to look for when you edit:

- **Lack of a Main Idea**—The college essay is often a one-shot deal, and the impulse to cram in as much as possible can be strong. If you start out talking about why you love debate and finish with a discussion of your relationship with the debate coach—who also happens to be your English teacher—you may need to sharpen your focus and expand on one or the other.
- **Weak Verbs**—How strong and precise are your verbs? List every one of them in your essay and see how good they are. Too many "to be" verbs are a bad sign, as in, "Jessica's dance across the floor was graceful." Better would be "Jessica danced gracefully across the floor." Best would be "Jessica glided across

the dance floor." Notice that a strong verb—"glided"—provides a much more vivid description than "danced gracefully" or "was graceful."

- **Passive Voice**—Sometimes, the person doing the acting disappears altogether, as in, "It is clear that the job must be done." Even if the sentence were to say, "The job must be done by Tom," it would still be convoluted and passive. An active sentence would say, "Tom must do the job." Notice, too, that passive voice uses a "to be" verb. Avoid it.

- **Failure to Use "I"**—Most students have had at least one teacher who told them never to use "I" in a paper. (Instead of "I think," you might say something like "One can conclude.") But in a college essay, always use "I" when you're talking about yourself. It is far more honest and direct than cloaking yourself in phony third-person omniscience.

- **Double-Dipping Adjectives**—If you describe a "cool, clear, sparkling mountain stream," you've overdone it. Instead of using two or three adjectives at a time, choose the one best, as in "the sparkling mountain stream." Go back over your essay and see how many times you used one adjective versus two or three. Were two really necessary? Sometimes the answer is yes, sometimes no.

- **Too Many Simple Sentences**—A few simple sentences are great for effect—just make sure that your entire essay isn't made up of them. A bunch of simple sentences merely list disconnected ideas; compound and complex sentences establish relationships between those ideas and allow you to explore nuances. For instance: "I had a headache. I went home." Or again: "I went home because I had a headache. " Or finally: "Though I went home with a headache, it wasn't as bad as the one that sent me to the hospital last year." The first example makes no connection between the headache and going home; the second describes a cause-and-effect relationship; and the third retains the relationship while adding more perspective.

- **Wordiness**—Even good essays are full of words that aren't necessary. Any word that does not add insight or specificity should be cut. Likely candidates include clauses like "as you can see" and "it is obvious that" and words such as "basically," "perhaps," and "additionally." Scrutinize your essay one word and one clause at a time. Is everything necessary? If you think your prose is wordy but have trouble cutting, ask a reader to mark words and passages that seem superfluous. It is always easier to cut someone else's essay than to cut your own.

- **Messed Up Tenses**—When in doubt, use the present tense rather than the past. When both the present and past are technically correct, the present is more immediate. When we refer to the essays in this book, we say that the author "writes" about a particular subject rather than "wrote" about it. While this may be a matter of preference, it is crucial is to avoid inconsistency among tenses from one sentence and paragraph to the next.

- **Trusting the Spell Check**—It won't catch some of the most common errors, like when you write "an" and mean "and," when you leave out a word, or when you write "there" and mean "their." Definitely do the spell check, but don't make it a substitute for human editing.

- **Unwillingness to Start Over**—Sometimes it takes three or four hours of work, and maybe even a complete first draft, to realize that your topic isn't working. Some students can't bear to let what they have written go to waste, and end up with an inferior essay. Don't be afraid to cut out entire sections or chuck the whole thing—even if some of it is good material. Two really good pages that don't mesh will make a worse essay than one good page standing alone.

When you finally think you're ready to click on "send," hit "save" instead and come back again for one last review. The vast majority of essays, even the good ones, include at least one misspelling, typo, or other error. Only after you have proofread yet again, and found nothing, should you consider yourself done.

Part Two:
Real College Essays That Work

The rest of the book consists of essays from our 109 student contributors, each with a one hundred-word introduction from us. Where the essay was written in response to a particular question, we have repeated it in italics.

You may want to simply browse the essays, but for your convenience, we have divided them into fifteen categories according to their topic. The topics include:

1. Academics
2. Science and Science Fiction
3. Hobby or Interest
4. Athletics
5. The Arts
6. Camp Counseling and Community Service
7. Racial and Cultural Differences
8. Politics and Religion
9. A Significant Experience
10. Humor
11. Family and Relationships
12. A Moral Dilemma

13. Personal Growth
14. Travel
15. Why I Love First Choice U.

Not every essay fits neatly into one of these categories, and we could have included many of them in more than one. Our intent is not to pigeonhole the essays, but merely to promote ease of use.

You'll note that some categories include more essays than others. Rather than solicit essays in various categories, we simply sought excellent ones and let the chips fall where they would. The results confirmed what we already knew: that some topics are more likely, on average, to yield excellent essays than others. The right student can produce a fine essay regardless of the topic, but an essay about drama is much more likely to lead to the self-examination that makes a good essay than, say, an essay about athletics or a political issue. We offer our thoughts about each category in brief introductions preceding the essays.

We would like to call special attention to category fifteen, the "why us?" essay. In today's competitive admissions climate, many colleges want to know why you are interested, and they may use the depth of that interest in their decisions about whether to admit you. Too many students spend hour upon hour on their main essays and then crank out the "why us?" essay without sufficient thought and relevant specifics.

We recommend browsing the essays in all of our categories for ideas that may prove useful when you begin your own writing. Even the best writers are influenced by the work of others, and the essays in this book provide a broad sample of excellent material from which to draw. Take note of the techniques and themes that resonate with you. Experiment with the literary structures you see in these pages using material from your own life.

Though we hate to mention it, the same rules that apply to plagiarism in the classroom also apply here. Don't even think about copying paragraphs, sentences, or even phrases from the essays in this book. In addition to being wrong, it is counterproductive to try to graft the details of someone else's life onto yours. A book like this is a particularly bad place to plagiarize because it has wide circulation. But even if you are tempted to grab an essay from a dark corner of the Internet, don't do it. Every year, candidates who are otherwise qualified are denied admission because of doubts about their essays, or because phrases in them match those in essays in a book or on the Internet.

With that, we turn you loose on our smorgasbord of essays. Enjoy!

Academics

Nothing is more impressive than an essay that shows deep mastery of an academic subject. We mean the sort of mastery in Essay 2, which combines creative analysis of a difficult poem, superb writing, and an anecdote demonstrating the student's contributions to class discussion. Colleges are primarily academic institutions which covet the rare student who will make a significant intellectual contribution. One other pointer about the scholarly essay: it helps to write with a sense of humor, or at least with a hint that you don't take yourself too seriously.

1

SPEAKING HIS LANGUAGE(S)

A well-chosen quote can be a great way to start an essay, and author Ilya Alex Blanter provides a brilliant example in the one below. The opening is light, the body is serious, and the conclusion reaches back deftly to the beginning. On the surface, the essay describes Ilya's passion for languages. But a closer look shows that he uses the languages to illustrate various facets of his life, from his background in Russia to working with kids from an underfunded school. Above all, the essay shows Ilya's rare passion for learning that surely made an impression on every admissions officer who read it.

Essay by Ilya Alex Blanter

"I speak Spanish to God, Italian to women, French to men,
and German to my horse."—Charles V

I don't speak German. Horseless, and with two cats that understand only Russian, I never had the need. Besides, languages don't fall into neat categories for me as they did for Charles. But they do have a place in my life, and recently I have come to better understand just how important a place it is. As this year's High Holidays approached, it came to me: on those days, I would be using five different languages.

I love such days. Enclosed on both ends by my native Russian—the language of my family—and founded upon my probably even more "native" English—the language of my friends and school—those days don't stop there. They take me through Latin at school and Hebrew at my temple, two languages with such different histories: one that went on to seed countless others and has now all but vanished, the other battered for two thousand years to near extinction and yet now the vibrant language of millions of people. Those days also feature my fairly recent and much cherished addition, Spanish, the language that lets me connect with people in a small Mexican town and in a San Diego marketplace.

Now I love those five-language days, but it has not always been that way. Years ago, even two languages seemed to be more than I could handle. Fluent in Russian at the age of two, thrown into an English-speaking world, I was confused and disoriented. How much I hated English, and a year later, when it had become my own, with what vengeance did I turn on my Russian! Only relentless and often painful pressure from my parents kept me truly bilingual through all those early years. At the time, I resented them and their demands; only later did I realize how much of a gift they had given me.

Languages are my passion and they are my life. It amazes me that, having grown up speaking English, just last summer I could still pass for a native in Russia, where I have not lived in over fifteen years. I am thrilled that I was able to study *The Aeneid* in its original text; deeply moved that I could read ancient Torah scrolls at my Bar Mitzvah, the first person in my family in at least three generations to do so; and excited that I was given a chance to use my Spanish to teach math, science, and drama in a volunteer program for kids from underfunded, understaffed, and often just neglected Oakland schools.

> **I am thrilled that I was able to study *The Aeneid* in its original text.**

I have made the transition from resentment to love, and these days I dream about going for more. I don't know which language lies next on my path, and, luckily, I don't have to make that decision now. But I do know that this is the path I want to take—through college and beyond, into my career and into my future. Should I explore Italian or Portuguese? French or Catalan? Maybe even German? Well, in that case, I'd better start saving up for a horse.

Ilya Alex Blanter attends Princeton University.

THINKING OUTSIDE THE URN

Not many seventeen-year-olds can truthfully say that they are passionate about any poem, let alone one like John Keats's "Ode to a Grecian Urn." Author Kate Flanagan shows her passion with delightful creativity. Notice her skillful rhythm in using dialogue to drive her story forward: she opens with a paragraph of description, then uses a quote; then another paragraph of description, then a quote. All of the italicized lines are from the poem, as well as "beauty is truth, truth beauty." Says Kate, "I edited this paper as I have all my English papers. I read it out loud a few times, wrote alternative beginnings and endings, and worked with the length. The hardest part of all these application essays for me was the length factor. I overwrite everything."

Essay by Kathleen Flanagan

What can you bring to the Rice community, in past experience, background, etc?

Now I was at the front of the classroom, using what little artistic coordination I had to draw a great big figure on the board: yes, those had to be eyes, an L-shaped nose, wrinkled eyebrows, a gaping "O" for a mouth. I added little stress lines on either corner of the cheeks, just to show how intent my hastily composed figure was on examining this *"Sylvan historian, who canst thus express a flowery tale more sweetly than our rhyme."*

I sat down tentatively.

"Kate," my English teacher said, "I asked that the class draw the images Keats evoked inside the Grecian Urn."

I examined the board carefully. Figures of centaurs and trees and altars and young lovers in the heat of the chase were contained within the vessel she'd sketched a few minutes earlier. My figure loomed to the right of the urn, eyes open, sort of worried-looking now that I thought about it.

The class was silent. I'd done it again. I had gotten...*too creative.*

"Well, Ms. Erskine," I started hesitantly, "how could this urn mean so much if no one was there to observe it, to remember the history behind the '*marble men and maidens overwrought,*' to imagine the '*burning forehead,*' the '*parching tongue*'? Who would be there to feel the woe, the '*old age that shall this generation waste*'?!"

> My honors English class was looking at me as if I had an urn tattooed on my forehead.

Silence, still. On top of being too creative, I'd gotten all passionate about it. My honors English class was looking at me as if I had an urn tattooed on my forehead. I prepared myself to live through it this time, just like the other times I'd gone out on a limb and fallen flat on my face, while the teacher looked at me as blankly as the students.

But suddenly, Ms. Erskine beamed. "I was hoping someone would say that! The point of this poem is to measure not just art, but time and our own humanity...."

I had gotten lucky that day—my teacher understood me.

I have to agree with Keats that "*heard melodies are sweet, but those unheard are sweeter.*" My ideas are often considered unconventional; because of that I have learned to be brave, and to stand up for the way I see things. I can usually make my case, whether anyone else gets it or not. I have a commanding voice and I ask to be taken seriously. And while it is sometimes hard to risk the pride I've gathered over seventeen years for a single opinion, I get a rush when I put myself out there.

I'm always up for a challenge—be it taking an AP Biology class to a semester abroad in England, to working hands-on with a cadaver at a university summer school. It's not that I don't get scared, but being afraid motivates me to accomplish my goals. I value passion, dedication, and the quest for knowledge. My perspective is international; I find the glass ceiling of language and culture barriers easily broken, especially if you refuse to see them. Perhaps my attitude can be attributed to growing up in the most diverse city in the country; but I think it has more to do with having an open heart and big eyes.

So, if I dare to put myself in a nutshell:

I am in a "mad pursuit" to understand life and education and humanity in the world, believing that "beauty is truth, truth beauty." If you are loyal to one, you'll find both. Let me add that to the Rice community. Let me grab the moment, taste the adventure, and immerse myself in the environment of a university renowned with a love of knowledge and the pursuit of truth. I'll take on whatever burdens are necessary to keep this spark alive.

Kathleen Flanagan attends Rice University.

3
BACK IN ASTRONOMY COUNTRY

For true scholars, an essay about your academic passion makes perfect sense. It helps if there is a hands-on element to it, as in this essay about going to Astronomy Camp. Author Chris Limbach has the love, and he also has experiences in which he is an actor rather than merely an observer. With references to planetary nebula and the SSP-3 photometer, he establishes his credibility. But the clincher is his second theme. He is a scholar, but also a social animal who appreciates camaraderie in his quest. A scholar who delights in sharing with others is much more appealing than one who stays sequestered in the lab.

Essay by Chris Limbach

After a pleasant, early morning flight I had finally reached my destination. As I stepped out of the plane and toward the arrival gate I caught a gust of hot, dry, desert air. I knew I was back in astronomy country, where over 80 percent of the nights are clear and the Milky Way's frothy band arches majestically across the black sky abyss. Another magical week of learning under the star-laden sky awaited; my return to Astronomy Camp was long overdue.

Hosted by the University of Arizona and organized by Dr. Don McCarthy, the camp draws young astronomers from all over the United States, and many times from countries beyond. My first venture to the camp was in June of 2002, after I had just completed my freshmen year. The camp had been a Godsend, reinvigorating my desire to study astronomy and the universe. In 2004 I returned again, this time more knowledgeable, ready to delve into the research projects that are the heart of the experience.

Early in the week I met with a small group of campers, and together we proposed three different research projects to the counselors. One studied the majestic dance of two binary stars through photometry with an SSP-3 photometer. Another focused on the light curve of a far-flung asteroid. The third sought to analyze the behavior of beautiful yet mysterious "flyers" in planetary nebula through spectroscopy. Each of these projects was researched throughout the week. Data was gathered and analyzed, and conclusions were made and presented to the whole group. The thrill of doing research permeated my thoughts during the whole camp, and the investigative experience was thoroughly satisfying. Even this, however, was not all camp had to offer. A large part of its influence on my character lay elsewhere.

> **Astronomy isn't just about what's in the textbooks. It's about people, and it's about everyone's search for the truth in our universe.**

Daytime activities gave me the chance to bond with other campers, and I became good friends with many teens who were strangers only a few days before. The love of astronomy brought us together, and it was a great source of fun and excitement. We participated in many activities, including the construction of a scale model solar system and imaging the sun at the hydrogen alpha wavelength. We also cooked and cleaned for each other, and supported each other's research projects. Without the sense of community, the experience would not have been the same. A love for anything cannot be sustained without someone with whom to share it, and astronomy is no exception. It was my fellow campers who had the greatest impact on me during camp, and they are fantastic people I will never forget.

Astronomy isn't just about what's in the textbooks. It's about people, and it's about everyone's search for the truth in our universe. No matter what one's experience level, there's a universe waiting to be explored. Investigation through original research marks the foremost thrill of inquiry and discovery. Often, however, is it the people investigating with you that are the most interesting and important of all. Astronomy Camp taught me that.

Chris Limbach attends the University of Arizona.

4

A PASSION FOR LATIN

Latin is the last subject that most students would choose for an essay—which is why it's a great topic. Author Andrew Rist is a true Latin junkie, and he makes a convincing case for the importance of Latin in his life. Though his national honors are impressive, Andrew's commitment to Latin while attending three different schools stands out even more. Says Andrew, "The only advice I would give people writing essays is to follow their passion. Otherwise your essay will be lifeless."

Essay by Andrew Rist

I can say with certainty that there is nothing that has more of a positive effect on my life than Latin. Of course other things have grabbed my interest over the years, like poetry, math, singing, and women, but my true passion is for the Classics. I never would have thought that a civilization that lived over two thousand years ago could have excited me, but I have learned that many of the problems and concerns of Classical society are still widely applicable to our modern society. For example, in Plato's *Republic*, Socrates seeks the true definition of justice. Just like Socrates, we could never actually put such an abstract idea into a few words, but we still seek simplicity, as Socrates did. In Classics I see the basis for the majority of Western Civilization, and I yearn to explore it further.

I stumbled into this odyssey of classical discovery that I now call my life in the seventh grade. My Latin teacher was unusually eager to urge students into participating in Latin Club. I admit that she forced me into it, but from the very first time I competed I never regretted it. In middle school, Latin filled the void in my mind that was begging me to care about something, anything, so I kept working at the Classics, hoping I could keep the void full.

After middle school, I faced the inevitable transition to high school. My transition was rocky. Austin High is a huge school where I knew only a few people. On top of my trouble fitting in at this impersonal school, I found that the Latin program at Austin High was weak. My teacher had other problems to deal with and most of my classmates were too high to care. I realized how truly blessed I had been at my middle school. I decided to take more of a leadership role in the Latin program than I had in middle school. Unlike my middle school, Austin High tended to send only two or three people to Latin conventions. I was in charge of making sure the three of us got where we had to be during conventions. My freshman year was also the first year I won a spot on the state-bound Certamen team, which became a nationals-bound Certamen team when we won out over teams from San Antonio and Houston at the State competition. In this game of buzzers that tested both thumb-speed and Classical knowledge, I excelled, and our team took Third Place at Nationals. It was at Nationals that I had a close look at the students of St. Andrew's Episcopal School. Due to necessity, I traveled to Kentucky with St. Andrew's for Nationals. It felt like I fit with them. They impressed me with how close all the students were, both with each other and with their teachers, including one that, like me, was new to their community.

By the end of that summer I knew that I wanted more than anything to be a part of the St. Andrew's community. I toured the school, but even before that I think I was decided: if at all possible I wanted to go to St. Andrew's. Thanks to the efforts of my parents and the Latin teacher I enrolled at St. Andrew's for my sophomore year, and I have never looked back. As a result of this change I started working harder in every subject at school, thus my grades went up, even in courses that were more intellectually challenging than the ones I had previously taken at Austin High. I also improved in my favorite area. At the Texas State Junior Classical League convention I was shocked to find that I had been named Texas Latin Student of the Year for having the highest score on the decathlon, a test that tested a range of subjects related to Classical

> The only advice I would give people writing essays is to follow their passion. Otherwise your essay will be lifeless.

civilization, such as Latin grammar, mythology, history, and literature.

My junior year was even better. Although classes were even more difficult, nevertheless I enjoyed the challenge and continued to excel. In Latin, where some thought I had little room to improve, I continued to climb. Again, I was named Texas Latin Student of the year; I got a 5 on the Catullus-Ovid Latin Literature AP; but the achievement I am most proud of came during the summer at the National Latin Convention in Richmond, Virginia. Not only did my Certamen team win first place, taking home the Maureen O'Donnell Traveling Trophy, but I had the highest score on the national decathlon, which came not only with a $500 scholarship, but also the title of Best Latin Student in the Nation. My parents, Latin teachers, and friends could not have been more proud.

Rome may have fallen 1,500 years ago, but I cannot help but think that the Classics live on. People still want to know the meaning of justice and they often consult Plato in their search. I want to find the answers in Classics like so many before me. The Classics may not have been my first love, but they will be something that will stay with me forever.

Andrew Rist attends Harvard University.

5

A CLINIC ON HOW TO BE CONCISE

The ability to write to a word limit can be an important skill in college admissions, and author Annie Sykes offers a superb example with the following essay. The question is Princeton's and calls for a "brief essay of about 250 words." In a mere 254 words, Annie gives a real sense for her love of reading as she packs in specific references to a variety of books and authors. Her kicker to end the essay is particularly deft; Anna and Count Vronsky are characters from *Anna Karenina,* a Tolstoy novel generally considered superior to his more famous *War and Peace.*

Essay by Anne R. Sykes

What would you do if you were given a year to spend any way you wish?

If I could have an entire year to do anything I pleased, I would spend it indulging myself in every book that years of required reading have prevented.

I have a long history of sneaking my pleasure reading; as a ten-year-old, my parents often caught me awake long after bedtime with a flashlight and an *Anne of Green Gables* book. More recently, my mother, knowing my weakness, actually bribed me with a stack of books from her book-club list—one book for every college essay I finished. With a whole year to read the books I choose, I could finally be open about my "habit."

> My parents often caught me awake long after bedtime with a flashlight and an *Anne of Green Gables* book.

Reading provides me a way to learn and to escape. I can read *Reviving Ophelia* and learn about the development of adolescent girls, a subject that fascinates me. I can read *Anna Karenina* (which I've been trying to finish for the last three years) and be transported to 19th-century Russia. I can finally find out why my sister laughs out loud when she reads David Sedaris's latest collection of stories. It's thrilling to me that just by opening a book, I can visit a faraway place, learn something entirely new, or simply forget the details of my everyday life for an hour or so.

While I don't deny that I've gained much knowledge through the reading I've done in school, with a year off to read the books I want I could not only expand my mind further—I could finally find out what happens to Anna and Count Vronsky!

Anne R. Sykes attends Wake Forest University.

Science and Science Fiction

T his pair of topics may be akin to lightning and the lightning bug, but at the core of both is a love of science and technology. Essays in this category do not lend themselves to extensive self-analysis, but instead succeed or fail with the author's creativity and analytical insight. In this section, we include a straightforward reflection on the value of science (Essay 8), an essay on AOL Instant Messenger (Essay 7), the story of a student who built his own robot (Essay 9), and one of the University of Chicago's far-out science-fiction topics (Essay 6).

6

BEAM ME DOWN, SCOTTY

The following is a run-of-the-mill University of Chicago essay. In other words, it's about as wacky and way out as you can get. If you like this sort of thing, U of C could be for you. Author Nolan Frausto says that he picked this question because "it was the only one I couldn't think of an answer for." Go figure. So how should you approach an essay like this? The same way Nolan does. Make logical deductions, imagine, tell a yarn, and generally go for broke. Throwing in a reference or two to Euclid or Karamazov, as Nolan does, would be a nice touch.

Essay by Nolan Frausto

In a book entitled The Mind's I, *by Douglas Hofstadter, philosopher Daniel C. Dennett posed the following problem: Suppose you are an astronaut stranded on Mars whose spaceship has broken down beyond repair. In your disabled craft there is a Teleclone Mark IV teleporter that can swiftly and painlessly dismantle your body, producing a molecule-by-molecule blueprint to be beamed to Earth. There, a Teleclone receiver stocked with the requisite atoms will produce, from the beamed instructions, you—complete with all your memories, thoughts, feelings, and opinions. If you activate the Teleclone Mark IV, which astronaut are you—the one dismantled on Mars or the one produced from a blueprint on Earth? Suppose further that an improved Teleclone Mark V is developed that can obtain its blueprint without destroying the original. Are you then two astronauts at once? If not, which one are you?*

The brain: an almost indecipherable (at least to me) mass of neurons. Some extend an infinitesimal distance in the brain while others run through the length of the body. Each neuron is constantly sending and gathering tiny electrochemical signals which travel along a nerve axon, shooting along at incredible speeds towards its destination. The signal travels towards the nerve ending and spreads quickly through the thin, branch-like dendrites extending into other cells. The electrochemical signal interacts with the cell connected to the dendrites and cues a reaction from that cell. This happens in billions of neurons every second, spreading out from the brain and spine, each neuron interacting with certain cells to obtain or transmit information. This entire system of electrochemical signals provides an interaction that, in total, induces feelings, thoughts, and a perception of the physical world.

If the Teleclone Mark IV were to make a perfect copy of me, with my memories and feelings and brain all exactly the same, there would in fact be another me, yet would this clone actually be me? This question essentially becomes: Is there such a thing as a soul? Is there a defining characteristic that exists in a person and makes him indistinguishable and nonreplicable? Is there a part of someone that acts as a link between the spiritual world and the physical world and is the source of all consciousness, character, and quality in any specific creature? I don't believe there is. The human soul is the human brain. Each thought, feeling, and perception of reality stems from the billions of nerve impulses traveling through the billions of nerve axons throughout the brain. Thus, the defining characteristic is not the soul but the brain. As Francis Crick stated in his *Astonishing Hypothesis*, "You, your joys and your sorrows, your memories and your ambitions, your sense of personal identity and free will, are in fact no more than the behavior of a vast assembly of nerve cells and their associated molecules." If this is true, then the clone made by the Teleclone Mark IV from my atomic blueprint would in all reality be me. This seems to be the only logical and scientific conclusion that can be made.

Yet even so, there is something wrong with this conclusion. There is some base human awareness that screams "that cannot be!" Something seems fundamentally wrong with this concept, and my initial reaction was to think, "Wait a second…the clone would not be me, I'm me!" I once read a science fiction series by Tad Williams called *The Otherland Series* that dealt with the same subject. In the book there was the ability to create a digital brain, which a person could transfer his memories into and thus live forever. The whole concept of digital immortality as suggested by the book didn't feel right. Though it makes logical sense, my brain (or soul?) refused to accept it. If the Teleclone Mark V were to make a clone of me and leave the original me still intact, I

> If the Teleclone Mark IV were to kill me and create my clone simultaneously, would I technically be dead?

know I would not be the clone. Our perceptions of reality would immediately diverge, and we would cease to be each other at that instant. My perception would still be through my own eyes and brain, not that of the clone's. I would still exist in a singular awareness and thus perceive reality as my own self. Yet if perception originates from the brain, and the clone and I both had atomically identical brains, then what would define what *my* perception would be? What quality would differentiate me from my clone? And moreover, if the Teleclone Mark IV were to kill me and create my clone simultaneously, would I technically be dead? Logically no, but somehow still yes. The original me would have lost perception. Or would have he…or I…or it? Though my original brain would have stopped functioning, my brain would still exist. Wouldn't it? Does that matter?! What is going on!?!? WHERE AM I?!?!?!

It is, all in all, a very confusing situation.

The whole question inevitably settles on the existence of a god: a subject that is so far beyond me that I don't even know where to begin. I have often wondered about the nature of existence and reality, and, even though I'm almost eighteen, I have reached no definite conclusions. As Ivan Karamazov once said (and I agree) "[there are mathematicians and philosophers who] even dare to dream that two parallel lines, which according to Euclid can never meet on earth, may meet somewhere in infinity. I have come to the conclusion that, since I can't understand even that, I can't expect to understand about God." I, likewise, can't expect to understand whether it is my brain, soul, or God that defines who I am. But even though I may not know the answer to the question, I do know who I am at this instant, and that no one else has the exact same memories, thoughts, and feelings that I do. While I still continue to seek answers, that thought gives me comfort while I do so.

Nolan Frausto attends the University of Chicago.

7

TAKING AIM AT HIS GENERATION

Sometimes a great topic is staring you in the face—especially if you are in front of a computer screen. In devoting his entire essay to AOL Instant Messenger, author Jared Olkin demonstrates yet again that the best topics are often close to home. Says Jared, "The idea of writing about AIM came to me almost instantly—I didn't know specifically what I wanted to write about it, just that it was a good symbol." It is also a good topic because it allows him to show a mature understanding of himself and his generation. The essay ends with an especially good kicker that shows Jared's skill as a writer.

Essay by Jared Olkin

AOL Instant Messenger (AIM) is emblematic of my generation. AIM symbolizes many of my generation's positive attributes, but also symbolizes many of our negative ones, too.

Analyzing AIM by taking each part of the phrase, one at a time, reveals much. The first part, AOL, represents the consumerism we Americans hold to as dearly as the Victorians held to their sense of modesty. But it also represents a vision; even the term "America On-Line" conjures images of an entire nation connected to one another. And that vision is my generation's, for there is nothing that we want more than to feel connected to something larger. That is one positive aspect, as is our comfort with technology and our ability to feel connected even when those connections are electronic. But there is also a downside to this feature of my generation. While we may not literally "Bowl Alone," we do often engage in parallel play rather than truly engaging with other human beings, and this has created the potential for an unraveling of the social fabric as we grow older.

Consider the next word, Instant—what a word! Instant connotes no delay, no line to wait in; there is only the now. It is the notion that everything can be acquired or achieved at any moment. Not only that, but advertising's constant message of "act now" has fostered in my generation an inclination to leap from one thing to another, trying to get our "instant fix." This need for an instant fix verges on being a clinical disorder—my generation has essentially diagnosed itself as having ADD (Attention Deficit Disorder). Individuals have verbalized the disorder ("I ADDed"), just as they took the term "AOL Instant Messenger" and felt the need to shorten it to AIM, an acronym of an acronym! The positives here are energy, enthusiasm, and pace. The downsides are a lack of patience and not being willing to invest the time to delve more deeply or relish a nuance, if doing so implies that we need to slow down.

> **I would love to explain in more detail, but I just got IMed.**

Finally, take the last word, Messenger. A messenger is like a servant, doing all of the work transporting goods. And herein lies one of the biggest problems of my generation—we expect. We expect things to be handed to us without having to work to get it. We always expect there to be a messenger at our service. We expect absolutely everything. To us there are no privileges, only what we already have and what we do not yet have. We respond as though it is a tragedy that anything should fall into the latter category. We are spoiled by what has come so easily, and it is not clear if we have the will or perspective to overcome the challenges that will inevitably come our way.

AIM symbolizes both the positive potential and the troubling shortcomings of my generation. Thus, AIM also represents what those who aspire to be future leaders need to recognize and address in order to tap my generation's energy and adaptability, while helping us to build or compensate for our tendencies toward impatience, passive entertainment, and a sense of entitlement.

I would love to explain in more detail, but I just got IMed.

Jared Olkin attends Tufts University.

8

SCIENCE AND THE UNIVERSE

The essay here was written for the Amherst supplemental question, which asks students for "original, personal responses" to one of five quotations (including this one). Author Joseph Ross begins the essay with a nice insight—that science can often raise questions rather than provide answers. Another high point is the last line, which ends the essay with a flourish while highlighting the difference that scientific understanding can make in how we perceive the world.

"The Value of Science" by Joseph Ross

"I like science—but only a little. What I love with all my heart is the universe. The world as revealed by science is far more beautiful, and far more interesting, than we had any right to expect. Science is valuable because of the view of the universe that it gives."

George Greenstein
Sidney Dillon Professor of Astronomy
Amherst College

Through science, humankind is attempting to unravel the mysteries of the universe. Yet when I study scientific truths, I inevitably end up with more questions. Each little piece of knowledge I learn is analogous to a single brushstroke on a grand masterpiece. I agree that science is valuable for the perspective that it gives on the universe. Undeniably, science reveals the complexity and grandeur of the universe; from the smallest subatomic particle to the largest galaxy. At the same time it highlights the things we have yet to discover. A telescope may expand my sight into space, yet I know that I am only seeing a small portion of what the universe has to offer.

Science is important, not solely for the perspective it gives me of the universe, but for the understanding it offers. Science provides concrete knowledge on existence. For example; atoms are the building blocks of all things, and the stars are made of gas. I do not find this knowledge less important than my realization that I am bigger than an atom but smaller than a star. While what we now know about the universe may seem trivial, I realize science has made immense strides in the last hundred years. Science has the potential to become as great as human ingenuity and accomplishment can make it. As technology and scientific process advance, I can only speculate as to what science will achieve in the distant future. Science is a magnificent tool as it has the potential to unveil the universe. And while I realize that such is unlikely to fully unfold in my lifetime, my respect for science is in no manner diminished.

> **Science helps me appreciate the splendor of the universe, and it provides the means to explain it.**

Although science has so far failed to disclose a complete picture, partial understanding is better than none at all. Science helps me appreciate the splendor of the universe, and it provides the means to explain it. Both the universe and science contain limitless potential and are fountainheads of imagination and curiosity. As being somewhat adventurous it is only natural that I have great love for both. The universe and science are physical and intellectual playgrounds that have no boundaries. Yet the universe and science are inconsequential without each other. Otherwise, science would have nothing to investigate, and the stars would simply be lights in the night sky.

Joseph Ross attends Bucknell University.

BATTLE OF THE ROBOTS

Engineers are not known for writing brilliant college essays, but if all of them had topics as good as that of author David Wu, they might do better. The story of E2V2's epic battle against Chromedome is hard to top, but most students of a science/engineering bent can tell about a lab experiment in their past that went well or horribly wrong. The advantage of writing about a lab—or a robot battle—is that both provide a sequence of events that gives structure to the essay. In the case of David's essay, the robot battle leads naturally to a discussion of making the robot, and then to the significance of the project.

Essay by David Wu

"E2V2" was my own creation and I would drive it in BattleBotsIQ 2003, a national robotics competition. I felt my body tense for the battle against the spinbot, Chromedome. Before the match, I had reviewed and decided my strategy against spinbots—attack it before it spins up and then keep hitting it. I believed the two-pound titanium plate mounted at the front of my robot should be able to absorb the shock from the hits. The match started; I drove E2V2 quickly to strike Chromedome before its spinning shell reached high speeds. E2V2's agility and unrelenting ramming soon partially disabled Chromedome's weapon and drive system. Subsequently, E2V2's vertical steel blades severed Chromedome's electrical wiring and caused it to start smoking; the opponent was totally immobilized. After forty-nine seconds of collisions, flying sparks, and strategic driving, E2V2 was declared the victor.

My peers and advisors nominated me to lead this extensive robotics project. Creating a BattleBot was daunting. However, I willingly accepted the responsibility to be the team leader. My team and I analyzed weaknesses in our previous robots, watched videos of matches, and built prototypes. After exploring many options and understanding scoring strategy, my team decided to make a wedge-shaped robot with a pair of vertical steel blades to inflict maximum damage on opponents. We would adopt aggressive driving strategies to deal with different types of opponents.

Besides using engineering design programs like AutoDesk Inventor and AutoCAD, I learned to use Feature CAM to write manufacturing procedures. There were instances in which I had to modify programs because of the incompatibility between computer software. My advisor instructed me in the use of the CNC Milling Machine. It was fascinating to watch the various drills and bits convert my computer programs into components for E2V2.

> **I drove E2V2 quickly to strike Chromedome before its spinning shell reached high speeds.**

After initial assembly, our robot didn't function properly. The team spent a lot of time troubleshooting and consulting with advisors. Gradually, we identified the problems and corrected them accordingly. For example, we changed the location of the antenna to enhance its reception of radio signals from the controller. The team constantly explored options to solve problems and adopted necessary changes while assembling the robot. Pride and excitement can only partially describe my emotions upon the completion of the robot that consumed so much of my time.

Eventually, E2V2 placed seventh out of seventy-two participants. At the closing ceremony, the robot's polished titanium armor and steel blades reflected the flashes from cameras that celebrated the success of E2V2. And, I was overjoyed.

David Wu attends the University of Michigan.

Hobby or Interest

E ssays in this category tend to be whimsical or low-key, though they can still contain important lessons. Among others, the range of topics includes bowling (Essay 18), stamp collecting (Essay 10), and making airplanes out of balsa wood kits (Essay 14). Interest or hobby essays tend to be more successful than those about athletics because the goal of participation is self-fulfillment rather than winning. Two of our authors (Essays 13 and 22) chose to divide their essays into chunks by describing a series of things they like—a good strategy if you are at a loss to find an overarching theme.

10

WHEN STAMP COLLECTING IS COOL

This essay is for every applicant who thinks that having a near death experience—or making a diving catch in the championship game—is a prerequisite to writing a great essay. Alex Callen takes a mundane hobby, stamp collecting, and makes it come alive with skillful use of personification in his opening. The fact that stamp collecting is off-beat and a little nerdy works to his advantage because he can show himself to be a person who follows his passions regardless of what others may think. Among the hundreds of newspaper editors and varsity team captains, a stamp collector stands out.

Essay by Alex Callen

When I was ten years old, I met Vince Lombardi. I saw him at the post office. He was sitting quietly with George Marshall and Humphrey Bogart. Vince cast a triumphant smile in my direction. His excitement was so contagious that I could not help smiling with him. Mr. Marshall, however, seemed to stare right through me. His solemn gaze conveyed little more than that he had very important things on his mind. Then I looked to Humphrey Bogart, who, with a suave movement, simply cocked his head to one side, and sat there, just looking good. The three men seemed nice enough, so I took them home with me. Yes, they had all been dead for many years, but I didn't really mind. In my room, armed with a pair of tongs, I gingerly slid each of them into the slots of homemade album pages, next to stamps of bright blue jays, waving flags, bursting flowers, a crooning Elvis Presley, and scores of others, which I had acquired over the past two years.

Philately caught my attention very early in my life. My grandfather hooked me with a stamp from the 1960s that commemorated the sesquicentennial of the Erie Canal. I was drawn to the small colorful pictures like a crow is drawn to shiny objects. I started saving every stamp that I could find. The hobby quickly developed into more than a haphazard accumulation of pretty paper labels. A closer examination of each stamp revealed new cultures, new languages, new people, new geography; new worlds, each competing to quench my inherent thirst for knowledge, steering my imagination to new heights.

As a group, stamp collectors have been categorically branded as wealthy, reclusive, boring, moldy old men. However, I've been an avid philatelist since age eight, and, as a seventeen-year-old in high school,

I don't fit the stereotype very well. It is true that few young people collect stamps. Though I know some exist I've never met another stamp collector my age. More often than not, my peers express disapproval for the hobby. In fact, when I told a friend that this essay would be about stamp collecting, he laughed and said, "Man, you're going to have a tough time making *that* sound cool." I pointed to a pile of trading cards on his desk and replied, "Hey, at least I don't collect Magic cards" (Magic is a fantasy card game similar to the Pokemon game that swept the country a few years ago). I understand how some could perceive the slow, tedious processes associated with stamp collecting, like sorting, classification, grading, and organization, as exercises in monotonous futility. I, for one, not only welcome the procedural structure of these processes, but also embrace the rare opportunity for uninterrupted solitude that accompanies them, using it to develop my patience and allow my imagination to lead me through exciting childhood realms of exploration and adventure—winning Super Bowls, rebuilding post-war Europe, making films—which are markedly absent from the high school experience.

When I was ten years old, I met Vince Lombardi. I saw him at the post office.

I don't think I will ever be able to make philately "sound cool," but at the same time, I don't feel like I need to. It's not about being "cool." I'm a philatelist, because stamp collecting gives me pleasure and peace of mind.

Alex Callen attends Cornell University (NY).

11

WHY DEBATE? FUNNY YOU SHOULD ASK...

After devoting countless hours to the activity of their choice, many students come up blank when asked why they find it meaningful. Author Christopher Childers has no such problem. In no particular order, he tells us that debate a) gives him a better understanding of his father, b) helps him develop deeper friendships, c) allows him to have substantive discussions that he would never otherwise have had, d) lets him compete on an even playing field with others from all walks of life. How many diving catches or game-winning home runs ever opened the door to all that?

Essay by Christopher Childers

Of the activities, interests, and experiences listed on the previous page, which is the most meaningful to you, and why?

My coach always tells me that there is some reason why we, as debaters, can take four weeks out of our summer vacation, away from our friends and our families, to enclose ourselves in lecture halls and cramped dorm rooms to learn the depths and intricacies of debate. He has never told me what this reason is, but now that I'm beginning my senior year and I have attended three of these camps, I think I finally understand why. Debate, by definition, is simply a discussion over opposing view points. So what makes it so interesting? What makes it meaningful? Simply, it acts as a forum and a gateway into realms of discussion you would never encounter otherwise. No other activity exists where individuals of any age, any ethnicity, any background, any height, weight, sex, or color can voice their opinions on an equal playing field.

Debate has also affected me in other ways; I can't tell you how many times I get in debates with my father over controversial topics such as abortion, gay marriage, stem cell research, etc. These conversations, although intense and often times frustrating, allow me to understand the assumptions my father makes, and often they provide me insight into my father's adolescence. I can trace his beliefs back to their root causes, and this ability has allowed me to finally understand what makes my father tick. Being able to argue with somebody over opposing viewpoints allows you to create amazing relationships, whether they are friendships or rivalries. I value my relationships inside the debate community as my strongest. Finally, I think debate emphasizes and improves the art of conversation; debate acts as a retreat from the daily discussions of, "Dude did you see my new Mercedes?" and, "Oh my gosh, did you see *The O.C.* last night?" and it expands our communication into deeper, more thought-provoking interactions. So when somebody asks me, "Why do you go to debate camp?" I simply smile, shrug my shoulders, and talk, until they can hear no more.

> **Debate acts as a retreat from the daily discussions of, "Dude did you see my new Mercedes?"**

Christopher Childers attends the University of California at San Diego.

12

A GENERATION OF COUCH POTATOES? COUNT HER OUT.

Colleges want doers—the kind of people who are efficient with their time and have an agenda to accomplish. Author Sarah Ferguson is just that sort of person, as she explains below in an essay for Princeton (with a suggested limit of 250 words). The essay begins with a reference to the ultimate teenage time-waster—TV—and moves on to the many things that she *does* spend her time on, from writing poetry to taking an Italian class.

Essay by Sarah Ferguson

Tell us about yourself in such a way that we will have a good sense of who you are.

I don't watch television. When my friends burst into the senior room, screaming at the top of their lungs about *Real Worlders* MJ and Sarah or the Steven-Kristin-LC love triangle on *Laguna Beach*, the only reason I know what they're talking about is because I hear about it every week. My friend Wes's idea of a perfect afternoon is one spent in his basement, playing video games and watching a movie. Much as I like Wes, that's not my idea of a perfect afternoon. Don't sit in front of the TV, make something. Write a poem, plant a garden, start a painting, make a collage, take some pictures, bake a cake.

My goal in life is never to waste my time. Anonymously quoted smart people say time is money, time is precious. To me, life is about using time in the best way possible. I've always taken the initiative to do what I want to do, and enjoyed making choices about how I spend my time.

> **Write a poem, plant a garden, start a painting, make a collage, take some pictures, bake a cake.**

When I'm home from school, rehearsal, Italian class, done with homework and other obligations, I am still productive. "Doing something" means more to me that fiddling with random activities to kill time. To me, it doesn't mean watching TV, or talking on the phone, but rather reading a book and gaining knowledge, creating something beautiful with words, paint, or beads, helping a friend with homework or a problem, or discussing that awkward topic with my mom that I've been dreading for weeks.

College is a chance for me to find even more things to do with my time. I'll have studios to take advantage of when creating artwork, museums to browse, library stacks to explore, and new people to meet and make friends with. And I will do something, trust me.

Sarah Ferguson attends Princeton University.

13

A FEW OF HIS FAVORITE THINGS

For students who want to take an unconventional approach, consider what we call the "list essay." Below is one variation, in which the author takes "seven wonders" and tells why they are meaningful to him. In the first of these, he finds meaning in something that is seemingly mundane, a lump of clay, and thereby shows his unique point of view. There is a danger here; choosing a trite subject, such as hugs or chocolate layer cake. Instead, go with something like calluses or dual-density midsoles and tell a meaningful story about yourself.

"Seven Wonders" by Christopher John Hallberg

Wedged Clay.

Most people think that clay is clay, that mud is mud. Well, as a matter of fact, this is simply not so. Wedged clay is rolled and twisted at a factory to remove air. This clay is much smoother and easier to work with than ordinary clay. It's the best invention since sliced bread for the potter. For myself, working with clay on a potter's wheel is one of the most meaningful uses of my time. When working with a wheel, the clay must remain centered at all times. This centering action takes an infinite amount of concentration. As I transform the clay into a usable bowl or cup, I am reminded of my ability as a human being. That is the ability to create, whether it be something as simple as an creating an eating utensil or creating a new interest in a needy child.

Calluses.

Beginning guitar players are often limited to the length of time they can play by soreness of their fingertips. This is caused by the force needed to press an unfriendly steel string against the fret board. Eventually, the body adapts to the steel string by forming calluses on the fingertips of the left hand. These calluses are wonderful for two reasons. The first is the immediate result that the player can now play for extended periods of time. For me, music is a way to relieve stress. With a demanding schedule, it is necessary to relax occasionally. Music helps me remain focused. The second is that music has a way of moving people by speaking to our hearts. Its nearly impossible to hear songs such as Bob Dylan's "Like a Rolling Stone" and not feel moved. Music provides a universal connection among all people that is undeniable.

The Internet.

My father constantly reminds me how lucky I am to be growing up in this time. With the explosion of the Internet so much information has become instantaneously available. My worldview has increased dramatically as a result. Now it is possible to access first-hand accounts of many important events in the world. Global communication has been completely revolutionized. It is now possible to have an electronic pen pal in a third world country. We are all able to benefit from its ability to connect us as a people.

Furnaces.

To be able to come home everyday after school in the bitter Wisconsin winters to a warm home is something that I take for granted. Every year as it gets colder I often think about those that do not have a warm place to go at night. It becomes very apparent that it is a blessing to have a heated home. Its nice to know that I can go to sleep at night and not have to worry about waking up in the middle of the night freezing. Furnaces in Wisconsin are wonderful.

> My legendary days as a track and field star came to an abrupt halt in third grade.

Dual-density midsoles.

A small minority of the running population suffers from a collapsed arch in one or both feet. I happen to be a member of that cursed minority. My legendary days as a track and field star came to an abrupt halt in third grade as I rolled my ankle coming off of a hurdle. I became flat-footed from that day forward and it became extremely painful to run more than a hundred yards at a time. Then I was introduced to running shoes specially designed for people who need arch support. They are equipped with dual-density midsoles. I am now able to run for miles without any foot pain. I consider running so important because it helps give meaning to my life. When I am out pounding the pavement at six in the morning, I know that something special occurs in the repetitive motion of running. It causes me to reflect and gives me joy in knowing that I am accomplishing something even though it is as small as traveling a route that I have traveled many times before. Through reflection I discover what brings joy to my life and where I need to change and grow.

Smiles.

These are such an important part of our everyday lives! Everyone knows that being greeted with a smile is mood altering. Imagine how powerful flexing a few additional facial muscles can be! The best part is that smiles are free and universally accepted. In any language a smile can be felt in the heart.

Star-shaped stickers.

In second grade our teacher, like many others, would place star-shaped stickers on the wall next to our names when we accomplished something notable. I feel blessed because as I grow I realize more everyday how thankful I am for the great education and motivation which has been given to me. I often wonder what life will be like after high school. At Marquette High School our spirits are nurtured with many opportunities for growth. I know that as I leave MUHS I can only hope that I will continue to be blessed by a Jesuit education at Marquette University.

Together all of these wonderful items reflect who I am as a whole person. The wonderful items all relate to being a better person for others. The clay, music, and running help me to better understand who I am and how I can help others more. The Internet and furnace help me to see how fortunate I am and how I can work to make others just as blessed. Finally, smiles and star-shaped stickers, how could we live without them?

Christopher Hallberg attends Marquette University.

14

TAKING FLIGHT WITH MODEL AIRPLANES

In the age of Xboxes and iPods, there is a certain charm in an essay about rubber-band-powered airplanes made out of balsa wood. A quixotic topic such as this is the perfect way to catch the eye of an admissions officer, especially when you have invested as much time and effort in the planes as author Brian Inouye. Brian is also an athlete, but in his words, he "quickly ruled out the clichéd 'learning from losing' or 'making the big play' sports stories." Says Brian, "Although my premise paralleled one of the overdone sports stories, I thought it was interesting that I learned the same lesson in something not involving athletics whatsoever."

Essay by Brian Inouye

Every first Thursday of each month I always look around the Van Muren Hall gymnasium looking at the sixty- and seventy-year-old men and wonder what I am doing there with them. They have lived through world-shaping events like World War II, the Korean War, and the Vietnam War, yet I sit there and interact with them as if there were no differences at all. The reason? We simply share a similar hobby. For the last four years, I've built rubber-band-powered balsa airplanes alongside many of these old timers. It began in eighth grade, when I was randomly selected to be the model airplane builder for my Science Olympiad team for the event known as The Wright Stuff. In this event a competitor builds a tissue-covered, balsa plane to achieve a "best flight time." I was quite hesitant at the outset due to my lack of knowledge about the subject, but decided to forge ahead in order to help my team. In a stroke of good fortune, I stumbled over a phone number at a nearby hobby shop for the captain of the local flying club. After a simple call and meeting, I started working with my mentor, Chris Borland, a retired man of about sixty years of age.

I have never been a very dexterous person. When I was younger I engaged in sports activities and played with action figures, forever imagining new adventures. I never played with Legos or blocks like many other children which might have enhanced hand-eye coordination and fine motor skills. Plane building requires many minute changes of details that only calm, nimble, and patient hands can make. None of which I have. Numerous times I broke a plane by sanding too roughly or glued my fingers together while really trying to glue two pieces of wood. Most of these events ended with my driving an Exacto knife into my building board and a shout of expletives. Not until recently could I claim that I can adeptly use my hands. I have needed to take my time to build planes, gluing the pieces ever so precisely and making everything perfect. At first I was frustrated with myself since my mentor would finish a plane in four hours and it would take me twice as long, but he had also been building planes since he was a child. After realizing this, I became more accepting of the time and patience needed to build planes and began to allot a greater amount of time for building. Instead of doing fast, shoddy jobs, I sacrificed my regular basketball television viewing time and replaced it with spending more time building planes and perfecting my techniques. I also endured long nights to finish planes the same day I started, hoping to limit the variables such as humidity that could skew the structure while having to concentrate even more because of my fatigue.

> **Most of these events ended with my driving an Exacto knife into my building board and a shout of expletives.**

This last year I spent more than fifty hours constructing four working planes for the regional, state, and national Science Olympiad competitions. I say "working" because I constructed many more planes, however only four were perfect enough for the competition; the others were abandoned. Through all this work, I almost gave up after the regional competition due to a horrific showing. My two best planes simply did not take off the ground as the balsa wheels got stuck in the carpeted floor of the Grand Ballroom at California State University at Sacramento. Finally, after my second failed flight I took the plane, sat down, and cried. I hated my plane. I hated myself for failing both my team and myself.

In retrospect it was this failure and embarrassment that became my motivation for the rest of the year. Constantly remembering that rare emotional breakdown and failure of my airplane to even lift off the ground, I was fueled to do better. I pledged myself that I would not fail again! I spent days and nights building planes, scrapping them if there was even a minor flaw. Finally, I rebuilt a plane, tested it, and took it to the national competition. My life, my self worth, and my pride were all tied up in this mixture of balsa wood and tissue paper. Upon arriving at the competition site I froze in fear when I noticed the carpeted surface that covered the center of the Ohio State University indoor track. Trembling, I tried to focus, remembering what my mentor said before I left Sacramento. "Just have fun." Recalling those three simple words cleared my head of doubt and fear and also cleansed my soul as I then casually strolled out onto the carpeted area and flew my plane. It stayed up for four minutes and nineteen seconds, twice as long as any of my planes have ever flown! I was elated and felt vindicated when I placed sixth in the national competition and was awarded a bronze medal.

Tackling this odd, anachronistic hobby has changed my life in many ways beyond doing well in the national competition. Studying and receiving good grades have always come fairly easily for me and it wasn't until this challenge that I learned to persevere and at the same time be patient and calm under pressure. My hands never seemed skillful enough and my luck never seemed to be there at the right time. I had to overcome many failures, but in the end, everything came together.

Brian Inouye attends Stanford University.

15
THE SHOES MAKE THE ESSAY

It's the simple stuff that makes a great essay. If you run out of ideas, try spinning a few stories out of the shoes in your closet. With each different shoe she describes, author Amanda Lewis reveals a different facet of her personality. On one level, the essay functions as an engaging way of telling about each of her extracurricular activities. But Amanda also demonstrates her ability to make creative analogies, and that she has an eye for detail in her closet and in her life.

Essay by Amanda Lewis

Don't you just hate those days where you find the perfect outfit, but don't have the right pair of shoes to complete the look? For me, deciding what shoes to sport depends upon which facet of my personality I wish to reveal or activity I'm about to partake in. Each day I face a dilemma—do I show the flashy, fun side or the conservative, chic side? When viewed compositely my eclectic shoe collection seems to create a convoluted image; but in reality they each represent an important component of my character. In order to better understand me, you have to simply look through my shoes. For instance, my saddle oxfords are not in the closet because I think they're stylish; no, they're here because they are a mandatory article of my school uniform. However, certain aspects of the shoes reveal much about my identity. As a student at Saint Mary's Hall becomes a senior, they experience the tradition of receiving their blue ties. This blue color represents the leadership and importance of being a senior, and therefore I wear this badge of leadership and connection to historical tradition in the form of my blue shoelaces. Other interesting shoes are my cowboy boots, since, of course, every Texan must own a pair of cowboy boots! These reflect the rugged nature of my personality, one that isn't afraid of ranch work or attending country dances with my friends.

This infuses southern flavor and shows yet another dimensional and integral part of my persona.

Extracurricular activities, readily apparent in my volleyball shoes and dance shoes, also play a large part in my character. The scuffed volleyball shoes look worn from seasons of use and reflect my ongoing passion for the sport, which I've played since I was five. My variety of dance shoes reflects the different dances I've done— ballet, jazz, Flamenco, Irish. Ever since beginning to dance in order to entertain my family at the age of three, dancing has become an important and defining trait of my identity, as can be seen by my collection of dance shoes. The final important part of my character is the fun and exciting side that appears during the weekends. My pumps and complicated strap shoes show the vivacious girl who enjoys mingling and socializing. Serving as a stark contrast to the flashy footwear, my clogs depict a person who enjoys comfort. Much of my time is spent in them, testament to my personality—despite having a busy and engaging life in many different ways I always find time to relax and enjoy life! A typical day progresses as I put on the saddle oxfords for school, changing into the dance shoes for dance during the day, prepare for volleyball practice with athletic shoes, and finally returning home to embrace the comfortable confines of my clogs. As you can see I utilize many of these shoes on a daily basis as I partake in different activities and show a variety of aspects of my personality.

My pumps and complicated strap shoes show the vivacious girl who enjoys mingling and socializing.

Amanda Lewis attends Johns Hopkins University.

16

PÉTANQUE, ANYONE?

After reading countless essays about soccer and basketball, imagine how refreshing it would be to see one about Pétanque. Don't know what that is? Join the club—or read the following essay by Marc Masbou. His description is superb, as when he describes the arc of the ball as a "gentle parabola," thereby showing that he knows as much about math as about writing. Says Marc, "Getting different perspectives helped me vastly improve my essay. However, don't be afraid to disagree with advice other people give you. Take it all in, and then make an honest decision as to what you think is best."

Essay by Marc Masbou

Jot a note to your future roommate relating a personal experience that reveals something about you.

The rusted ball rests in my hand. My sandals shift in the gravel. My right arm lies loosely at my side, swinging gently. I'm crouched near the ground, concentrating on a little wooden ball ten yards away. I pull my arm back, then swing it forward as my body rises. The heavy ball flies away in a gentle parabola, and scatters pebbles when it lands with a thud...right next to the wooden ball. "*Oui!*" I exclaim as I do a little jig.

> **I'd much rather quietly place my ball in a prime location than push others out of the way.**

What am I doing? I'm playing the classic French game of Pétanque. The goal is to get as many of your balls as close to the wooden ball ("cochonnet") as you can. I play Pétanque every summer, when I visit my family in France. Simple as it may seem, Pétanque is actually quite complex. Over time, it has taught me about myself and others. There are two shots in Pétanque. The first is a "pointé," where the player tries to place his ball near the cochonnet. The second is a "tir," where the goal is to displace an opponent's ball. Some people, like my brother, win by using a "tir." I have always been a "pointé" shooter. I'd much rather quietly place my ball in a prime location than push others out of the way. A "tir" is all power and little accuracy, while a "pointé" is the exact opposite. However, both shooters are needed for a great team. If you're a "pointé" person, then we've already got something in common. If you're not, let's play Pétanque!

Marc Masbou attends Stanford University.

17
A LIFE IN LETTERS

Just as AOL Instant Messenger can be a great essay topic (Essay 7), so too can the process of old-fashioned letter-writing. Author Francie Neukom eloquently conveys her love of language as she describes her interactions with various pen pals. Says Francie, "My friends would always laugh at me for preferring old-fashioned snail mail to the phone. They rolled their eyes when I said I was writing a college essay about it. However, I knew that my true self would shine through if I wrote about something I was head-over-heels in love with, and writing letters is one of those things. Sometimes the things that make us dorky or weird are the exact qualities that will make us stand out from a pile of fifteen thousand other application essays."

Essay by Frances Patricia Neukom

My mom is already telling me that I will have to clean out my room and throw away most of what fills my desk drawers. I am a very sentimental person and keep large quantities of what friends have given me over the years, so it will be hard for me to decide what to discard. The one thing I will never throw away, though, is my letters.

I first began seriously writing letters when I was in fifth grade and found my first pen pal, a cheery girl named Cate from Virginia. We were referred to each other through a magazine and began avidly writing. Cate was not much like me, as she loved horses and hiking while I preferred dogs and writing. Our geographic differences amused us—she couldn't believe I'd never seen a snow storm and I was perplexed when she started playing lacrosse, a sport seldom heard of on the West Coast. But we learned about each other through our letters and I grew close to her—this girl I'd never met who lived three thousand miles away.

She was followed by many others: a girl who lived in West Virginia, another Kate but spelled with a K, who wrote me a letter when she read a story I'd published in a kids' magazine; an elderly lady I knew from Kentucky, Ginny; an old friend from camp, Georgina. I wrote to Frances (named after me), the daughter of a Welsh pen pal my mom had when *she* was my age. I even began writing to a girl who left my school in eighth grade and lived right over my back fence. Although I saw Sarah occasionally, the way we described our unfolding high school experiences to each other was through our letters. She described her public high school events, like making Homecoming floats, while I told her of my small-school happenings, like the annual lip sync. In my letters, I expressed more and more of myself, igniting my lifelong love of writing. My letters were always keys to self-discovery—I learned who I was through those scribbled sheets. And I kept almost all of my pen pals' letters.

In this world of word-processing computers and instantaneous e-mails, letter writing seems a bit quaint to most people, an activity of yesteryear. But I never see it that way. I have always told everyone I can write much better than I can speak. Sometimes when I need to discuss a serious subject with a friend, I find it easier just to sit down and write a letter. With a letter, you have time to reflect on the issue at hand, mull over the precise words to use, and eliminate the constant need to keep the conversation going. Letters are permanent things—they don't vanish into the air like the spoken word. If someone pays you a compliment in a letter, you can save it for when you need it.

I don't type letters. As much as I love computers for their many advantages, typing seems so impersonal. Everyone uses Times or Helvetica to aid the reader in legibility. But letters don't need to have every word be understood—they speak for themselves. You can tell more about someone by their handwriting than printed papers. For instance, my Welsh pen pal would always adorn her curvy handwriting with doodles in the

> **My friends would always laugh at me for preferring old-fashioned snail mail to the phone.**

margins, something you couldn't do on a computer. Besides, question marks and exclamation points are so much more effective in hand-written form.

My letter-writing ability has carried over into other aspects of my life. At the end of the year, everyone wants me to sign their yearbook, for I am able to recount the private jokes I've shared with my classmates better than most. People are delighted to receive my postcards, even when I have spent only a weekend in Lake Tahoe, because I don't waste space telling them the lake is beautiful and wishing they were there. One time I got an eleven out of ten on an assignment from a particularly demanding teacher because the assignment was to write a letter from someone else's point of view.

I have lost pen pals over the years. Cate didn't write me for a while and then wrote back recently, describing in detail how she'd gotten drunk at a Creed concert. I felt as if she had become a different person than the girl I grew to know through letters and didn't write back. The elderly lady died a few months ago, and I still cry when I come across cat note cards of hers, filled with her distinctive cursive handwriting. My Welsh pen pal had family problems and never wrote back, no matter how many letters I sent her, pleading for a response, even a short one. (Her mom even stopped writing to my mom.) But I've kept a lot of them, and added some new ones. I am dreading next year a bit, considering how many friends I will want to write long letters to, even though most of them will probably send me only mass e-mails. But I know I will never join their ranks, for letters have allowed me to discover more about myself and other people than any activity ever has. My letters I could never throw away.

Frances Patricia Neukom attends Stanford University.

18

HOW TO SUCCEED BY NOT TRYING TOO HARD

After reading countless essays that belabor the significance of a soccer game or a school play, admissions officers will welcome the following one from author Scott Pelletier. He uses his enjoyment of that most mundane sport, bowling, to write an interesting essay that succeeds partly because it doesn't break a sweat. In no particular order, the essay shows that Scott a) cares about others, b) has a good sense of humor, c) can tell a good story, and d) doesn't take himself too seriously. Only near the end does he relate that his performance really does matter a great deal—he was very nervous during Sectionals—and that bowling has helped him build self-confidence. After his understated essay, it is a believable conclusion.

Essay by Scott Pelletier

A ball is rolled down the lane. Confidently, I turn around; there is no need to see the result. A perfect strike. I stroll back to the bench, receiving high-fives from not only my teammates, but the opposing team as well. Bowling has been my most satisfying extracurricular activity. Turning with a smile on my face to my teammates knowing I threw a strike, without having to see it, feels amazing. On the other hand, it can prove a little embarrassing when a pin is left standing.

When I was in ninth grade, I tried out and made the freshmen basketball team. Spending almost the entire season on the bench was not an enjoyable experience. While my spirit to play was strong, my height of 5'2" was an impediment. The next year I decided to try bowling instead of putting myself through another year of warming the bench. Bowling is an equal opportunity sport, where it doesn't matter if you're short, fat, or even deaf, dumb, and blind. It is the only sport I know of that you can eat french fries and play cards during practice. Bowling matches and practices are always fun as we never have to do strenuous wind sprints and no one ever gets injured. My teammates and I get to relax and have fun.

On good days, it is satisfying to know that I can throw a strike on any shot. My best game to date is a 266. On the other hand, I have also experienced the "agony" of getting a gutter ball. We often joke with each other about throwing gutter balls; claiming it "hit my leg" to use as an excuse.

It is amazing to see how although as individuals we don't have a lot in common, yet as teammates, we bond. The team is very supportive; we cheer when someone does well and give encouragement when one of us throws a bad shot. I have never quite experienced that kind of team sportsmanship before. As a varsity bowler, I enjoy helping the younger JV bowlers perfect their game. I have spent numerous practices working with one freshman in particular to improve his approach to the shot (unfortunately, my efforts had limited success).

It is the only sport I know of that you can eat french fries and play cards during practice.

My own game has improved as well. Sophomore year, when we went to the Westchester/Putnam sectionals, I was really nervous and I did not bowl up to the expectations I had for myself. In contrast, junior year, we qualified again and I averaged fifteen pins better than my season average. My skills, along with my confidence, had significantly improved. This newfound confidence has spread to other areas of my life. Recently, I had to give a speech for Mu Alpha Theta (Math Honor Society) and I was pleasantly surprised with the ease I felt at delivering the speech. While bowling is not as glamorous as football or basketball (no cheerleaders), for me it will always be wonderful way to spend an afternoon.

Scott Pelletier attends Columbia University.

19

A SAILOR SURVEYS THE HORIZON

A lot of overworked metaphors make the rounds in college essays—as in "I realized that the big game symbolized my quest for meaning in life"—but such essays can be good when they are done right. Author Christopher Pirrung masterfully explains his love of sailing—and convinces the reader that it is a pretty good metaphor for his life. He understands the importance of using terms like "outhaul," "boom-vang," and "jibe-turn" even if most readers won't know what they mean. Notice, as well, the graceful way in which he weaves in comparisons of sailing to charting a path in life. He doesn't belabor the metaphor at the beginning. Instead, he makes a brief reference to it in the third paragraph, subtly setting the stage for more extended reflections in the last paragraph.

Essay by Christopher M. Pirrung

Leaning backward in my one-man laser, I hike out hard in an attempt to keep the sailboat from capsizing, the tiller clutched hard in my left hand and the main sheet sliding through my right. These strong thermal winds are exciting yet challenging. I have been waiting for them for some time. As I leave the protected harbor and venture out into the bay, the swells grow and the horizon appears. Sailors know that Little Traverse Bay is one of Lake Michigan's best protected harbors, yet the horizon to the west gives the impression of vastness equal only to an ocean.

The race is about to begin as I try to assess the wind shifts and puffs. Everyone has the same boat and most racers are equally experienced; the key to winning resides in tactics. The right side of the course appears better because of the ten-degree wind lifts, but the windward mark is slightly to the left. What is the shortest course? Which side does the wind favor? There are a thousand options. I must tighten the outhaul, downhaul, and boom-vang to change the sail shape to de-power up the sail; the winds are strong today. So many variables make small-boat racing the most exciting and rewarding challenge.

Just like a sailor, I am at the real beginning of my life. Decisions I make now will affect who I shall become. Although slightly jittery, I must go forth with confidence and hope. On that race day, the wind favored the right side so I head out on port tack. Before long I noticed the wind shift left and I took the lead. Feeling proud of my successful tactics, I am the first to round the windward mark. Downwind, however, is anybody's game. You never know what a wind puff will bring. The left looked windy, so I pointed the bow slightly left. I caught a puff and enjoyed the ride for some time but when the puff died, I decided to jibe-turn the boat suddenly and unstably. The race makes me think of the infinite variables I face at this time. Sometimes I become passionate about my physics class and decide to dedicate my life to the study of hydrodynamics and naval architecture. Not long after however, I may meet a prominent man and become inspired to be an entrepreneur.

> Feeling proud of my successful tactics, I am the first to round the windward mark.

Sailing is a metaphor for my life right now because there are so many variables and paths to take, each of which can produce successful results. So many options lie at the beginning of a race, yet a sailor who initially heads right may cross the line within seconds of a racer who headed left. There is no correct path to take, just knowledge mixed with gut feeling. I may catch a puff and head right, but as the puff dies I must decide to push forward or tack. Once you start a race each decision affects your place but one thing is for sure: you can't finish a race on one tack only. Small-boat racing is a process of intellectual exploration where knowledge and curiosity lead you; a university should be no different.

Christopher M. Pirrung attends the University of Virginia.

20

BART, MTC, AND ME

When a student is passionate about an interest, and has taken the initiative to pursue that interest, an essay can almost write itself. Author Chris Ramirez is an excellent writer, but he merely needs to describe what he has done to learn about, and work on, issues related to public transportation. How many high school students attend public hearings or participate in conferences dealing with long-term transportation goals? Chris is already a functioning professional in his field of interest, which gives him all the fodder he needs for the ultimate "show, don't tell" essay.

Essay by Chris Ramirez

It was a thrill to land my dream job this summer as an intern with the Metropolitan Transportation Commission. As long as I can remember, I have been fascinated with everything associated with transportation. My commute to high school on the Bay Area Rapid Transit System (BART) and the city bus system puts me on the front lines as a user of public transit. This daily use has increased my awareness of how transit systems work and the impact transit policy decisions have on people. Last year in Journalism, my concern prompted me to interview other student commuters and write an editorial for the school newspaper on how proposed reductions in transit services would affect our own school community. I also wrote an English essay in support of equality in policymaking and environmental justice when allocating access to public transportation services.

Outside of school, I have been a member of several transit advocacy groups consisting of people from all walks of life. I have attended multiple public hearings and participated in the Transportation 2030 Conference, which set transportation goals for the nine-county San Francisco Bay Area for the next twenty-five years. Because of my involvement, I was featured in the Metropolitan Transportation Commission's annual report. Although it was exciting to see my photo on the cover, more importantly, this experience led to my summer internship at the regional planning agency.

At MTC headquarters my assignment placed me in the Legislation and Public Affairs Department working primarily on the awards program, honoring people and projects that have helped to make transportation more efficient. I solicited nominations, wrote summaries for the awards jury, and coordinated the many video shoots for the film featuring award winners. Working with the nominees and hearing their personal stories gave me a first-hand view of their perceptions on current transportation issues as well as visions for the future. At the same time, I served as an intern with BART in the Amtrak Capitol Corridor Management Section. My position enabled me to gain marketing experience working on their "Kid's Ride Free" and "Capitol Corridor Month on BART" promotions. Both internship positions provided a great opportunity to work with transportation professionals. Instead of looking from the outside in, as a transit user, I saw the process from the inside out. I learned that operations and management solutions are more complex than fixing one immediate problem, and that one must consider the ramifications the solutions have in the broader context. My internship allowed me to attend meetings with commissioners, write articles for the agency newsletters, and observe policy decisions being made. This experience convinced me that a career in a transportation-related field is something I want to pursue.

> I served as an intern with BART in the Amtrak Capitol Corridor Management Section.

To help make this dream into a reality, I intend to major in Urban Studies or Public Policy with an emphasis in transportation. Transportation issues encompass environmental, political, socioeconomic, legal, and economic concerns. I plan on taking courses in these areas as well as researching successful transit systems in other countries. Gaining this broader perspective will be important to my understanding of how mass transit can improve our lives by reducing congestion and improving air quality.

The "smart growth" concept that is currently gaining attention interests me. The idea is to create "transit villages" that will provide a variety of housing options and services within walking distance of public transportation. I feel this is a critical time to make good and equitable transportation decisions and believe the University of California, with its wide range of focused disciplines and commitment to quality education, will provide me with the knowledge necessary to participate in making those decisions. I am excited to be a part of the future transportation planning challenges.

Chris Ramirez attends the University of California at Davis.

21

TAKING CARE OF HIS BABY (WITH WAX AND A POLISHER)

Author Pavel Sotskov has written what is known as a process essay. In his explanation of how he cleans and waxes his car, Pavel shows logic, dedication, and attention to detail. Process essays naturally lend themselves to specifics, and Pavel gives us plenty. For instance, we learn that he washes the top of the car first because the water will flow down and loosen the dirt on the lower parts. A little compulsive? Perhaps. But anybody who devotes this much thought and effort to the car will probably excel in other areas, too.

"How I Use the Orbital Polisher" by Pavel A. Sotskov

Every Sunday morning until the weather drops below freezing and my parents do not let me use the hose, I wash my car. This may seem like an ordinary job to some, but to me washing a car requires a distinctive technique.

No matter how tired I am, every Sunday morning I wake up, brush my teeth, put on my blue sweatpants and red sweatshirt, grab the keys to the car, and head out into the driveway. Not even the puppy follows me outside; he likes to sleep till eleven o'clock on Sundays. I pull the car out into the driveway and position it just right so that the morning sun is blocked by the thick leaves and branches of the tall maple, and so I can easily walk around the back end.

I then attach the longest hose I can find in the basement of my house to the water spigot, and fill my large gray bucket with just enough soap that when agitated by the pressure from the hose the mixture I am left with is half a bucket of water and half of foam. I let the multicolored sponges soak for two or three minutes. Each sponge is used for a specific task: the yellow for the car body, the red for the wheels and tires, and the orange for cleaning the squashed bugs off the bumper. When the sponges are properly saturated I use the hose to soak the car and begin washing. Contrary to what my parents believe, there is a specific order of washing that must be kept in order to achieve the best quality wash. First, I wash the roof, then the hood, trunk, and only afterwards do I scrub the doors, bumpers, and finally the wheels. In this order the soapy water flows off the top of the car and loosens the dirt on the lower parts, which are then easier to wash.

After everything is washed and rinsed I dry the car off using a white towel to make sure I have not missed any dirty spots which would rub off onto the bleached towel. At this point, the sun is already higher in the sky, so I move the car forward to escape direct rays which warm the paint.

When the car is completely dry I begin to apply the wax again, starting from the roof and working down towards the bottom of the car. The wax dries in two minutes, which gives me just enough time to wax the car if my arm is working at close to the speed of sound. Normally, it takes me a bit longer than that to wax the whole car, so I finish with the waxing in closer to fifteen minutes. I use the orbital polisher to polish the hood, roof, and trunk, while the rest I do by hand, as the polisher does not do a good enough job on curved surfaces. After polishing, I buff the whole car by hand until the paint sparkles, the wheels shine, and the tires look wet.

Not even the puppy follows me outside; he likes to sleep till eleven o'clock on Sundays.

I vacuum the interior, and clean all the map pockets which accumulate fascinating rubbish throughout the week. I rub lotion into the dashboard to protect it from the sun and I wash the windows where my puppy has mashed his wet nose while riding on the seat.

I keep this precision and order every Sunday.

Pavel A. Sotskov attends Dartmouth College.

LIFE AS A MESSY DESK

If you can't figure out one angle from which to describe yourself, try three. Or twelve. That's what author Christina Xu does in the essay here, which surveys various items on her desk. The fact that she is of Asian descent allows her to explore the relationship of typical American items to those of the East, and thereby delve into her dual identity. She also manages to touch on her interest in philosophy, science, art, and music, with specifics about each that bolster her credibility. Says Christina, "I rewrote this essay probably twenty or more times—an entire month's worth of second-period study halls was spent in my history teacher's office, discussing this essay and how to improve it."

Essay by Christina Xu

Display dagger. Teddy bear. Cheesecake.

I love cheesecake. In fact, a slice of this delicious dessert is on my desk right now, impaled by a pair of chopsticks. These odd juxtapositions of East and West occur frequently at my house; my mother puts peanut butter into her moon cakes, and my dad uses the coffee maker to boil chrysanthemum tea. My two halves, however, have created a greater whole. I am able to think in both Eastern and Western terms, and I am comfortable with the philosophies of Plato and Lao Tzu alike, though I do admit to dicey moments in *The Republic* and the *Tao te Ching*. Raised in two cultures, I am able to connect to many others. I can be at home at a football game, a Chinese karaoke party, a Japanese tea ceremony, or a French soirée. I am capable of shoveling snow with Buddha.

Jade necklace. Post-it notes. *School of Athens*.

On the other side of my desk lies a copy of *A Brief History of Time*. When I was younger, my room was littered not with dolls, but with books about every topic. I idolized the versatile Leonardo Da Vinci, who seemed capable of everything. As I've grown older, I've sometimes felt like a penniless artist forced to meet the expectations of a patron rather than work for my own interests and needs. It is difficult to emulate Da Vinci in a society that emphasizes specialization. Artistic creativity, however, is not a thing to be controlled and confined—and neither is my mind.

Dancing vampire doll. *Rush Hour.* Army Men.

Last summer, I went to an astronomy camp in the hills of North Carolina, even though it had no significant "practical value." There, I saw the Milky Way for the first time. While listening to a professor point out constellations with familiar names and alien shapes, I marveled anew at the joy of learning for its own sake, with no agenda and no assessment. When I am asked about what I want to do with my life by friends, parents, and college applications, I imagine Da Vinci tinkering with this invention, sketching out that painting, examining yet another plant; choosing a major probably would have driven him insane. I may have been born six centuries too late, but no career can possibly define who I am. I will be the business major who can solder a circuit and paint portraits, the engineer who can recite British poetry and speak in five languages, the artist who knows calculus and can break two boards at once. I will be a Renaissance woman.

Newton's thermometer. Sheet music. CD spool with two discs remaining.

"We Didn't Start the Fire" is a work of genius—each line corresponds to a year of Billy Joel's life, and the major events of each year are organized with rhythm and rhyme. A good songwriter like Joel weaves together all the disparate tones, beats, and lyrics of the song into a melody that organizes but does not constrain. As I look through my CD collection, full of the delicately beautiful strains of Prokofiev and the head-banging bass beats of Rammstein, I am reminded that my life, too, must have a melody to keep it valid. Each of my tunes is a singular cacophony, but united they make great harmony. I am composed of many

> **I rewrote this essay probably twenty or more times—an entire month's worth of second-period study halls was spent in my history teacher's office.**

passions, many faces, many reflections, and the Tao teaches me to let my different parts go their own way. I am neither yin nor yang. I will simply stay in the center of the circle and direct the symphony.

Sheets of white paper. Keyboard. Me.

Christina Xu attends Harvard University.

Athletics

More lousy essays are written about sports than any other subject. Part of the problem is that sports are not about personal reflection or expression—like, say, the arts—and attempts to find lessons on the playing field tend to ring false. It is no coincidence that only three of our writers make athletics a central theme. Essay 23 is by a football player who gains self-confidence and a new identity from being a respected member of the team. Essay 24 is by a soccer player who is also an artist, and who makes the case that soccer really is like art. Essay 25 describes how a water polo player makes the best of the fact that she is not a particularly gifted player.

23

A '5'5" NOBODY,' AND HOW HE BECAME A TEAM CAPTAIN

Essays about athletics often fall flat, but that doesn't mean it is impossible to write a good one. Author Michael Asmussen's essay succeeds partly because of obvious sincerity: he has no great epiphanies after the championship game, nor does he offer any platitudes about hard work and self-discipline. Michael felt like a nobody until success in football made him feel like somebody. His story is endearing partly because he is so self-effacing—as when he was shocked to be named a team captain. And if you're going to write a football essay, it never hurts to talk about the time you cried.

Essay by Michael Asmussen

When I first came to St. Andrew's-Sewanee, I had pretty much led a common life for a child in my area. Athletically, I played baseball, basketball, and soccer. There was peewee football down the mountain in the valley, but on top of our little plateau there never was much interest in getting a team together. So I entertained myself by playing pick up football with my friends. I played soccer in the fall and it was always fun, but there was always something missing. It wasn't until I first came out for football during my eighth grade year that I finally discovered something that created a spark inside of me. In soccer, I had played every position, and there was not one niche for me. However, in football, I was a lineman. That was the one position that I played, and it was a position for which I was well suited. I had finally found something that could be all mine. This was my chance to do something on my own and to finally follow my dreams.

I had always been somewhat big as a child. So when I joined football it was only natural that I would join the linemen. My friend was a lineman, and I did not see any reason why I shouldn't play that position too. There was still only one problem. Although I was big for my age, I still wasn't all that big. At five foot five, and one hundred and fifty pounds, I was dwarfed by all the players that I went up against. My first year was frustrating because I did not get a lot of playing time. It was not until my freshman year that I finally began to get playing time, and bit by bit I improved. Finally, in my sophomore year, I cracked the starting lineup. When our starting noseguard was injured, my coach called upon me to fill the spot. I took over that position and held on for dear life. I never relinquished my spot on the defensive line, and worked as hard as I could to fend off any challengers. I was the lone sophomore starting that year and it created in me a sense of pride. That feeling of accomplishment inside of me carried into my junior year, where, after an intense summer, I took over the job of being the starting center on the offensive line. I was one of the iron-men of our team. I would start both ways and would get very little break from my jobs. I held these titles proudly as I knew that with them came a certain level of respect from both the coaches and other players. It was not until my senior season that I realized exactly how much respect I had earned from both the coaches and players. When the results from the elections were tallied, I was told that it was almost a unanimous decision that I had been selected as one of the three team captains. I was shocked to hear this because in years past the captains had often been the more popular players, which was a group that I never saw myself a part of. My coach told me that he was totally confident that the players had chosen the absolute best examples for them to follow. This was when I realized how much of a different person I was in comparison to when I began on the team as an eighth grader.

I almost never came to this realization. When I came home as a seventh grader in spring of 1996 and told my parents that I wanted to join the football team, they bordered upon adamancy in their desire to keep me from playing. Their biggest worry was that I might get hurt because I was so small. It took a great deal of coaxing and cajoling to get the permission that I desired. And once I got this permission my journey was not over. That August, when my first preseason started, I was utterly unprepared for what I was about to face. It was easily the hardest three weeks that I have ever experienced. To this day, I still remember constantly thinking of how I could be at home with my friends rather than suffering under the hot sun on the practice field.

But when it came time to peel my soiled jersey off my shoulder pads one last time, I cried.

But, before I had started, I had made myself a promise that I would see this commitment through. I would treat it like all the other commitments that I make and never give up on it. The first year was almost as aggravating as the three weeks of preseason. Every game, I would stand on the sidelines and watch as my friends were constantly sent in to give the starters small breaks. By the end of the season, I had begun to have serious doubts about ever playing again, but my friends told me that I just had to put the time in, and someday my time would come. When my time finally arrived, I experienced the greatest sense of accomplishment that I have ever felt. I had worked hard and shown all those around me that I deserved notice. Every time I pulled the jersey over my shoulder pads, I felt that maybe something great was about to happen. I had earned everything that I had gotten and done it all on my own. This was my accomplishment and nobody else's.

I think, however, that the biggest realization came when I took the jersey off my shoulder pads for the last time as a St. Andrew's-Sewanee Mountain Lion. It was the hardest thing that I had ever done as a player. I had been able to last through the three weeks of sheer hell of that first preseason. I had even been able to play through discouraging games when we were not only out-manned but also out-sized. But when it came time to peel my soiled jersey off my shoulder pads one last time, I cried. I cried because I realized how important football had been in my life. Football was the first pursuit that I had ever made on my own. Everything else that I had done had always been tried by my older sister and older brother first. But football was my own special accomplishment. I had spent five years of my life devoting myself to something that was entirely my choosing. I think that it had the most impact on my life over everything else I have done. It taught me to follow my dreams, and that through hard work and determination anything is possible. But most importantly it had become an outward and visible sign of my inward and invisible determination. After all, who would have thought that a five foot five nobody could have developed into one of the most respected players on the team? I certainly never did, and I am sure hardly anybody else did either, but that is exactly what I think drove me to succeed.

Michael Asmussen is a graduate of Dickinson College.

24

SCORING POINTS WITH ATHLETICS

We've warned you about the pitfalls of sports essays. Here's one that avoids them. The author gives a fluid description of scoring the big goal in the big game, but what comes later is at least as interesting. Games and goals are not of lasting importance, and though the author speaks of familiar standbys such as hard work, camaraderie, and teamwork, they aren't the bottom line, either. "The game of soccer is not so much a sport as an advanced art form," he writes, and proceeds to show how soccer "is an amoeba of continuous, fluid motion." Through the game, the author becomes a much more interesting person than the run-of-the-mill player who kicks the winning goal.

"The Beautiful Game" by Sam James

Glaring floodlights illuminated the brisk autumn night, steam rose from the sweaty players, and screams rang from the abnormally large crowd. With less than ten minutes left to play, the game remained a scoreless draw. I was the only freshman on the field, and I had been running on sheer adrenaline for nearly the whole second half. The ball floated into the penalty box, and I instinctively darted to meet the beautifully arching cross. With a slight jump and a deft touch off my right cleat, I watched the ball as it sailed just beyond the out-stretched arms of the goalkeeper. That goal proved the winner as we rallied past the top-ranked team in the state.

> The game of soccer is not so much a sport as an advanced art form.

Rarely does success and meaning in life come without toil. While last-gasp goals and hard-fought victories stand out in my memory, the importance of my soccer experience cannot pertain to any one set of events. It includes countless hours in the backyard, early morning timed runs, hard-fought losses, agonizing poor performances, and all the small but sweet accomplishments on the practice pitch. I have cherished the entire evolution of my twelve-year career, and the lessons I have learned that transcend the game of soccer. My experiences with soccer have taught me the importance of dedication and perseverance, the value of camaraderie and teamwork, and the ways to harness raw emotion. More importantly, however, my involvement in soccer has provided me with valuable insight on life. The game of soccer is not so much a sport as an advanced art form. It requires a combination of mental, physical, and technical ability, accentuated by instances of innate skill and creativity. Whereas most sports require strict rules, carefully calculated plays, and numerous breaks, soccer is an amoeba of continuous, fluid motion. On the field, soccer players are given the liberty to be artists, perpetually adjusting and tending to the movement of play. Life itself is continuous motion. The "beautiful game" has taught me to be an artist in everything I do, forever tending to and sculpting the events of my own life.

Sam James attends Tufts University and the School of the Museum of Fine Arts.

25

HARD WORK PAYS OFF (SORT OF)

If we had a nickel for every essay that talks about the importance of hard work to achieve a goal, we'd be too rich to worry about writing this book. But what about when hard work doesn't pay off? That's the predicament in which author Michelle Tessier finds herself. Michelle's soul-searching in response to failure is much more interesting than exhilaration in response to success would be. In the end, Michelle discovers goals other than winning or being the best, and in the process, she learns (and tells the reader) something important about herself.

Essay by Michelle Tessier

After deciding it would be fun to play a sport in high school, I joined my school's water polo team as a freshman. Although I had never been particularly athletically inclined, I threw myself into the sport with total energy and enthusiasm, hoping to be a starting player. I worked incredibly hard, arriving at practice early to swim extra laps, and staying after everyone else had left to work on my technique. But no matter what I did, I was still only an average player. Why couldn't I score more goals? In school, I knew that when I completely immersed myself in the material and devoted extra effort to my classes, good grades usually followed. I had become accustomed to my hard work and dedication being rewarded. So I was naturally disappointed when devoting the same tremendous amount of effort to water polo did not yield similar results.

> I realized that if I really wanted to participate in an activity I loved, I could not let my embarrassment or false pride stand in the way.

I began to ask myself, why was I doing this? It was embarrassing and even somewhat humiliating for me to participate in an activity that I couldn't do as well as others could. I could not help but be frustrated when my coach yelled at me during practices, benched me during games, or when I saw the weekly sheet of statistics being tacked up by the pool for all of the players to see. I even began to wonder whether participating in water polo was worthwhile if it were something at which I could not excel.

However, I would never allow myself to quit. For even though I was not the best player on the team, I am not a quitter and the truth was I love playing water polo. I enjoyed the physical challenge it gave me, swimming as hard as I could until every muscle in my body ached. When I didn't get to play, I took pleasure in analyzing our game strategies, sometimes discussing ideas with my coach, even going so far as to very subtly suggest his strategy was wrong. I was amazed to learn I could actually enjoy the time I spent on the bench, often inventing cheers to support other players. I realized that if I really wanted to participate in an activity I loved, I could not let my embarrassment or false pride stand in the way. And because I refused to give up, participating in water polo has been simultaneously one of the most frustrating and yet rewarding experiences of my life. I found the determination not to walk away from something that was especially difficult for me. And although I was raised with the notion that every goal was within my reach if I simply worked hard enough, I now understand that I don't have to do something better than everyone else in order to be successful.

Michelle Tessier attends Georgetown University.

The Arts

S ome of the best essays in this book are about art, drama, or music. The arts are a vehicle for personal expression, and writing about them can be a great way to reveal an author's personality and passions. Performers, in particular, have great material because getting on stage is itself a dramatic moment. Our authors are mainly actors and musicians, though one student (Essay 39) writes about the effect of a performance that he saw.

26

MAKING THE ESSAY YOUR STAGE

The following essay is a superb example of the you-are-there genre. Author Ross Bercun writes of making the audience live his "Actor's Nightmare" (the title of the play), and through his essay, he transports the reading audience to his shoulder for the performance. From "the moment the light hits my eyes," Ross's concrete description of being on the stage *shows* his passion for drama more effectively than he could ever tell about it. His writing is full of skillful touches, such as when he loops back at the end to give a second mention to the cute girl, the old woman, and the seven-year-old. Says Ross, "My advice for future students is to write about something they are passionate about because it will make the words flow out of them."

Essay by Ross Bercun

There I sit, just having eaten a big bucket full of butterflies. They are fluttering about inside my stomach. A warm ball of energy gathers in my chest, and all other problems of the past day, week, and year disappear. All that exists is my moment and I.

Most people despise the winged creatures stored inside their bowels; I, however, believe they give me the energy to pull upon every skill I have, all the potential in my system, to come together and put on the performance of a lifetime. I peek around the corner of the dark, velvet curtain like the corner of a dog-eared sheet of paper, ever so slightly. I see family, friends, teachers, neighbors, and strangers. I see the cute girl in the third row turning off her cell phone, I see the homely older woman looking around the crowd for a familiar face, and I see the seven-year-old whose parents had dragged him along to the theater. I will speak to all of these people; make them live in the world I do. For one night, these people will live my *Actor's Nightmare*.

With the starting note of the opening music, the stage goes dark, and the audience takes a collective breath. They enter into my world. For every second that passes until my entrance, the butterflies double in number. Then finally, I enter. My ears connected by my smile and my muscles moving by rote, the light hits my eyes and the audience disappears; only memory lets me know that they are still present. I breathe in a diaphragmatic breath and release my voice, letting my breath and tongue conduct the symphony that is my song. The ensemble of this piece works together as one, our voices in sync with each other and our harmonies immaculate up until the final note. The stage returns to the blackness that had occupied it only minutes before; the difference is the audience. They are no longer silent, but have erupted into an awaited applause.

Without one remaining butterfly, I return to my place backstage with a hum in my body that could only be created by a thrilling performance. My anticipation tells me that the fire has not left my system; I am ready for the encore that is my next entrance, my main entrance.

Up until then I am dragged through the play without my conscious mind, though it has been playing my upcoming scene in my head over and over ensuring perfection. The previous performances had been good, better than I had expected. But this was closing night, and I had to be perfect. In what seems like a split second, it is my turn to go on. The lights dim and rise again like the trail of the sun on fast-forward.

I close my eyes, breathe, and then step onto the stage, back into the light. The audience's silence notifies me that I have their undivided attention. I am no longer Ross. I am George, living in a world unfamiliar to him. The audience is no longer in the theater. They are backstage with me, living George's nightmare—living my nightmare. With every panicking nerve in George's body I act my part. I am my part.

Before I know it, it is time for a soliloquy. My soliloquy. No other person on stage, no prop on stage. All alone, just me and my audience. I deliver every line from my soul; I don't have to struggle to remember my lines because I say them naturally. They flow like glass water down a plastic stream. I

For one night, these people will live my *Actor's Nightmare*.

connect with the homely old lady, I connect with the cute girl, and I connect with the child who no longer would need to be dragged by his parents to the theater. A drop of sweat drips into my eyes and stings, a pleasant sting. I drop to my knees to end my monologue, and the silence from the audience tells me that I have succeeded in creating their life within the play. For this night, they only exist in my play.

Looking back, I was always upset that I didn't get a final bow, but that's how it is written in the script. Sure, it bugged me the nights before that I wasn't allowed a bow, but those were merely *good* performances. Tonight I needed one—I needed a bow. As the audience applauded the other cast members I could hear the restrained applause that was being saved. Saved for me. At the moment I was to bow, the applause would tear free like an angry dog from a weak leash. I never got to know what those dogs sounded like. I remained still, "dead" on the floor as the cast gestured to me. The lights dimmed for the final time and a disappointed audience fell silent.

Ross Bercun attends the University of Arizona.

27

EXPLORING A "MUSICAL UNDERWORLD"

One of the best ways to be funny in a college essay is to use the stream-of-consciousness technique. Author Ciarán Bradley does it to perfection in the first paragraph of the following essay as he describes the degraded condition of the lowly mandolin player. Self-mockery is often effective because the author is laughing at himself; he does not risk offending anyone. Says Ciarán, "The most compelling stories are the simple ones about seemingly everyday stuff, that when told a certain way, or considered from a different angle, all of a sudden are refreshing."

"The Plight of the Mandolinist" by Ciarán Bradley

They say that being a mandolinist is a curse. It is incurred by a genetic defect that dooms one to be at the bottom of the musical totem-pole for life. Once you are in, there is no way out. Together with the accordion, kazoo, and banjo, the mandolin is part of a class of instruments that are the black sheep of the musical world. It is a runt among giants like the piano or guitar; meant only for trivial occasions like garden parties and serenading ladies at their windows. I will be forever punished for deciding to become a mandolin player. I have joined the ranks of the so-called musical in-elite. Sometimes I have nightmares about arriving at the gates of Hell and Satan taking me to a new level (one that Dante was not aware of), reserved for bad polka bands and the Clancy Brothers. It has taken a lot of courage for me to accept these challenges that I am faced with because I play the mandolin, but I am not afraid. I am willing to accept them with pride. I scoff right back at those who scoff at me. Deciding to learn how to play the mandolin has been a great musical experience that has opened my eyes to another aspect of music.

There is a joke that musicians tell about violinists: "How many violinists does it take to screw in a lightbulb? One, he holds onto the bulb and the world revolves around him." For many years, I was one of these violinists. I thought that there were no other important instruments besides the violin. We got to play all the great melodies, and in orchestras we were right at the edge of the stage so that the audience could see our fingers move with such speed and agility. My view quickly changed, however, when I learned to play the mandolin. As I ventured into the musical underworld, I discovered that there were many other instruments which I had never even heard of. What were these mandolin family instruments? Who were the people that played them? Were they musicians as well?

It all started about five years ago when I took a notion that I might learn another instrument in order to give me something else to do during one of my summer holidays. My mother set up lessons with a family friend who had been cursed with the mandolin craze some years before. I hardly even knew what one looked like, yet before I knew it, I was at my first lesson. The mandolin is a small instrument that originated in Eastern Europe many centuries ago. It later became popular among the Western European upper class, and found itself in the parlor corners of the rich, musically ignorant bourgeoisie. Though respectable composers such as Vivaldi and Beethoven dabbled with mandolin compositions, it suited these people better as mantle ornaments than musical instruments. It really did not become popular until the turn of the century when everyone started to learn the instrument because it was small, quaint, and

The most compelling stories are the simple ones about seemingly everyday stuff.

was an easy alterative to playing the violin. In fact, one of the first things I learned about the mandolin is that it was tuned exactly like a violin. What luck! I could still play all those wonderful violin melodies, but in a new interesting context. I was hooked, and I decided to keep playing this instrument, unaware that this decision would affect me for the rest of my life.

I continued to play the mandolin, naively thinking that my repertoire would only consist of Vivaldi sonatas. Then one day, my teacher told me that he was going to take me to one of his Milwaukee Mandolin Orchestra rehearsals. This was when I started to get suspicious. I wondered if I had made a good decision in pursuing this mandolin playing with such zeal. I did not know what I was getting into. The Milwaukee Mandolin Orchestra is an eclectic group of musicians who had each stumbled upon the curse in their own way. Some were of the Bluegrass background. Some were on the rebound from earlier punk-rock escapades. Still others, like myself, were classical musicians. They met in a south-side basement as though they were sixteenth-century heretics hiding from the Spanish Inquisition (in the form of the classical musicians such as myself who would find out about these mandolins). Their repertoire dated back to the turn of the century when the mandolin was at its high point and was comprised of catchy little marches and foxtrots that, in their own way, deserved recognition from the masses. These brave men and women were the last remaining survivors of the mandolin craze. Some of them were actually old enough and had lived during the craze in the 1930s; others were there to carry the torch into the twenty-first century. I soon found myself playing right along side them, enjoying the shenanigans. I made my second crucial decision to remain playing with them and since then I have not looked back.

Playing with the MMO has turned out to be a wonderful, fulfilling experience. Recently I was named an official member of the group, being the youngest member to join since 1900. I have met very interesting people through my mandolin and have found myself playing concerts with the group in parts of Milwaukee that I never knew existed. I am very glad that I made the decision to play the mandolin, because it has made me aware of another genre of music of which most people, even professional musicians (the ones to whom the light bulb joke refers), are not aware. To those who look down on the mandolin, I would have to say that they cannot judge something they know little about. If nothing else, at least I will be able to serenade a lady at her window some day.

Ciarán Bradley attended University College Dublin, Ireland.

DRAMATIC FLAIR

This essay requires a little background. The author, Alexander Dominitz, directed a play at a local elementary school. The reader can figure out the context as the essay goes forward, but the author relies on the rest of his application to fill in nuts and bolts information (such as the fact that the production was his idea, and that he convinced the principal at the elementary school to endorse it). Note the skillful pacing. The essay covers the length of the show, and Alexander uses digressions into his own thoughts to give the reader a sense that time is passing. Says Alexander, "They're asking you to write about yourself…The subject you know best. Just write from the heart and everything will be all right."

Essay by Alexander Dominitz

"Please turn off all cell phones and pagers. Thank you, and enjoy the show." As the echo of my voice subsided, I seized the walkie-talkie that lay resting on the stool and raised it to my mouth. "Justin," I whispered, "kill the lights." I had just enough time to nod to the sound crew, signaling them to start the overture, before the stage went completely black. As Mendelssohn boomed from the speakers, my fingers fumbled around in the dark until finding the curtain chord. I began to pull downward, hand-over-hand, until the curtain revealed the court of the Duke of Athens. Kelsey's voice sounded from stage right: "Now, fair Hippolyta, our nuptial hour draws on apace…"

Breathe. As I leaned against the stage door, the journey that had brought me to this moment replayed in my memory: months of planning with the school's administration—outlining goals and creating schedules; hours of meeting with the faculty—enlisting the art department to build sets and begging English teachers to postpone projects; weeks of rehearsals, preparing the kids for the rigors of "opening night"; even the video that I wrote and filmed over a marathon-like weekend in order to advertise the endeavor. And finally…all my pessimistic friends who challenged my excitement with their disbelief: "Junior high school students? Shakespeare?" Then I thought, "But just look at them now!" Nina projects on stage—the smallness of her voice ceases to inhibit her performance. Chris watches his blocking—his awkward stance a distant memory. Amber now gestures with purpose—gone are the nervous habits that once characterized each movement. Garret knows every single line by heart—no longer will I be making the 10 p.m. house calls to help him memorize. But what about Brian? Little Brian…. I just don't know. Always so quiet and shy…have I reached him?

The Mendelssohn sounded again: time for intermission. I resumed my scurrying, taking down trees and bringing on columns, fixing loosened safety pins, freshening up faded makeup, and answering questions from the crew: "When do you want the spotlight in 4:1?" "What about the throne and the benches?" "Have you seen my donkey ears?" Suddenly, I felt a tug at the leg of my jeans. I turned around, and there was Brian, looking up at me with round, brown, hopeful eyes. In his usually timid voice, I heard a tone of determination. "Was that good? What can I do better for the next act?" I hugged him, reassured him, sent him to his entrance place, and rushed behind a curtain before anyone could see my tears of joy.

End of Act 5. As the lights came up for the curtain call, the audience rose in standing ovation. The faculty advisor tapped me on the shoulder. "It's your turn…get out there!" I looked out at the stage apron from my post at the curtain, smiled, and shook my head. "No," I said. "This is their moment."

They finished their bows, and as the curtain closed, all twenty-five seventh and eighth graders

> Hugs, laughter, and tears gushed from everyone—actors, technicians, and stagehands alike.

jumped up and down shouting, "We did it! We did it!" Hugs, laughter, and tears gushed from everyone—actors, technicians, and stagehands alike. I just stood there and watched, not daring to disrupt the spectacle, for I was witnessing the burst of elation that only those who have just created something beautiful can know. This was my bow. I did not need the audience's reaction to gauge the impact. I could see the results for myself. I can teach. I can inspire. I can touch lives. That's all that matters.

Alexander Dominitz attends Yale University.

29

WHEN DAD MAKES LIKE JOHN TRAVOLTA

No potential essay topic is richer than the relationships with your parents. The trick is not sounding labored or predictable. No admissions officer wants to read one more essay about how much somebody's dad means to him or her. And since the essay should really be about you, not somebody else, you don't want line after line of description about your parent. The following essay sings because in the process of telling about her dad, the author actually tells about herself; her enthusiasm, her sincerity, her patience, her joy in dance, and her affection for her dad are all lovingly conveyed.

Essay by HollyAnne Farris

"OH MY GOSH! I have a whole new appreciation for the art of dance!"

Who said that? The voice sounds familiar, but those words…they didn't just come out of the mouth of my dad, did they? They did, and wow, how long have I waited to hear something like that from him? Years… fifteen to be exact!

For fifteen years, the only things my dad has known or said about my life at McMillan School of Dance were things like "You mean you're only going to wear that thing for one night and we have to pay for it? Why can't we just rent it!" or "This recital is too long. We can't leave after your dance?"

That all came to a screeching halt the day I asked him to dance in the "Daddies" dance during our annual Jazz Shoppe Winter Recital.

Jazz Shoppe is a select group of dancers who train rigorously two days a week for approximately four months to learn twelve to fourteen different dances. This is in addition to the regularly scheduled classes we attend to prepare for the spring recital. Jazz Shoppe consists of a mini company, a junior company, two senior companies, and the infamous Daddy Company. I have been a member of the senior company for five years and this year, my dad officially became a member of McMillan School of Dance—Daddy Company.

As hard as we try to make each of the dances entertaining, the most popular dance of the Jazz Shoppe is the "Daddy Dance." It's hard to compete with eight or nine middle-aged dads, all dressed as John Travolta wanna-bes, complete with gold chains and open collars, shaking it to the Bee Gees's "Saturday Night Fever!" Some people come just to see the dads perform.

How he came to be a member of the Jazz Shoppe—Daddy Company is just short of a miracle. One night, on a whim, I asked him if he would be interested in dancing in the Jazz Shoppe, thoroughly expecting him to take one look at me and say something like "You're kidding, right?" But much to my delight and amazement, he said yes. I figured what better way to incorporate the one man who has always remained faithful to me into something that I love and take pride in!

So, in October, the practices began!

Every Tuesday, the daddies would go to the studio for an hour and a half to learn their ONE dance. Practices seemed to get more frustrating as they slowly learned more and more sections of their ONE dance (keep in mind I was learning twelve). Needless to say, there I was, attending their practices and videotaping our teacher. Each night I would pop the tape into our VCR and review, rework, and re-teach the Saturday Night Fever number with my dad.

The audience went nuts! They even had a few catcalls made to them.

Finally, it was performance night! While I was busy making sure I had my suitcase full of my own costumes, my dad was busy making sure each of his gold chains, which we had picked out exclusively at our local Super K-mart, were positioned just right and that his collar was standing up at precisely the right angle.

Then it was off to the auditorium!

While backstage, I glanced over and I could hardly believe what I saw. My very self-confident and self-assured father, pacing up and down in the wings. He was nervous. Finally we were experiencing some sort of role reversal. Now I was the one calming down his nerves and reassuring him that he was going to do just fine. I even heard myself saying to him, "Just go out and do your best and everything will be fine!" Where and from whom had I heard that before?

And then, the end result of many long days of practice was finally here! It was time for the infamous "Daddy Dance." The lights dimmed, the curtains opened, and there they went, eight "John Travoltas"—gyrating across the stage, nailing the dance! The audience went nuts! They even had a few catcalls made to them.

In less than three minutes, the dance was over, but a change of a lifetime occurred. Not only was he the best one out there, it was as if he became a different person on that stage. It was then I knew he could finally relate to me and my passion for dance. He now knows how I feel when the lights go down and the curtain parts and I become one with the stage and one with the audience. Who would have thought that the appreciation of dance would become a common link between us?

It was so great to be sharing something so special with someone I love, my dad. I was so proud that that was my dad out there, shining in the limelight! We will always share that memory of Jazz Shoppe together and will continue to do so as long as we both dance!

HollyAnne Farris attends Texas A&M University.

30
MUSIC IS HIS MUSE

Starting with a drug analogy is potentially risky, but author Troy Gabrielson pulls it off with a mixture of sincerity and concrete description. The essay is about his love of music, and he is especially honest about his insecurities as he auditions for a high school band. Telling details, such as when he imagined that classmates were scheming against him, make the narrative endearing and give it an air of truth. Says Troy, "My idea to write about music as a drug came to me one night as I was frustrated and avoiding work by playing solitaire. Once I had thought of the idea, the essay came out fairly easily."

Essay by Troy Gabrielson

Music is my drug of choice. I have become addicted to it—listening, practicing, performing, analyzing, thinking about past gigs and those that I will soon play. The thought of music and the continually playing soundtrack in my head give me a high that other junkies pay hundreds to experience. Like other users, I have deepened my fixation with each new encounter.

I entered the Hamilton High School Academy of Music as a freshman. In the weeks, days, and hours before my audition for the academy's jazz program, I considered the training I had received in middle school, and I hoped my ability and knowledge would save me from what I feared would be a disaster. After the audition, I felt pessimistic about my chances for getting into a jazz group. Waiting for the call from the jazz teacher, I wondered if I would be able to find my niche in high school if I didn't get into jazz band. I wondered if my three years of concert band and jazz ensemble during middle school and intense practicing for the big day had been futile. Then the director called and told me he had accepted me into the intermediate jazz band. I was thrilled.

During the first several months of the ensemble, I dreaded going to the class. Although I was used to being the best trumpet player in middle school, I was intimidated by the talented musicians around me. For several weeks I kept my distance from the other students. My adjustment to the class and to the new people came gradually, and by the end of the year I felt completely comfortable.

When the teacher promoted me to the advanced jazz band the next year, I plunged back into the canyon I had spent most of ninth grade climbing out of. As I walked into the rehearsal room, I experienced the same wave of anxiety as in my freshman year. My delusions that the band secretly schemed about me slowly evaporated with each month that passed.

Playing and performing with jazz ensemble for the past three years has bolstered my confidence and decreased my self-consciousness, both in and out of music classes. And my long, often frustrating practice sessions, during which I brutally criticize my playing, impel me to play better. When I practice or play in school groups up to my true ability, I experience the greatest sense of accomplishment. The burdens of practicing pay off, and my confidence swells.

> **My idea to write about music as a drug came to me one night as I was frustrated and avoiding work by playing solitaire.**

Music is my drug of choice. I will forever crave it. Fortunately, the supply is limitless, and it's cheap. There are always more etudes to master, more solos to play, more concerts to look forward to, and more artists to discover. Music has sustained me through high school and given me a reason to get up every morning. It's even better than a drug.

Troy Gabrielson attends Whitman College.

31

THE ORGANIZATIONAL MAESTRO

For a textbook example of organization, check out the following essay. It begins with a snapshot of the moment of completion with the author, Steve Hall, reflecting on a year-long series of arts productions that he has organized. The second paragraph steps back in time to trace the development of his involvement in music, and then his transition from performing to organizing. After recounting his impressive experience as producer, he concludes by going back to where he was in the introduction, thinking about his next project. Says Hall, "My advice is to place yourself in the shoes of the reader. If you were reading about two hundred applicants, what would make this person different?"

Essay by Steven H. Hall

While standing backstage sipping my nth cup of coffee, forty hours awake and counting, I tried to think of what I'd do next. A year's efforts organizing Breakin' Curfew would soon draw to a close with the fall of the curtain; after this last band finished and the packed theater emptied, I'd have to begin again—with nothing. What would I do with myself? An hour later, I was sitting in the middle of a big empty stage with pad and pen, wheels turning on the next project: new ideas, new work, new people, new bands, new music. More music. Even better music.

I can remember no time in my life in which I was not making music. When I was young, I played *all* the time. In second grade I began piano lessons; by seventh it was drums and guitar. Guitar and drums. All the time. Drums and guitar. By thirteen I was a budding musician with an insatiable appetite for performance.

High school provided me with a world of opportunities to play. As a freshman, I played drums in the top jazz combo. We rehearsed constantly, played competitive festivals and endless gigs. I soon joined a rock band of upperclassmen and began to write, record and perform with them as well; every night that wasn't a jazz gig became a rock show. Several good bands needed a drummer, so I joined another. Then another and another. By my junior year, I'd played with twenty-three bands, appeared on thirteen albums and sold a thousand copies; I was going to be a famous musician, no doubt about it.

As my passion for music grew and evolved, so did my enthusiasm for academics. I had the good fortune to attend Ann Arbor's Community High School, a school which is very supportive of the arts, but academically demanding too. My teachers helped me find a balance between performance and classes; time-management became a full-time job. I excelled in most subjects, developing a particular passion for English and literature.

Through performances and recordings mid-freshman year, I learned about a remarkable organization called The Neutral Zone— a multifaceted local teen center that provided a substance-free environment with a focus on art, slam poetry, and lots of music. They sponsored a Youth Owned Records program, which produced albums and hosted shows. I came to hold a variety of positions in the organization, finding great rewards in producing and promoting younger bands. Through developing my management and organizational skills, I discovered that this work provided me even more satisfaction than performing did.

I can remember no time in my life in which I was not making music.

I started to focus on becoming an organizational mastermind, proficient in structure, communication, and problem-solving. More and more engaged in community service, I became Facilitator of the Teen Advisory Council and, then, the Teen Fellow on the Board of Directors and Executive Committee, for which I even received a nomination for Ann Arbor Young Citizen of the Year. The more work I did for the community, the more my desire for performance faded.

Then came Breakin' Curfew. Now my largest endeavor, Breakin' Curfew is a collaboration between The Neutral Zone and the University of Michigan Musical Society (a venerable fine arts presenter with a 136 year tradition) to present the flourishing local youth music, poetry, and dance to the community. I joined as a Teen Curator in September 2003. As the year progressed and the curatorial process evolved, as I booked acts and directed rehearsals, wrote press releases and distributed fliers, hawked tickets and designed light plots, I began to find my niche: to encourage talents greater than my own—to bring things together and make things happen.

I've started producing Breakin' Curfew again for this year. Moreover, I created my own class based around an internship I have with the University Musical Society, learning their methods for producing concerts and shows while refining my own. Coming from a school such as Community High, I'm applying to Brown University because I'm eager to find my new balance between education and music in a more diverse setting, to expand my academic interests, and explore a new artistic environment. I'm not sure where these past experiences will take me, but isn't that the way to approach the adventure of college? I'm eager to make things happen, to work like a dog, to get out the pad and pen, and get the wheels turning—to begin my next improvisation and see where it goes.

Steven H. Hall attends Brown University.

MAKING A MUSIC ESSAY SING

A short essay about a "meaningful activity" can easily become run-of-the-mill. This one avoids that fate because the author, Peter Liu, delves beneath the surface of his involvement in music. At age seventeen, it takes a big man to admit that he listens to classical music; Peter shows a sophisticated understanding of how various forms of music can make him a better musician. Forming a new band is always more impressive than playing in an existing one. Without bragging, Peter makes clear that he is a guiding force behind his band. Says Peter, "Creativity can't be rushed; it's best to let ideas stew and mature in your head before sitting down to write."

Essay By Peter Liu

Of the activities, interests, and experiences listed on the previous page, which is the most meaningful to you, and why?

I started playing piano at the ripe old age of ten, but there was an advantage to learning music when I became more mature. Classical music is an acquired taste, and the time to develop that taste enabled me to tolerate the unavoidable lessons on basic notes and rhythms.

While many fellow pianists struggled to stay interested, I found that I could motivate myself by choosing pieces I enjoyed listening to, which led me to accept more and more challenging material. Although my friends teased me endlessly for listening to classical music CDs, the habit exposed me to the greatest of my hobby. I would try to learn the pieces as well as I could, and play along on the piano as I listened on the headphones. Many selections on the disc required finger technique far beyond what I was able to do, but the result was often too moving, too lithe to keep me from trying!

Last year, my friend and I started a new funk band at school. This was particularly exciting, because I could finally use my ability to play popular music. After listening to Duke Ellington for years, I look forward to being able to improvise on the keyboard, without following sheet music. Fortunately, there were enough eager electric guitarists at school for us to form a five-man group. Although the guitarists never had formal training, I feel we make a perfect fit: their wide-eyed, teeth-gnashing antics onstage encourage me to be more spontaneous, while my classical training helps give structure and musicality to our pieces. I believe Fat Cat Fusion has been a hit at school functions because of our dedication, if not outright talent.

> **Their wide-eyed, teeth-gnashing antics onstage encourage me to be more spontaneous.**

Peter Liu attends the University of California at Los Angeles.

33

PLAYIN' IN A ROCK-AND-ROLL BAND

Not many musicians would choose a karaoke night as the highlight of their careers—or the topic of a college essay—but author Emi Meyer does it with flair. She begins by sharing her high-brow interests in film and food. Having amply demonstrated her sophistication, Emi spends the rest of the essay on karaoke night. She scores several nice turns of phrase, as when she "pumped an internal fist" over the chance to play rock. Ultimately, this essay is about being part of a community, and how music can bring people together.

"Karaoke Night" by Emi M. Meyer

When I brainstorm the activities I enjoy, a theme becomes apparent. Many of my pursuits give me insight into another way of life and provide fuel for my eager imagination. For example, I seek out films that transport me to an unfamiliar era or region of the world. My favorites from this year's Seattle International Film Festival include: *The Story of the Weeping Camel,* an enchanting Mongolian documentary, and *The Twilight Samurai,* a poignant Japanese production. Restaurant hopping is another way I savor exotic cultures. My epicurean friends and I pick out an interesting venue described in the newspaper. In November we discovered a quirky café that fuses Japanese and American cuisine, where we sampled curry spaghetti topped with a hamburger. For my most recent fun activity, however, I choose an event that occurred at a home front— my school.

One morning in early December, Bobby tapped me on the shoulder: "Do you want to play with us on Karaoke Night?" I grinned and pumped an internal fist. I have played classical piano for over a decade. I have recently become a budding jazz musician. Yet secretly, I had hoped for the chance to rock. So when Bobby invited me to join the band for the senior-class fundraiser, I jumped at the opportunity. During lunch that day, I entered the music room to pick up a program. The clamor of smashing drums and screeching guitars threatened to knock me over. I listened to the songs: "Love Me Two Times" by the Doors, "Carry On My Wayward Son" by Kansas, and "Long December" by Counting Crows. It was a genre of music I had never performed, and there were only two days to learn. But I was thrilled to give it a try.

The next day became a throbbing blur of rock-and-roll. I woke up early to listen to the CDs. I rushed to the senior lounge keyboard between classes. I frantically worked out the chords in the music room at lunch. I sought out Mr. Hurlbut, our choir teacher. He helped pick out the chord changes and rhythms. The imagination with which he interpreted what he heard inspired me to play the songs more freely, without worrying about replicating the original. By three o'clock that day, I felt confident.

On the day of Karaoke Night, the band rehearsed some songs. Almost every senior stopped by the music room to listen in or try an instrument. When I returned to school that night for the event, I was excited but relaxed, for the event felt like everyone's joint project. There was a big audience that included students, parents, and teachers.

> **Bobby tapped me on the shoulder:**
> **"Do you want to play with us on Karaoke Night?"**

As soon as I stepped on stage, I heard *"Yeah Emi! Woooo!"* and thunderous cheers for every musician. The band members had confidence in me that I could wing the accompaniment. And I had confidence in them that they would keep me from becoming lost in the choruses. With constant encouragement from the audience, we accompanied various singers. Some were amazing. Others sang just for fun. But after every performance, the whole audience would give a standing ovation. Every instrumental solo was received with hoorays. We were having a great time, united in the energy of loud music and temporarily free from the stress of college applications.

Ours is a small school where the senior class consists of fifty-nine students. There are only a few non-whites, including "hybrids" like me. When I was about to move up to the ninth grade, I almost transferred to a large public school because I wanted more diversity. Near the end of my high school years, however, I have come to appreciate my school. Although we lack racial variety, we are rich with ideological diversity, including political, religious, and sexual. The rigorous academic load teaches us how to think on our own. The individuality of each student is respected. More than anything else, I value the connection between my peers and me. We have known each other since we were twelve!

Karaoke Night was terrific because the whole senior class rocked. The event embodied the exceptional camaraderie at our school. I will cherish it as a sweet memory as I begin my college career to explore the unknown and exotic in coming years. Perhaps ten years from now, we will have an Alumni Karaoke Night. Wherever I am, I will definitely come back for it.

Emi M. Meyer attends Pomona College.

34

FINDING YOURSELF IN A PAINTING

Most people have at least one print hanging in their bedroom, but few scrutinize it to the extent that author Kate Newton has reflected on Renoir's *Dance at Bougival.* It helps that she also had it on the wall in her elementary school art room, but this essay is all about Kate's ability to identify with the woman in the red hat, and to see her idealized self in the image. Note the nice kicker in the last sentence that gives the essay an exclamation point. Says Kate, "When you are writing about something that is personal, you have to go with your gut first. You can always go back and fix what needs to be fixed."

Essay by Kate Newton

Choose and describe a particular piece of art and explain its significance to you.

All six of my elementary school years were spent in the same art room. Miniature tables and chairs sat surrounded by walls covered by prints of paintings and sculptures created by some of the greatest artists of all time. When my young eyes wandered around the room, which was often, I found my attention constantly drawn to a painting of a woman in a red hat. Something about it heightened my curiosity and it became not only my favorite painting, but my fascination. Upon leaving elementary school, I bought a print of my own to hang in my room at home.

The longer Renoir's *Dance at Bougival* hung on my wall, the more hidden details I noticed, and my once inexplicable fascination with this particular work of art became more apparent. The lady in the red hat represents a side of myself not often seen, one that dances in the street without a care in the world. She embodies passion and love of life through such simple touches as a red hat and her expression of contentment. She dances on for the world to see, completely absorbed in the moment. Living for the moment and for the sake of loving life has always been a wish of mine that I continue to bury in the back of my mind because I've been told it's not "practical" or "responsible." Renoir's painting constantly reminds me not to completely let go of that spontaneity.

Dancing is an act of passion; it is an act of freedom. Sometimes I search for this type of freedom in life, but at times, it can only be found in the subtleties of artwork. Renoir's *Dance at Bougival* was created when Impressionism was a prominent form of painting, my favorite period. Paintings were not meant to be perfect or precise; they were merely meant to inspire feeling and movement to try to capture the essence of life. The vibrant colors speak for themselves and the brush strokes display the passion felt by so many during the late 19th century. As I look closer, the background slides out of focus and the floor seems to blur below the figures, giving the painting a weightless, dreamlike quality where time seems to stop in that one blissful moment.

When you are writing about something that is personal, you have to go with your gut first.

Even when school becomes stressful or events in my life don't come out just right, I will forever hold a piece of myself in that painting of the lady with the red hat. She exists in a small world of color and light, where time and space have no meaning. All eyes are drawn to her as she floats freely across the canvas, the red strings woven through her dress like the passion her life embodies. Even though some days I walk right by it without a second glance, deep down I know that her life in that painting is sometimes the one I secretly wish to explore on the most dreary of days when all I really want to do is wear a bright red hat and dance like no one is watching.

Kate Newton attends Wake Forest University.

35

AN ANCIENT CATHEDRAL AND THE GRATEFUL DEAD

The key to author Harry Russin's essay is the fact that it is really about him, not about the Chartres Cathedral or the Grateful Dead's "Dark Star." The foundation of his essay is the ability to make an unexpected comparison between two reasonably well-known but very different works of art. His intellect makes the essay interesting, but his passion makes it soar. "I would hardly count listening to the Grateful Dead as a life-changing experience, but exploring that music is an artistic celebration for me," says Harry.

Essay by Harrison Russin

Describe a character in fiction, an historical figure, or a creative work (as in art, music, science, etc.) that has had an influence on you, and explain that influence.

Two works of art have made me shiver. Chartres Cathedral in France and "Dark Star" by the Grateful Dead continue to fascinate me every time I think of them. As art, the two specimens are completely opposite to each other. Chartres is a masterpiece of human ingenuity, architecture, creativity, and order. "Dark Star" is an exercise in improvisation, a constantly evolving work of group invention and lateral thought. However, both compositions represent me as a person and as a thinker.

I recall the first time I saw Chartres in an art history video. The cathedral's spires rose out of the television screen and I beheld the gothic cathedral as if it were frozen in time. Like a Bach fugue, the flying buttresses and vaulted arches contain intricate designs that made me wonder if their complexities were due solely to the architect's genius and planning. The colors in the stained glass windows are simply irreproducible, their kaleidoscopic light playing on the limestone floor. Although each window by itself contains a relatively simple rendering, thousands of the windows create a complex scene that is crowned by the rose window with its incredible Chartres blue. The symmetry and complexity of Chartres appeals to my analytical mind, but the Transcendental and creative features invite my soul to appreciate the cathedral as a work of art.

From my viewpoint as a musician, "Dark Star" is not as much a song as an experience. After starting to play the album *Live/Dead* for the first time, I felt as if I had wandered into a previously unknown part of my mind. The opening notes made me think I was eavesdropping on a concert that was just starting. Immediately my ears entered orbit and I was trapped between Phil Lesh's bass and Jerry Garcia's growling guitar. I entrusted my mind to the band, and they treated it to an improvisation that was so orchestrated, so complex that I did not believe it was a spontaneous performance. The palette of the electric guitar painted fantastic peaks and subtle valleys of modal, dorian riffs and harsh-sounding chord progressions. Every time a new theme was introduced, the band played until the motif evolved into a work of art that cannot be frozen in time. "Dark Star" does not include the complex planning of a cathedral, but I cannot attribute its artistic value solely to genius; like Chartres, there is something more. I am not claiming that Chartres and "Dark Star" are equally enduring works of art, but juxtaposing a gothic cathedral and a piece of modern popular art makes me recognize different interpretations of different art forms.

> **I was trapped between Phil Lesh's bass and Jerry Garcia's growling guitar.**

Chartres and "Dark Star" stand contrary to each other. However, I am composed of both elements—order and improvisation. I have a need for organization and subjectivity. I used to be in love with science because solutions are either right or wrong. I still admire science, but literature, history, and the arts have captivated me. The power of the mind enthralls me because, through science, it defines life; but through art, it relishes life. I have realized that, as Ralph

Waldo Emerson wrote, "Empirical science is apt to cloud the mind." My mind is not formulaic, but I still need standing ground—a floor or launch pad. I have entered the labyrinth of the arts. I still marvel at the intricacies of Chartres, but I am longing to improvise.

Harrison Russin attends Swarthmore College.

36

HER FAVORITE CHARACTER IS...
THE NARRATOR?

When author Alise Smith was asked to choose a character in fiction to expound upon, she picked not a famous hero or villain, but the anonymous narrator in *Joseph and the Amazing Technicolor Dream Coat.* An unconventional choice to say the least, but as we've noted more than once, anything that piques or surprises in the world of college essays is a good thing. With her exceptionally polished prose, Alise shows a wonderful feel for the hearing and telling of stories, and for her role as one who watches the world and describes it.

"The Narrator Backstage" by Alise C. Smith

Describe a character in fiction, an historical figure, or a creative work (as in art, music, science, etc.) that has had an influence on you and explain that influence.

Sitting backstage in the cool blue-gelled silence before a show, I sometimes find my mind wandering. It's not that I'm bored or anything, but after all the hectic running around that goes on before a show, it's nice to have a moment to just relax and think, even if it really is only a moment.

As I wait for the curtain to rise on opening night of our summer community theatre production of *Joseph and the Amazing Technicolor Dream Coat,* I find one of those moments, and I take full advantage of it. For the past four weeks, as part of the tech crew, I've helped build, paint, hang lights and microphones, write light cues, work out mic schedules, fly set flats, and do all the other random jobs that need to be done before a show can begin. And now it is opening night, and I can feel my excitement growing like a bubble inside of me.

One of the reasons I've always loved this show is because of my favorite character. It is not Joseph, or Jacob, or Potiphar, or even

Pharaoh. Nope. It is the Narrator. I smile to myself as I think of the weird looks I'd probably get if I told this to anybody. "The Narrator?" they'd ask. "What a boring part!"

But I beg to differ.

The Narrator is someone I can relate to. "How?" one might ask. The answer to that really lies with my family. I'm the oldest cousin on both sides, so for as long as I can remember, I have been left in a rather awkward position. Even as a child, I often felt too old to play with my little cousins, and I usually ended up hanging around the adults. The typical kid may shudder at the thought of sitting and listening to a bunch of old folks gab about "boring grown-up stuff," but as the years passed I grew to relish it. Sitting with the grown-ups opened my eyes to a world completely different from the world I experienced as a child. It gave me a totally different perspective on life as I listened to jokes about practically any subject: complaints about work, debates about politics, and even discussions about romance. But, most of all I loved to listen to the stories. When Grandma told about her sister sneaking off with her boyfriend, or Dad told about his broken back, or Grandpa told about the pesky squirrels in his garden, or my aunts and uncles laughed about the crazy teachers they once had, I felt like our history, my history, played itself out right before my eyes. I watched in fascination.

Listening to all those stories had quite an impact on me. They really made me pay attention to the rest of the world. I watched and listened, and as I grew older, I started to realize that everybody has a story to tell, no matter how mundane his or her life may seem. And it wasn't just my family either. The people I passed every day in the halls of my high school, the people I saw on the street, the people living in the houses I sped past on the freeway, all the people in all the countries in all the world had a story. They only needed someone to listen. And then if that someone told someone else and that someone else wrote it down, and yet another someone read that... The stories could go on forever. I wanted to tell all the stories I'd

> **I felt like our history, my history, played itself out right before my eyes.**

heard. I wanted to be the one to write them down, so that they would not be lost, but instead remembered as long as there were people to read or listen.

So I'm like the Narrator, I think, as the actors begin to fill the backstage, and my moment starts to slip away. I watch the world around me and tell its story.

Alise C. Smith attends American University in Washington, DC.

37

AN INFATUATION WITH ART

An intriguing title gives an essay extra pizzazz, especially when the title is echoed by a line in the main body (that usually comes near the end). Author Emily Stein chooses some particularly nice words, such as when Mrs. Reed "glides" to the front of the room, or when her mind "swam" with visions of beautiful colors. The last paragraph is the longest, and not coincidentally, where Emily builds toward an emphatic statement of her passion for art. In her last six sentences, she offers a textbook example of how to begin with the concrete and move to the abstract.

"Lavender" by Emily Stein

I tentatively grasped the plastic blue handle of the fattest brush. Its firm but compliant bristles tickled as I pulled them along my palm. I looked around nervously, waiting for my first oil painting class to begin. The intimidating, white primed canvas rested on my easel, boasting its potential. Fresh, plump paint tubes in every color but black sat in a neat line, echoing the rainbow. My water cup was half full. I was ready.

I thought about the conversation that had resulted in my registration for the class. A month before, my mother and I had discussed what a long, boring summer it would be without anything scheduled. So I had decided painting would be the best waste of my time. I had always enjoyed art classes in school anyway.

At noon exactly, a woman with spiky red hair cut close to the scalp glided to the front of the classroom. Her neck and wrists were suffocated by silver bands inlaid with jade, and a vibrant French scarf was wrapped carelessly around her neck. She was the teacher, Mrs. Reed.

Promptly, she introduced the paints. As instructed, I squeezed thick pearls of each color onto my palette. Mrs. Reed began moving her brush delicately, dipping it into her water cup, dropping a few beads of water onto her palette, and mixing a touch of aquamarine blue into the small pool. Then she introduced other colors to the melee, her wrist making loose, consecutive circles. Somehow she managed to produce the most beautiful lavender I had ever seen. Mrs. Reed firmly placed the tip of her brush, which was now saturated with watery paint, at the top left corner of her blank paper and pulled it down an inch.

"Lavender," she explained. I looked at the paper, at its glistening purplish-white stripe. Suddenly my fingers itched to make lavender, too. And this was only one shade of one color. My mind swam with how many beautiful colors must exist, waiting to be solidified on a canvas. Mrs. Reed set the other students and me free, challenging us to see how many colors we could discover. Then we learned how to sketch and block in still lifes, to see the delicate contours of the apples, and the tiny details of the iris's petals. I began to see everything around me in a different way. I had found my euphoria. Stepping into

As instructed, I squeezed thick pearls of each color onto my palette.

that classroom, I had not known what an addiction I would have to painting. Yet even now, three years, many paintings, and a few awards later, I am still the last to leave the art room. I go into art stores just to run my hands along canvases and admire fat new tubes of paint. My world has morphed into landscapes as I drive, still lifes as I eat, and portraits as I sit in class. Through colors and shadows I have become more alive. I am grateful to my mother for making me attend that first class. It has changed my life forever.

Emily Stein attends Barnard College.

38

A FOOTBALL PLAYER GETS OUT OF HIS RUT

Everybody knows the groups that populate a typical high school: the jocks, the nerds, the artists, and so on. By the time students apply to college, most know their comfort zone and are reluctant to leave it. That is why author Will Thanheiser's story is so impressive. He begins with a remarkably self-aware explanation of why, as a smart athlete, he really didn't see himself as an actor. Despite his limiting self-image, he soon discovers that he enjoys acting and might even be good at it. He doesn't claim to have had an immediate transformation—who in real life actually does?—but instead stresses that his personal growth is an on-going process.

Essay by Will M. Thanheiser

Before last year I had always thought of myself as a very shy, uncreative, introspective individual. And I was happy that way. I had found my little niche in the Kinkaid society. I was the jock who excelled in sports and also managed to make pretty good grades as well. But I wasn't an artist. I hadn't taken an art class since eighth grade, and I only took it then because it was required. I didn't think I was good at acting, or drawing, or playing an instrument. So I never did. Truthfully, it was because I was way too insecure about myself to risk humiliation. I was a perfectionist. I wasn't accustomed to failure, and didn't really see a point in trying it out now.

However, it is required that each student receive a fine arts credit before graduating from my high school. So, I decided to take Children's Theatre my junior year. A couple of my friends were going to do it with me, and I had heard that hardly any artistic ability was needed. So I gave it a shot. I started out very timidly, not volunteering for improvisational exercises or looking for a big part in our major production, *Charlie and the Chocolate Factory*. I didn't want to make a fool out of myself. But for some strange reason, our teacher saw some sort of hidden talent inside of me. She had seen me play football in front of thousands of people, so she knew she could rid me of my stage fright. And besides, how could I be intimidated of children less than half my age? Slowly the whole acting thing grew on me. I went from speaking in my own deep-toned voice to adopting the personality and traits of one of the central characters in the play, Grandpa Joe. I found myself really enjoying performing for elementary students from my school as well as some underprivileged schools around Houston. And besides, they made me feel funny. They had no idea that I really wasn't a good actor or funny at all. They just enjoyed the show.

My newfound artistic confidence encouraged me to try other new things as well. I became a much more social person. Whereas I used to just hang out with a select group of friends, I began trying to associate with more and more members of my class, as well as meet new people from other schools. I began opening up more to my family instead of keeping everything bottled up inside of me. Now this didn't just happen right away, and I still hang out primarily with my same group of friends. In fact, our relationships were made even stronger. However, I am really trying to become a more approachable and personable young man. And I think I am doing a pretty good job up to this point. But this "transformation" is an on-going process, and I hope the college experience will only help to facilitate its development.

> **They had no idea that I really wasn't a good actor or funny at all. They just enjoyed the show.**

Will M. Thanheiser attends Princeton University.

39

WHEN JOCKS JOIN THE CHOIR

Author Alex Wellman writes deftly about his surprise at seeing senior football players "singing about being someone's buttercup." Everyone knows the role that cliques play in high school, and it is impressive when a football player such as Alex shows an awareness of the need to broaden his horizons. On his first reference to his significant experience, Alex does not write that his attitude was changed forever, but rather that he was "reminded of the importance" of being his own person. It makes sense to be low-key at first; after he has shared more of the anecdote, he can be more believable in making claims as to its significance.

"Me, Myself, and I" by Alex C. Wellman

It has been about eighteen years since I was born in New York City, and I have spent roughly the last eight of those years in what I still call a new home, here in Charlotte, North Carolina. My life has followed the clichéd and semi-charmed life of a teenager growing up in a very nice American neighborhood. I spend my falls playing football, and my springs running track. I spend my weeknights doing homework and my weekends at movies, parties, and friends' houses. Where I tend to stray from the cliché of the typical teenager is in my ability to be myself. It is with thanks to three random individuals, people to whom I never thought I would owe anything, that I was reminded of the importance of never compromising who I am just to make somebody else happy.

Somehow, standing 6'3," 200 pounds, and playing two sports religiously makes me fall into the category of the stereotypical athlete. Historically, high school athletes are supposed to make jeering remarks at kids who do not play sports and act differently from them. They are even supposed to poke fun at the kids who play sports, but do not get the playing time. I was never one to agree with this sort of thing, however, I almost did back in my sophomore year, because all of the other athletes were doing it. Well, all of them except these three seniors on the football team. These were all guys that were going on to play college ball somewhere and it is to them that I owe what will probably be the greatest lesson that I ever learned as a teenager.

It was during assembly, and all I was concerned about was getting to my break period, which was next. That was when Mr. Stallworth, the director of the drama program at my school, got on stage and said that there would be a special performance by the chorus. The audience groaned, because they knew this meant that break would be cut short. The stage lights kicked on, the curtain dropped and I will *never* forget what I saw next. The three burliest, meanest, and best seniors on our football team had decided to join the chorus. Seeing them up there singing about being someone's buttercup made me want to laugh until the tears ran, but I quickly decided it would not be wise to do so for fear of what might happen to my little sophomore self come practice that afternoon. What overcame me next was a sensation of profound respect for those guys. They had crossed a line that the Hollywood gods and the higher-ups in society had dubbed as a taboo. I had always thought of them as being the stereotypical jocks, but seeing them belting their lungs out on stage proved to me that they were indeed more than just athletes.

What those seniors do not and may never know is that they changed me for a thousand lifetimes over. Seeing them up there with students who I never thought they would associate with made me realize that the only barriers the human race struggles to cross are the ones it creates. Since I saw that performance, I have made a point of talking to and hanging out with kids who I would not have normally associated myself with because of that invisible line. Today, I realize that if I had held myself back from different people, I would have been going along with the crowd. In essence, I would have compromised my own morals and values because someone else thought that they just were

> Seeing them up there singing about being someone's buttercup made me want to laugh until the tears ran.

not good enough. Thanks to those three seniors, I know that it is ok for me to be the king of my own life, instead of the pawn of someone else's.

Alex C. Wellman attends Middlebury College.

Camp Counseling and Community Service

Working with kids, and learning from them, are the unifying themes in this category. Aside from an essay about working at a homeless shelter (Essay 41), and another about volunteering in Bolivia during the winter break (Essay 45), all of the following describe tutoring or mentoring children. Yet as Essays 40 and 43 remind us, the kids often teach valuable and unexpected lessons of their own. If you are involved in tutoring or community service, keep the focus on what you gain from the experience rather than what you give.

40

WISDOM IN UNEXPECTED PLACES

Colleges love applicants who can learn from those who are different from them. By highlighting lessons from the mindset of elementary schoolers, author John Ivey Eagles finds an ingenious way of showing that he can learn from anyone. This sort of openness is solid gold to institutions that place a high value on diversity. Direct quotes from his "teachers," a couple of wayward kids, add the concrete detail (and humor) that make this essay sing. Says Eagles, "I found it very helpful to put out a draft that I felt pretty good about and then leave it alone for three or four days and come back to it as a reader, rather than as an editor, to see what I thought."

"Alfred and Bill: Role Models for Life"
by John Ivey Eagles

I have spent the past four summers working as a volunteer and counselor at a summer camp for kids ages four to ten. Each week presents new challenges, opportunities, and surprises and I am often amazed at the wit, intelligence, and confidence that elementary schoolers can display. This year, it was the bright faces of two campers, Alfred and Bill, that provided the most humor, challenge, and surprise to me and the rest of the staff. While no child consistently behaves in a manner appropriate for adults, they often offer interesting and unconventional insights that have inspired me to try to redefine how I view the world.

Bill's father wore NASCAR T-shirts, hats, and socks, and he spoke with a thick southern accent; despite Bill's short hair, one could not look at him without seeing (imagining?) the faintest hint of a mullet peeking out from underneath his cap. Upon being asked his name, Bill would reply, his boyish, drawling voice raised to a yell, "I'm Bill who doesn't play by the rules," and in a much softer tone, as if beginning an unrelated sentence, add, "too much." It clearly articulated a desire for freedom, while not creating an inconvenient commitment to rebellion. I support questioning authority, finding your own path, and civil disobedience. However, occasionally the status quo deserves credence. Thus I am striving to be "John Ivey who doesn't play by the rules . . . too much."

> **Dat would be *tewible* . . . *Can't* you call my dad's fwiend? He knows our famiwy vewy well.**

Like Bill, Alfred was not one to be hemmed in by society's expectations. With amazing consistency, he would come in to camp with his pants or shirt on backwards, and sometimes he would return from the bathroom missing one, the other, or both. He spoke with an astonishing vocabulary and a voice that sounded like he had just learned to talk. The incident with Alfred that I found most inspiring followed his biting another camper's ear. The camp director was talking to Alfred, who was in time-out, explaining that he would have to call Alfred's mom. "No! No! Dat would be *tewible* . . . *Can't* you call my dad's fwiend? He knows our famiwy vewy well." Alfred knew he was beaten, but he never gave up. After his dad's friend, he suggested two grandmothers before the director ended the conversation. His persistence was impressive. No matter how far out an idea might have seemed, he was ready to suggest it as an alternative to something he found disagreeable. I have found that too many people are willing to give up too quickly on issues that are important to them. Like Alfred, I believe we should always suggest even that which seems impossible or laughable. The effort might turn into a compromise, or even be the best idea in its own right.

Alfred and Bill each demonstrated admirable qualities. Their behavior showed that kids often approach problems and questions from angles older people cannot imagine. The way children absorb and react to life can provide others with interesting ideas on how they can take the best and most unusual notions of children and apply them to make their lives more interesting and fulfilling.

John Ivey Eagles attends Haverford College.

41

DOING WELL BY DOING GOOD

There have been a lot of bad essays about the problem of homelessness. This one stands out because it chronicles personal experiences. Not many high school students have the moxie, as author Marisa Kaley did, to step into the role of coordinating a homeless shelter, even if it was only for one night per month. The first two paragraphs skillfully set the scene as the reader realizes only gradually (or perhaps not until the third paragraph) that she has entered a homeless shelter. Says Marisa, "My advice is to have someone you trust proofread the essay. No matter how many times you read it yourself, there will be mistakes that you miss."

"Hillcrest House" by Marisa Kaley

After climbing a set of dull looking concrete stairs, I entered the kitchen/dining area, a small space complete with a television and curtained windows. Two tables were set for the guests. Down a hallway were two bathrooms, one marked "Men," the other, "Women." In the second room were two rows of freshly made twin beds, each topped with a neatly folded pair of pajamas, robe, and slippers. A partition separated each bed from the next, ensuring at least a bit of privacy. My parents and I began heating dinner as we waited for the guests to arrive.

And arrive they did, crammed into one lonely van. Many knew the routine, entering with a shy, almost whispered hello and then proceeding to the showers. One by one men and women took their seats at the dinner table, eagerly awaiting a home cooked meal. Each was extremely appreciative of our efforts as hosts and no one forgot to use their manners. From my conversations, the guests were cognizant of current affairs and television programs, wanting to watch a variety of different shows while they ate. Everyone was easy to engage in conversation and seemed to want to talk, need to talk.

In May of 2001, I became the Freedom Plains Presbyterian Church coordinator for the Dutchess County Coalition for the Homeless Overnight Shelter. The shelter provides temporary, emergency housing for adults who are homeless, based on the simple philosophy that no one should have to sleep on the street. Our church is responsible for the fourth Wednesday of each month. A group of volunteers cook a meal for fifteen people. Two additional volunteers bring the food to the shelter and spend the night, during which time they serve the meal, do laundry, make breakfast, and otherwise take care of the guests.

As coordinator, my most challenging responsibility until September of 2003 was finding volunteers to stay overnight at the shelter, since many adults work on Thursday mornings. I had been fortunate to find volunteers as I could not host overnight until I turned eighteen. I was, however, still able to make a difference in my community. I wrote letters, called church members, spoke about the program at church services, cooked meals, organized donations, wrote church Bulletin and Herald inserts, participated in a training program, and visited the shelter during the day. In September of 2003, the host hours changed from all night to eight to eleven p.m. but the other tasks remain. I have since hosted on three nights with my parents and have had a much easier time finding volunteers.

I have gained a great deal as a result of my involvement with the shelter. I am working to increase awareness of the needs of the men, women, and families who are homeless to our church members and also to my fellow high school students. Last November, I organized a very successful supply drive at my high school and on Thanksgiving eve delivered two van loads of towels, sheets, blankets, pajamas, slippers, and toiletries to the shelter. I hope that my next supply drive will be even more successful.

Many of the shelter guests are the working poor. I have learned that their problems go beyond not having a place to live and include substance abuse problems, mental illness, and past incarcerations. I have realized how sheltered my life has been and that I have taken so many things for granted. I like knowing that I can help people in my city and feel more grateful for the things that I am so lucky to have. I can prove to those older and to myself that I am responsible, can handle a challenge, and can help improve people's lives even though I am just one person, and a teenager at that. I have been raised with the idea that those who have received talents and benefits need to give back. I am lucky to have had and to continue to have experiences that enable me to gain new perspectives and to develop additional skills. I have received so much more than I have given in volunteering in my community.

Marisa Kaley attends Wellesley College.

MAKE ME BARF

We won't spoil the final twist of this essay, but suffice it to say that sometimes an essay merely needs to be a story well told. The personality of the author, Sarah Lindsay, comes through loud and clear in her description of being a counselor at summer camp. Instead of lapsing into heavy-handed moralizing about camp and everything that it taught her, she shows the importance of camp by relating an anecdote. In the process of revealing her care for the campers and her camaraderie with the counselors, she demonstrates an equally important trait: the ability to laugh at herself.

Essay by Sarah Lindsay

"I don't do throw-up."

My own words were coming back to haunt me as I heard one of my campers yell, "Ewww, Bridger threw up." I froze. I forced myself to turn around and look. I glanced quickly, then immediately looked away. I stopped breathing through my nose so I wouldn't be able to smell it. I was horrified.

The one thing that I hate most is throw-up. Looking at it causes me to gag. Earlier that week I had been talking to my friend, Molly, who was a counselor in Cabin 3. She was telling me how she had had to clean up her camper's vomit.

"I would *never* be able to do that," I said.

"Well I didn't have a choice," Molly replied.

"I just…I don't do throw-up," I retorted.

Working at Camp Seafarer on the "Crystal Coast" of North Carolina for the summer was like a dream to me. I had gone there as a camper, and my experiences there have influenced my life greatly. The counselors were so supportive, and it seemed like they never ran out of energy. I was excited to have the opportunity to affect someone's life the way my counselors had affected mine. Being a counselor, though, was more work than I had anticipated. I was always exhausted, and it was hard to keep giving 100 percent of myself twenty-four hours a day. In the end, however, it was worth staying up with a homesick camper or saying a longer goodnight to the shyest girl to help bring her out of her shell. It was just so much responsibility trying to keep twelve ten-year-olds safe, while trying to help them have a great summer. Now my responsibility was spreading to the one thing I dreaded most, cleaning up throw-up.

I looked around at Bridger who looked like she was either laughing or crying. I assumed she was crying since she had just gotten sick. Then I noticed my co-counselors, Jessie and Liz, standing around. I looked at them, waiting for them to take the initiative and start to clean up. But they didn't even move towards it. Then Jessie made a move.

"I'll take Bridger to the health center," she said

Darn, I thought, *I should have volunteered to do that.* I glanced at Liz.

"Sarah, I'm busy. Why don't you clean it up?"

I couldn't believe it! I was stuck with doing the one thing I have always said I would never do. *All right, I can do this,* I said to myself. *What to get first?...Paper towels!* I went into the bathroom to find some, but we were out. *Okay, it's going to be okay. I'll just go to the cabin next door.* I got some paper towels from Cabin 9 and hurried back to my cabin. As I approached my enemy, the throw-up, I noticed a lot of girls were crowded around me laughing.

"This is not funny girls, Bridger's sick," I told them and they backed up, still giggling softly.

> **I looked around at Bridger who looked like she was either laughing or crying.**

All right here goes nothing, I thought as I started to fling paper towels down on top of the vomit. I then squeezed my eyes shut and went in for the kill, picking up the mess. I picked up the paper towels as fast as I could and threw them into the trashcan. I had done it! *I can handle this job; the late nights, exhausting days and all the puke that comes with it,* I celebrated. Then I noticed that now the whole cabin was laughing.

"Sarah!" Bridger exclaimed, "The throw-up was fake!"

I learned, that summer, that with responsibility comes great rewards, such as my campers' hysterical laughing over the fake throw up. Every smile and every hug made the draining job worth it.

Sarah Lindsay attends Vanderbilt University.

43

ASKED TO TUTOR, SHE BECOMES THE LEARNER

The following essay provides an excellent example of how to begin with a quote from the middle of a conversation and then loop back to the beginning of it to fill in the details. Author Lauren Mamer opens with the high point of the conversation with her ten-year-old pupil—a discussion of Nickelback. She then fills in necessary background information, goes back once more to Nickelback to begin the third paragraph, and then reaches all the way back to the beginning of the conversation in the fourth paragraph. The conclusion is also worth noting. Instead of waxing eloquent about what she learns from her experience, Lauren leaves herself "a good deal humbled" with no pat answers for next time.

Essay by Lauren Mamer

"Hey, Nickelback, I know that band. You like them?" I ask, leaning over Chipu's shoulder to look at the stickers and pictures she has all over the front matter of her binder.

"Yeah," she looks up at me with her big brown eyes and smiles, clearly as relieved as I am to find something in common. It's my first day tutoring at Webster Middle School. I'm working with Team Prime Time, an organization that provides a place for children to go after school where their parents can pick them up after work. It is housed in a large, dimly lit classroom, where tables are arranged in a haphazard circles around the room. Students are spread out, either in small groups or alone, around the tables, backpacks thrown down next to them, hunched over homework sheets or sharing textbooks. The linoleum floors in the big room make every whisper echo, so with twenty-five students trying to avoid doing their homework at the same time, quiet moments are few and far between.

"Oh that's cool," I say. "I listen to Nickelback all the time. What's your favorite song?" The conversation moves haltingly on from there as we both become more comfortable. Who knew it could be this hard to introduce myself to a ten-year-old? When I walked into Team Prime Time, I had no idea what to expect. I had not tutored young kids before, but I assumed there couldn't be much that I wouldn't be able to explain to a sixth grader. I later realized just how wrong that assumption had been. The coordinator, Mark, helped me get started by pointing out Chipu, a small, shy-looking girl with curly, dark hark hair tamed into braids, peeking out of a navy-blue hooded sweatshirt.

I walked over as she was doing her math homework. Actually, she had her book open to the correct page and was staring at her math homework (oh how well I know *that* feeling). "Hi, I'm Lauren," I said, as I discovered that 'I'm here to tutor you' can be an awkward idea to try and convey in a first conversation. After chatting about music for a bit, we got to work.

> I, on the other hand, found myself a good deal humbled with a new ten-year-old friend who has great music taste.

"So...what is your assignment?"

Chipu pointed to the required problems on the page. There were faded pencil check marks in the margin next to them from a former student who evidently had done the same assignment. Looking down at the page I quickly read the problem.

"Okay, it looks like they're asking you to find which of these numbers in the list is a prime number," I said. "Right," I immediately thought to myself, "read the directions back to her; clearly that's not the problem." Luckily for me, she let it slide.

"So," my valiant second attempt began, "did your teacher go over how to do anything like this in class?"

Chipu shook her head.

"Okay, well a prime number is a number whose only factors are one and itself," I said. She looked at me blankly. "Does that make sense?" She shook her head no.

"Do you know what a factor is?"

"No," she answered simply.

"Oh, okay. Well a factor is a number that divides evenly into another number with nothing left over. So let's try 4. 2 is a factor of 4 because it goes into 4 exactly twice with nothing left over, see?"

"Sure," she said, nodding.

"So a prime number is a number like 5 where only the numbers that are factors are 1 and itself, 5."

She nodded.

"So is 6 a prime number?"

"Yes," she said decisively.

"Are you sure?"

"No," she responded. Clearly if yes made me second guess her response then no must be the correct answer. I remember so clearly using that trick when I was younger. I tried to explain it a different way to little Chipu but received a similar response. Clearly the concept of prime numbers was a bit beyond the Chipu-Lauren team, so back to factoring for now.

"So those factor things. Do you know how to find them?"

"No," she shook her head emphatically.

"Okay, you divide the number whose factors you want to find by the numbers below it and see if they go in evenly with no remainder. So if you have the number 8, you divide it by 1, then by two..." Eventually we made it all the way up to 8 this way. "So, 1, 2, 4, and 8 are factors of 8, see?"

Chipu nodded seriously. During the following pause we looked at each other and I realized my teaching skills were going to take a lot more practice before I made much sense to listen to.

"That didn't make any sense at all did it," I asked her.

"Nope," she responds honestly.

"Okay, let's try again," I said, trying to think of a better way to explain something so abstract and wondering how I had ever been able to grasp it.

By the end of "homework time," although we hadn't quite finished the math homework, she'd managed to get enough of a grasp of factoring, so she knew how to do the assignment. I, on the other hand, found myself a good deal humbled with a new ten-year-old friend who has great music taste.

Lauren Mamer attends Stanford University.

44

RUBBING SHOULDERS WITH PRE-SCHOOLERS

There is nothing easy about the question below, which comes from a scholarship application at the University of North Carolina at Chapel Hill. Even harder is answering it in 269 words, a feat that author Jillian Nadell manages to pull off. Jillian deftly captures the world of small children, and her role in it, without oversimplifying or trying to give it phony meaning. These are kids—exuberant, irrational, lovable kids. Her ability to describe them in minute detail is a sure tip-off that she is having a good time. Says Jillian, "The best advice I can give is to really make the essay represent you and your voice."

Essay by Jillian Nadell

Describe an occasion or activity in which you used your time, energy, and talents to serve someone other than yourself. What was your motivation for this service? Did you gain anything from the experience? Did those you served gain anything?

"I am the smartest boy in the world," one of the small boys in the class had said one day. So I asked him, "How do you know that you are the smartest boy in the world?" Then his face began to crinkle and a little angry voice replied: "I just told you! I know, because *I am* the smartest boy in the world." I could not believe that I was talking to a four-year-old.

When I walk in each morning, there is usually one smiling, and another crying for his mother, one unfortunately picking his nose, and another "violently licking" a fake

> **The best advice I can give is to really make the essay represent you and your voice.**

head of lettuce. But it's not just the cute variety of children that motivate me to volunteer at the Temple Emanuel Pre-School Camp in Greensboro, North Carolina, each summer; it is the joy that I gain from seeing their faces light up when I walk in the room. It is a great feeling to know that you can make a child's day, just by telling him/her a story about fire ants.

Ralph Waldo Emerson said, "It is one of the most beautiful compensations of life that no man can sincerely try to help another without helping himself." From me, they gain a friend and a teacher. They remember, at least for a while, that I was the one who read them stories, and taught them songs, and pretended to be a princess or dinosaur along with them. And every time I run into them I receive a huge hug and kiss, and that in itself is enough compensation and motivation to continue going back each summer.

Jillian Nadell attends the University of North Carolina at Chapel Hill.

45

A DIFFERENT KIND OF CHRISTMAS

Author Mary Plumb tells a remarkable story. Instead of a traditional Christmas vacation, her family packs its bags and heads off to work in a Bolivian orphanage. Mary vividly portrays the joy she found there and skillfully contrasts it with the materialistic Christmas she left behind. It would have been easy for her to lapse into heavy moralizing, but Mary lets her experiences show everything that needs to be said. The essay is punctuated with vivid vocabulary—words like "grumbling," "pranced," and "gallantly"—that add texture to the narrative without making it seem thesaurusy.

Essay by Mary Plumb

"I do it for the joy it brings 'cause I'm a joyful girl. 'Cause the world owes us nothing, we owe each other the world."—Ani Difranco ("Joyful Girl")

In the fall of my junior year, my mother announced that she had signed us up for a mission trip to Bolivia for Christmas break. My first thought was, "That's impossible! But I wanted a new computer and some new clothes. How will we ever get all the gifts down there? Our suitcases will be too heavy!" I was careful not to say these selfish things out loud. We—my mother, my three older siblings, and I—would be working as volunteers at the Amistad Mission in Cochubamba, Bolivia, a city of over two million people that none of us had ever heard of. Were we really going to spend Christmas working in an orphanage in one of the poorest countries in the world? For weeks leading up to the trip, I worried about what I would do there.

The minute we arrived at Amistad (the Friendship Mission), my fears dissolved. The children must have heard the grumbling engine and grinding of the bus tires on the gravel road, for as the primitive bus turned the corner, I could see no fewer than fifty sets of luminous, brown eyes welcoming us. Immediately sprinting toward us, one little girl, Naomi, leapt into my arms and kissed my face before even saying, "Hola!" Never before have I felt so welcomed by anyone—and these were complete strangers! Excited by our arrival, the children directed us to the community center, really a basketball court, which had been decorated with a Nativity scene made of crumpled manila paper. Dressed in tomato-red traditional Bolivian skirts, the teenagers narrated the Christmas Pageant as the younger children performed. Small native children were dressed as Mary, Joseph, Jesus, the three Wise Men, and the shepherds. The smallest girls pranced in full white dresses with masks made of cotton balls to make them look like sheep. Having obviously rehearsed for a long time, they proudly serenaded us with Christmas carols in Spanish, their joyous enthusiasm unbridled.

> My first response was to feel sorry for him: surely he was ashamed of his deformity and the need to wear this weird gizmo.

One day, I noticed a boy named Marcelo with a strange-looking apparatus of red plastic, rubber bands, and metal covering his face. My first response was to feel sorry for him: surely he was ashamed of his deformity and the need to wear this weird gizmo. But he came strolling up to the community center without a worry in the world, and as I approached to comfort him, he unleashed a huge smile inviting me to come outside to play soccer with him and his friends. No one else seemed to notice or even care about the brace installed to fix Marcelo's cleft palate.

The mission residences included ten houses, "casas," each housing a "family" of eight children, with a "mamà" and "tìa" as caretakers. One afternoon I was invited to Casa San Francisco to eat lunch with one of the "familias." As guest of honor, I sat at the head of the long table with ten children sitting along each side. Over the wailing of the babies and bickering of the teenagers, the "tìas" attempted to say grace. Next, they passed out plates of rice, each with cooked carrots, peas and a small piece of flavorless chicken. As I was served my plate, three-year old Maria spilled her apple juice all over my food. The ensuing silence told me that they expected me to be upset. Knowing not enough food was left in the pot to replenish my plate, Eduardo, the eldest boy, gallantly offered me his. When I refused, he switched the plates anyway. During my weeklong stay, I noticed acts of generosity and kindness both large and small. These people had few material possessions to give, but during my week there, I received gifts beyond the tangible and became very attached to all of the children at the Mission.

Working hard from sunup to sundown was not exactly my original idea of how to spend my coveted Christmas holiday, but the week I spent working side by side with my family remains one of the best experiences of my life. We arranged activities for the kids—arts and crafts, trips to the park, and sports games. On Christmas day, when we helped the Amistad children host a fun-filled party for families living in dire conditions just beyond the Mission fence, our guests were overjoyed. The faces of both parents and children lit up as I handed each of them one simple present; filled with an appreciation for such simple things, these children deserved so much more, yet they were happy with what they had.

Not until several weeks after our return did I realize, "Hey, I didn't get that computer I had wanted so much, nor the new jeans." At the same time, I realized that I might have missed it all had I not gone on our Bolivia trip. The gifts I received last December from the orphaned children of Amistad added not a single pound to the luggage I carried home, for the lasting gifts they gave me were those of joy, of friendship, of growing up.

Mary Plumb attends the University of Texas at Austin.

46

TO CAMP, THIS TIME AS A COUNSELOR

Author Dana Waskover's essay starts like one thousand other summer-camp essays. But her ordinary beginning sets the stage for an unexpected twist. When she goes back to camp as a counselor, she finds out that life is a lot less fun and a lot more work than she remembered. Instead of exhilaration, she finds disillusionment—and a much more interesting essay topic than if she had had a wonderful time. The essay sparkles in part because Dana lets the story unfold without too much foreshadowing, which allows the reader to experience the letdown with her.

Essay by Dana Leigh Waskover

The summer of 2004 represented a meaningful and eye opening experience for me. I spent the summer as a counselor at an overnight camp, Raquette Lake Girls Camp, where I had attended as a camper from 1998 through 2002.

This picturesque camp is located on beautiful Raquette Lake, one of the larger natural lakes in the Adirondack Mountains of New York State. Seeing the lake brought back fond memories of the endless hours of fun and play I had as a camper. I remembered my first year as a camper and the challenge of passing the very essential deep-water test. Participation in all activities on the lake depended on whether or not I passed the test, which I did successfully.

The summers at Raquette Lake were a time of relaxation and play, of carefree days and nights in a setting of camaraderie and much happiness.

So it was with great joy and excitement that I returned to Raquette Lake as a junior counselor in June 2004. This was my first real job and I was thrilled to be back at camp. Enthusiasm for the camp experience heightened when I arrived several days before the campers. I learned that I would be assigned to live in a bunk for fourteen nine-year-old girls and that I would be spending my days as a swim instructor and lifeguard at the lake waterfront. I looked forward to this experience.

When the campers arrived, I realized that I would have a substantially different experience than I had expected. After one day I came to the sobering realization that I was not a camper any longer. I was hired help. I was expected to work from early morning through bedtime. I was responsible for the total well-being of my campers. This included waking them in the morning, getting them washed and ready for activities, helping them follow a healthy diet, overcome their homesickness, and smooth out their relationships with friends. I was friend, mother, and disciplinarian to fourteen children.

The lake, which had represented challenges and joy to me, became my workplace. I was stationed on the dock from after breakfast until dinnertime. My only break was for lunch, when I joined my campers and served them their food.

As a camper, if it were too cold or rainy, I would skip the lake activities and relax with my friends, all snuggled up in our bunk. As a counselor I could not do that. The summer of 2004 was one of the coldest and rainiest in camp history and I did not have the option to say that I did not want to stand on the dock because I was cold or wet. I endured the weather because I had made a commitment to the camp to work for the entire season.

The change in my status, from camper to counselor, being responsible for waterfront safety and the happiness of my campers, was both a sobering and maturing experience. I had to grow up. I had to take my responsibility seriously. All this responsibility, the hard days and long nights, did provide some satisfying relationships with my campers and other counselors, but the salary was not gratifying. I earned $750.00 for the entire summer's work.

> After one day I came to the sobering realization that I was not a camper any longer. I was hired help.

In retrospect, the summer of 2004 was an awakening for me. I know that I have the perseverance to complete a task that I agree to do, no matter how arduous or uncomfortable it may be. I believe this strength will serve me well during my college years, as I work hard at my studies, face many challenges, and begin to identify a career that will bring me emotional, intellectual, and financial rewards. Somehow, I feel that Raquette Lake helped me evolve from child to adult. Just in time for college.

Dana Leigh Waskover attends the University of Tampa.

Racial or Cultural Differences

If there is one kind of essay topic guaranteed to succeed, this is it. Colleges value diversity, and a student from a background different from the norm, especially a student who is willing to write about that fact, will add to the richness of campus life. We should hasten to note that essays on racial or cultural differences are not the exclusive province of minority students, as Essays 54 and 57 demonstrate. The biggest advantage to essays in this category is that they hit close to home. If you're writing about your race or cultural identity, you're writing about yourself.

47
CHATTING IT UP WITH A BAOBAB TREE

For exotic appeal, it is hard to top the following essay from author Prince Agbo. Prince is of African descent but grew up in France and French Guiana, and he uses the device of a palm tree talking to a baobab tree to represent the tensions in his multicultural identity. (Baobabs, native to Africa, are massive trees with trunks up to sixty feet in diameter.) Any writer can use personification; simply choose two objects to represent facets of a personality, sides of an issue, etc., pretend they are people, and let them go at it. The device generally works best when, as in Prince's essay, the objects have a common tie (such as both being trees) that makes the conversation plausible.

"Who Am I?" by Prince Agbo

As I am filing all those college applications, the question keeps coming back to me. Who am I? Where do I come from? Where am I heading?

Am I African? Am I French? Am I Caribbean? Or…soon an American college student?

As I reflect on my African roots, my French and Caribbean upbringings, and now, my new life in America, I could compare myself with a palm tree, being laughed at by an African baobab.

I will always remain deeply rooted in my African ground. Actually I am a palm tree here—a very hard to knock down palm tree. My neighbor is a friendly Baobab. He is my companion on this red ground. He is so tall and so powerful I sometimes get jealous. He is impressive, also. Who am I? Well, he may be tall, powerful, impressive, strong…whatever; at least I, the palm tree, did also grow up in France, unlike Baobab who will never see the French sun. Baobab does not like me thinking that way. He gets mad at me. Anyway, as he says, he absolutely does not need the French sun. His is the brightest, the yellowest, and the warmest sun on earth: the African sun!

> Baobab does not like my reasoning. Neither what I say, nor the calm I say it with.

The African sun has those qualities, for sure. But, dear Baobab, I also know about them. Indeed, it is the African sun that, a long time ago, made my first seed grow. It is also this African sun that gave me that strong color, and the red of my sap. Dear Baobab, I have experienced the virtues of the African sun. But I have also experienced the virtues of travel. Though I remain the same palm tree.

Baobab does not appreciate my comment. Blowing, bowing, his devil eye confirms his saying: the French sun would never make me as tall as him. He is right. I am not that tall, certainly not as tall as he is. But my branches are wide, so wide that I can embrace different cultures from all over the world. Plus, dear Baobab, may I mention that your flowers lack some vitality...some brightness? I keep on considering your flowers, and they definitely cannot compete with mine: mine are brightly, joyfully colored; they actually come from French Guyana, to be precise. I am the only palm tree with rainbow flowers welcoming so many butterflies.

Baobab does not like my reasoning. Neither what I say, nor the calm I say it with.

"Who do you think you are?" he asks me, screaming.

I am me. I am always the same. Wherever I go, whatever I go through. Today, my flowers are covered with Vermont snow. Tomorrow, who knows...? For sure I am small, but I am rich, rich with those different weathers I go through, with those new experiences that each season and each trip brings me. Baobab stares at me; he looks confused. Then he bows until he reaches my height and, delicately, he uses his height to protect me from the snowfall. What's next? Baobab is curious.

Well, dear Baobab, for now I am still a bit sleepy, but soon will come spring and my flowers will blossom, paving the way for a new adventure: America!

Prince Agbo attends Cornell University (NY).

48

TWO BIRDS WITH ONE ESSAY

Though technically about an activity, this essay speaks most eloquently about the applicant's ethnic identity and his dedication to it. There is both passion and precision in his description, and like many good essays about ethnicity, Romit Bhattacharya uses it to dispel stereotypes (e.g., "speaking Indian") while showing, not telling, the importance to him of his Indian identity. The fact that the activity described in the essay occurs at 11:24 p.m. makes it all the more real. This version was the author's fourth try at an activities essay. "I continued to write essays until I felt that what I wrote corresponded with what I truly felt," says Bhattacharya. "I truly felt a sense of frustration and exasperation, but also a deep commitment to the cause."

"Activities Essay" by Romit Bhattacharya

I'm tired and a little bit desperate. My clock angrily glares at me through its neon green dial. It's 11:24. The biology exam tomorrow will be murder. I resolutely pass over my textbook, and instead return to the screen where Pandit Jasraj stares back at me. I run through a quick checklist in my mind: I sent out the emails to the members, I typed up the biography for the program, I bought Styrofoam cups for refreshments. Homestretch. I tilt the graphic of the vocal maestro just enough to look funky next to the bold text, "Pandit Jasraj, Live In Concert!" O God, WHY am I doing this? All I want is some sleep.

Why am I the first person called to make flyers? Why do I even do it? It seems hopeless. Another event comes and goes in an auditorium we rent out for the night. Everyone listens to some music and discusses it over a samosa or two, but our goal is not furthered. India Center still does not have the funds it needs to buy itself an address, a place that all the varied and fragmented Indian communities can jointly call their "home." Here they will cease to be Bengalis, Marathis, Tamilians,

Gujarathis, or Punjabis. They will not identify themselves as Hindu, Muslim, Buddhist, Sikh, Jain, Jewish, or Christian. Here the community will build its own little microcosm to fit into the majestic mosaic of New York.

My friends often ask me if I speak "Indian" at home. That would make it all so much easier, and sometimes I wish there were one such language. But then it is that very diversity which gives Indian culture its multilayered richness. And although it means working extra hours to rally the community together, to shake them up and remind them to vote, to wake them up to the truth of harmonizing all their regional tongues to sing in one unified voice, I am willing to put in that effort. I want that united Indian voice to speak to every name on the membership list, and reach out and address each one's concerns. I want that voice to resonate in public parades and diversity shows, as well as reach into the corridors of Washington so that change can be brought about effectively. I want to strengthen and support the trembling immigrant voices with a vigorous chorus of "The Star Spangled Banner." Yes, I am willing to make my flyers bright and flashy, and send my emails with capitalized entreaties, and look out on that auditorium to see if the seats are packed and the donation boxes are jammed full.

> **My friends often ask me if I speak "Indian" at home. That would make it all so much easier.**

So I do not resent it when Mr. Ralph D'Souza calls me and asks me to pick up the famous Kathak dancer Rachnaji from the train station, or check the sound system on the stage. I put on my India Center volunteer badge, slip on a dark blue blazer, and go cheerfully on my way.

Romit Bhattacharya attends the University of Pennsylvania.

49

FIGHTING THE CULTURE OF HIP-HOP

Autobiographical essays are solid gold when the writer can talk about something other than the affluent suburban upbringing typical of most students at selective colleges. Author Danielle Brown writes about aspects of the African American community, and in the process, illustrates the challenges she has overcome. She complements her critique of the culture of hip-hop with her dedication to enduring role models within the African American community, which she illustrates with her anecdote about the young girl she is tutoring.

Essay by Danielle Brown

"Lynching was ritualistic public square violence, part of a sordid history of white criminality" (Hakim Hasan). Looking out of the car window onto Crenshaw Boulevard, I do not see an angry mob cloaked in white, dancing on one of the street corners. Nor do I see towering willows ornamented with dangling bodies. As I look out of my window I see young African American boys flaunting diamond earrings that make their earlobes droop; young men and women bumping the latest "Jay-Z" song while bringing their twenty-inch rim-spinning Escalades to a halt at the red light. In the past, African Americans had coped with several acts of hatred, particularly lynching. Today my community is facing a new dilemma—one that is self-inflicted and a killer among African American youth. The mortality rate caused by "hip-hop lynching" increases everyday in my neighborhood. Illiteracy, materialism, degradation of women, and praise of drugs and sex are preached to youth through negative hip-hop music, which causes them to carry these immoral ideologies over to their everyday lives.

The immoral ideologies that are taking over my community verify society's blind following after incompetent leaders. As Carter G. Woodson once said, "If you allow a people to control the way you think, you do not have to assign them an inferior status, if necessary, they will seek it themselves." To escape these negative influences, I have joined College Bound, a program designed to prepare minority youth for college and leadership in their community. As of now, I am participating in the Rites of Passage, a program through College Bound designed to prepare seniors for college and adulthood. Although I approve of College Bound's goals to reach out to minority youth and guide them to academic success, there are not enough programs available to help the growing number of troubled minority children.

The community in which I live has had a significant influence on my outlook on life. Turning away from the misleading hip-hop "role models" that many of my contemporaries admire, I look up to the individuals who actually made a difference in their communities; leaders such as Marian Wright Edelman, Malcolm X, and Carter G. Woodson. Although I have found means of escaping immoral ideologies that are invading my community, I have chosen not to become a refugee of my neighborhood, but to give back what I can.

Currently, I am tutoring for a junior high remedial English class at my school. With our instructed trips to the library, I have gone beyond the expected vocabulary reviews and grammar sessions, stretching my abilities as a tutor to also assist as a mentor.

> As I look out of my window I see young African American boys flaunting diamond earrings that make their earlobes droop.

As we all know, in every rosebush there are thorns. From the moment I stepped into the paper-strewn English class, I knew the boisterous creator of this tumult would be difficult to work with. Although Veronica's aggressive and unruly temperament in the classroom intimidated her peers, this wild chimpanzee morphed into a tranquil panda while studying in the library. It was while I was helping Veronica with her Martin Luther King Jr. project that I learned something shocking. Despite his mass popularity and having read his biography, Veronica knew nothing about Dr. King. Straying away from the project, I went into depth about how important it is for young African Americans to know their history and those that shaped it. Although I eventually gave her some basic facts about Dr. King, I used Veronica's carefree attitude towards her project to indicate to her that she was not doing well in school not because of an inability to achieve but her unwillingness to succeed.

By working with younger children and influencing them to go beyond what hip-hop music preaches to them and to work further than the limits they set for themselves, I feel that I am able to affect the outcome of many lives that would have easily been sucked into the downward spiral brought on by negative messages given through hip-hop music. Volunteering for a summer camp at Pan Pacific Park in the past was a truly rewarding experience because of the affect I had on the youth in my neighborhood. My volunteering and current tutoring experiences have encouraged me to continue working with youth in my neighborhood, and I plan to continue to reach out to the youth in the community I will reside in throughout my college life. At my future college I intend to major in archaeology and minor in English.

Danielle Brown attends Pitzer College.

50

WHEN TWO WORLDS COLLIDE

Anybody whose parents were immigrants can relate to—or write an essay about—living in two worlds. With the premium that colleges place on diversity, such essays generally hit the mark. In this essay, the author uses a phone conversation to introduce the reader to the way her American and Korean lives intersect. She adds depth by giving the reader a peek inside the Korean culture, at least with respect to the importance of speaking good Korean. "The trick is to be both while being one," she says, a pithy way of describing the challenge of living in two worlds at once.

Essay by Anonymous

"Hello 엄마! No. I'm at the movies. 극장! 조금있으면가." Translation: "Mom! No. I'm at the movies. The movies! I'll be home soon." If I'm with my friends, someone will ask: "What was that?" And I answer, "I was speaking in Korean to my mom." This answer is never enough, as I have learned. Only after a few rounds of saying odd phrases for their amusement is everyone's curiosity satisfied. "How do you say _____?" they say. I answer patiently in Korean. I am bilingual. Most of my friends have witnessed my trait in action many times. I speak English at school, and mostly Korean at home, but when the two are intertwined, the English and Korean are hard to separate. My internal Korean and the English, that has perhaps become internal now, blend smoothly. The blending of both languages occurs quite often and quite naturally, in and out of the house.

The problems arise when these two worlds start to fight with each other. One fights the other for more attention, and both struggle to pull me in and own me completely. Then these two different worlds can be quite confusing, especially when I blurt something out at the spur of the moment and it comes out in the wrong language. I might roll my eyes and with a sigh say, "Duh," to my parents when they don't really understand the connotation. Or I might yell, "안 돼!" (No!) while arguing with my friends. The fine line shrinks even thinner. Balancing is the challenge. When you are immersed in two completely separate worlds simultaneously, it is not a dichotomy or an absolute division. The trick is to be both while being one. The two entities are completely different but never alone. That is who I am. I have had to master this skill because I am bilingual and because I am a Korean living in America.

> **I speak English at school, and mostly Korean at home, but when the two are intertwined, the English and Korean are hard to separate.**

In the Korean realm, those who do not speak Korean can be rejected, ridiculed, or even ostracized. There is an unspoken expectation that a Korean must be able to speak his or her native language and still speak English. Although bad English is understandable, bad Korean is humiliating. Pronunciation, intonation, and grammar must be flawless. If it's not perfect, you are labeled a sell out or a "Twinkie," one who has yellow skin but feels white on the inside. So essentially, you are excluded from both. My friend Joel is the ultimate "Twinkie." Sadly for him, he speaks no Korean and his English is bad too; it has a tinge of an accent that shouldn't be there. Joel struggles with being "too American" or "too Korean" or not enough of both. He knows as well as I do that proficiency in both languages is very important: English is essential to live life in America, yet Korean is essential to retain our culture. That day when Joel asked me how I "found myself," I told him: "It's a blending of the two without compromising either, and I really think I've found the perfect balance. I'm in the best place that I could ever be: in both."

The author attends Duke University.

51

"I WANTED TO BE TRUTHFUL"

A great essay doesn't need to be glitzy. This one begins with a simple-but-effective rhetorical question and ends with a repetition of the same question. In between, the essay consists mainly of a retelling of life experiences, but the directness of the prose makes the story interesting and even poignant. The author's use of the third person in the first part of the essay is a subtle way of signaling her shyness to reveal such intimate details—a touch that adds both charm and sincerity. The paragraph that begins with "Looking at my application" reveals the likes and dislikes of a typical teenager and thereby shows (rather than tells) that she has risen above her challenging circumstances.

Essay by Nicole Clarke

So there's a girl. You've read her application, but do you really know her? You know that she works hard and that she dreams of going to Princeton, but does that count as knowing her? I'll tell you a bit about her. Then, you decide.

She was born on the small Caribbean island of Trinidad. Bright-eyed and smiling, she came to America with her mother, having no idea of the hard times she would have to face. She lives with her mother, and her father has never played a significant role in her life.

This girl has had hard times, especially on the home level. Her relationship with her mother has deteriorated to the point where it is non-existent. She has had to make decisions about the "big stuff" on her own. She has had to deal with the financial troubles of a low-class single parent family, the drama that is a prerequisite to being a teenager, and the lack of sleep that is sure to hit after pulling too many all-nighters.

*****

Surprise, surprise, I am this girl. But don't worry; my life has by no means been all bad. I play an active role at school serving as both

National Honor Society and Senior Class president. I spend my summers at math and science programs, and this year I've spent my free time working on an independent research project, and yes, to me these activities are fun!

This past summer I spent six weeks in Socorro, New Mexico, studying astronomy, physics, calculus, and computer programming at the New Mexico Institute of Mining and Technology. Aside from its academic benefits, the Summer Science Program or SSP also gave me room to grow as a person. Forging new friendships and developing certain characteristics that will stay with me throughout the rest of my life, this summer for me was when I "grew up."

People for years have been throwing terms like "mature" and "responsible" at me, but only now do I truly understand the breadth of these words. I am responsible for my own actions, my successes and my accomplishments, my failures and my mistakes, my hopes and my dreams, and the path by which I choose to reach them.

Looking at my application there are many things you won't know about me. I hate ice cream. I love meteor showers. I don't understand basketball. I cherish rainy nights. And, I believe in true love! I know one pair of socks can be worn more than once, although four times is pushing it. I absolutely adore bowling shoes, comfort and cuteness all packed into a "rental." I swear by true friends; they are angels in disguise. Sweatshirts should be an unchangeable part of the worldwide uniform. And snow days rock!

I know one pair of socks can be worn more than once, although four times is pushing it.

So my life has not been easy. But, as I continue on this path to what lies ahead, I believe—and invite you to do the same—that life will be what you make of it. You cry sometimes, you laugh sometimes, and many times you'll be ready to give up, but you will reap the rewards of your hard work and looking back, your personal growth will make it all worth it.

So tell me, do you know me now?

Nicole Clarke attends Princeton University.

52

REFLECTING ON THE FACE IN THE MIRROR

Most people can remember a reflective moment when they stopped to look at their face in the mirror. Why not write about it? Author Katie Hua describes such a moment as she pondered her disappointment at being ineligible for National Merit Finalist recognition due to her immigration status. The essay includes several elements of good storytelling: an anecdotal beginning, a flashback, and then a sound (*Whoosh*) that brings her back to the present. "My advice is to give yourself tons of time on the essay," says Hua. "The essay is supposed to show admissions people who you really are, and if you are frustrated and pressed for time, it probably won't reveal the real you."

Essay by Katie Hua

I stood still, facing the giant bathroom mirror. Whoosh. The bathroom door swung open, and a group of girls came in, chatting and laughing. I stared into the mirror. A blonde, clearly more than a head taller than I, strolled past, reaching for the paper towel dispenser. Another stocky redhead briskly walked into the stall right behind me. The two different hair colors contrasted sharply with my own under the fluorescent lights. We were all wearing the same cardigan sweater, the same blue plaid skirt, and the same brown leather shoes. My uniform was impeccable, as I had been interviewed by a newspaper not fifteen minutes before. The girl that stared back at me from the mirror was short and skinny. She had a long face with dark brown eyes, black hair, and a big forehead. She was a red belt in Tae Kwon Do; she was a co-captain of Robotics; she was the founder of the school's American Mathematical Competition team. But she was also an international student.

"When can I stop being an international student?" I asked myself exasperatedly. My memory flashed to the interview. A reporter came in and asked me some questions for the local newspaper after I had just been announced as a National Merit Semifinalist. I remembered how she asked me what it felt like to be a semifinalist. I said I was surprised and excited. I smiled a lot and said the things a good student was supposed to say, but what I neglected to mention was that I did not qualify to be a finalist because I lacked the proper immigration documents.

But I did not lack anything else. Were my other qualifications not good enough?

In the back of my head I remembered my first step onto the land of the United States at the age of twelve. I remembered how thrilled I was to be able to listen and finally understand a casual conversation in English; I remembered my American counterparts' excitement when they learned how to say some basic expressions in Chinese; I remembered how we traded stories of growing up on opposite sides of the globe. We laughed at each other's strange accents and customs; we learned from each other's experiences.

My mind wandered farther and farther back down memory lane to China as I stood still. It was as if I could still see my cousins and myself through the mirror, running around wildly while our blindfolded grandfather, with his hands grabbing the air and his back stooped, tried to catch us. Memories of grandpa brought warmth into my heart. I smiled, knowing that a part of him has been passed down to me; and, though he was no longer of this world, he would see through my dark-brown eyes and feel through my youthful hands.

Whoosh. The door swung open again, and the two girls walked out, still talking and laughing. I took a deep breath and decided that it was time for me to go. I ambled out and saw a beautiful sunny autumn afternoon through the window. One of my friends ran up to me, patted my shoulder, and cheerfully said, "C'mon, let's go do some homework and chat outside." "Sure," I said as I grinned back. "Hey! Let's see who can get there first!" She ran past me playfully, leaving behind her a trail of laughter. "Wait!" I yelled after her as I hurried to catch up: "Don't forget we still need to figure out that one calc problem!"

When I finally sat down on the cool green grass and squinted at the radiant sun, my heart was content. "I don't lack anything," I thought. "I don't need any man-made rules to qualify me. This is me. The complete me is right here, right now, basking under the glory of the sun. And that is good enough."

Katie Hua attends Princeton University.

53

WRITING ABOUT RACE

Though colleges highly prize racial diversity, students are often reluctant to write about it. The author of the following essay was no exception. "I did not want to write about race but it was an ethical dilemma I had faced many times and I knew I could write a good essay on the topic," says author Merri Martin. With a superb anecdote in her lead, Merri shows the impact that an essay about race can have as she delves into a variety of issues that cut close to home. Some students will find issues such as these too raw and painful to write about, but for those who feel comfortable doing so, writing on race can be a great way to tap deep emotions and powerful insight.

Essay by Merri Martin

Evaluate a significant experience, achievement, risk you have taken, or ethical dilemma you have faced and its impact on you.

"May I help you?" the blonde sales associate asked me for the fifth time after watching me like a hawk. Once again, I told her that I would definitely come to her if I needed anything. When I was younger, I naively thought that the clerks were being extremely polite or working hard to earn a commission, but now as a black teenager, I know better.

Luckily, I have never been the focus of blatant hatred of any kind, but I can remember countless subtle acts of suspicion. From wary salespeople to not so polite "friends," I have been the target of racism from people of all colors. In most cases, this racism was subtle and not intentionally hurtful, but it opened my eyes. Racism exists in all types of people, even minority groups. In fact, I've learned that this form can be more hurtful. I've been called "too white" or "not black enough" by people I considered friends (black and white), but I never defended myself. At first I was shocked that I was being attacked, and I immediately felt inferior and scared. When I was younger, I even started to believe these things were true, but I have since discovered who I am and realized what it truly means to represent and take pride in my heritage. I have also learned why people may be prejudiced and they are the ones who need to grow from new, diverse experiences. I also know that I can better express my feelings now, and I no longer keep those harmful thoughts inside.

Over time, I have come to realize that diversity means more than a mix of black and white people; it involves all skin types, cultures, religions, and backgrounds. I have become more aware of others' feelings and today, I am more appreciative of my environment and have surrounded myself with true friends who are knowledgeable and open-minded.

If I were again to be the direct target of racism, understated or blunt, I would do quite a few things differently. If someone I knew was doing or saying anything offensive, I would not stand by and let it

> **From wary salespeople to not so polite "friends," I have been the target of racism from people of all colors.**

continue, but rather I would present my point of view, which I optimistically believe would embarrass and enlighten many people without further prompting. I would also highly encourage this person to make an effort to get to know other people who they may have prejudged, since no members of an ethnic group are one-dimensional.

Dilemmas and confrontations like mine may be painful, but in the long run these experiences make us stronger. I am looking for a college that encourages these values and promotes understanding and acceptance. I know that Babson College is the best school for me because it actively seeks unique individuals who will bring something to campus, and I can't wait to begin college this fall in this diverse learning environment.

Merri Martin attends Babson College.

54

A FRIENDSHIP BRIDGES THE RACIAL DIVIDE

Author Matt McConnell is a white teenager whose life has been enriched by a black friend who comes from a more modest socioeconomic background. Matt's sincere desire to learn about his friend comes through, and his eye for detail (as in "chipped paint" and "firm handshake") make for an interesting story. A weak essay on cultural difference might show garden-variety sympathy, or even a more genuine empathy. A strong one, like Matt's, shows an author beginning to see the world through another person's eyes.

Essay by Matthew Wells McConnell

I've been raised in a somewhat sheltered environment, mostly surrounded by wealthy, white kids. Often, I pondered whether or not I was materialistic or blatantly ignorant of my good fortune much like many of my peers. Transferring from a rather small, Catholic school in Rock Hill, I noticed the different mannerisms— spoiled nature and flaunting of wealth—that a majority of the students possessed and I thought little of it because I was so young and naïve. As I started to mature, a fear sparked within me like the strike of a matchstick, fear that I was being unduly influenced and would develop the characteristics of some of my more sheltered and spoiled classmates. That is not who I wanted to become.

A couple of years ago, a black student named James came to my school, and we quickly became acquaintances. He has wielded such a positive impact on my life as no other single person could have done. Born in Queens, New York, he was the only child in his family, including his extended family, who was not born in Africa. He went to a boarding school in Nigeria, where his dad went through schooling, and moved to Charlotte with his dad, stepmom, and brother.

Before I met James, I had never experienced such a tight bond and strong friendship with a person of African descent. As our relationship blossomed, I was hit head on by a different world. For example, the first time I ventured over to his house, it affected me and altered the way I perceive certain things every day. As I stepped out of my car, I noticed the paint chipped away on the façade of his house and the metal bars in front of his windows. The furniture in his house was torn and antique-looking; some masked in tape in order to hold it together. My nostrils filled with the smell of home cooking as I entered a kitchen and dining room that could barely fit a family of four. James introduced me to his dad, who greeted me with a strong handshake and a thick Nigerian accent. His poverty-stricken family didn't enjoy all the luxuries that most of my friends and I enjoyed; yet, they were content with the little they had and not once did I ever hear James complain of his misfortune. He would always and still does call me for rides because his family can't afford to buy him a car. One spring, James went to the beach with my family and me. As we were running to shake off the restlessness of the long car ride, James turned towards the beach and stopped. He stared as the spectacle in awe and told me he had never seen the beach before.

I asked James about the discrimination he faces every day, and he shared with me numerous situations that opened my eyes to what he, and many other African Americans, go through each day. I

> He would always and still does call me for rides because his family can't afford to buy him a car.

invited him into my life and conversed with him about my white southern background and my Scottish descent. One day, James thanked me for caring enough to befriend him and make an effort to understand his situation and where he is coming from. Thus, our worlds collided by integrating in a spirit of harmony and trust. Barriers were broken. James bestowed upon me a gift that no other friend I had was capable of giving. He taught me to be thankful and grateful for my parents' hard work and for what they have given me. He showed me various ways to look at things from other perspectives and not conform to the common racial stereotypes.

Most importantly, he indirectly showed me how I could become a better person by crossing different boundaries and getting to know people who aren't like me, and experiencing new situations. I hope to continue to use this wonderful gift at Duke and in my life after college. I will be forever thankful for the contributions James has made, and this gift will never be forgotten.

Mathew Wells McConnell attends Duke University.

55

"I COULDN'T IMAGINE WANTING TO DYE MY HAIR BLONDE"

Kids can be cruel, and students who come from minority backgrounds often have difficult stories to tell. Such is the case for author Christina Mendoza, who has the added twist of being part of a racially mixed family. Her essay tells the story of how she learned to take pride in being Mexican American. Christina does not identify one turning point or significant experience, and her essay is the better for it. Instead, she describes a process of evolution in which she gradually learns to take pride in her mixed-race background.

Essay by Christina Mendoza

"Ha ha! Christina is a dirty Mexican!"

Growing up in a small, conservative community, it's easy to be shoved into your own category if you don't look or act like everyone else. My hair and eyes, instead of being blonde and blue like all of my Czech classmates, were chocolate and espresso. My last name had a "z" in it, and my grandmother called me "mija." By the time I was in grade school, the teasing began, and I was hurt and confused. Didn't all grandmothers call their grandchildren "mija"? Why did everyone except for me have blue eyes? And why was I being called "dirty Mexican" when I was cleaner than the boy who made the remark?

After an afternoon of teasing and tormenting from my classmates, I asked these questions to my mother, between sobs. By this time, she had become extremely good at giving me the "you're unique and beautiful" speech, but it was hard for her to truly empathize with me because neither she nor my father knew how I felt. She was a Caucasian who grew up in California; he was a Mexican American who grew up as the majority in San Antonio. I was the product of the two—the "half-breed" daughter who was raised in the small town of Seymour, population 2,800.

My other family members didn't seem to have any trouble fitting in. My father's ethnicity is well respected. He is the only doctor within a fifty-mile radius who can speak Spanish. My sister was the beauty queen of our town—her sleek, glossy hair and olive complexion were the envy of every girl. My little brother received the recessive genes (fair skin, blue eyes), so he looks like everyone else in Seymour. I felt I was stuck somewhere in the middle of my siblings, stuck in the middle of two cultures, and not accepted by either.

Time does have a way of healing things. I didn't just wake up one morning and think, "I'm proud to be Hispanic," but as I have matured, I have learned not to be ashamed of my ethnicity. Instead of hiding who I really am, I have embraced my Mexican heritage and have become proud of it. Finding out about the many opportunities that are available to students of Hispanic descent has motivated me even more to delve deeper into my culture.

> **My assailant said in a mocking tone, "I wish I could be a smart Mexican."**

Looking back, I couldn't imagine wanting to dye my hair blonde to feel better about myself. The blonde girls are unique in their own way, but diversity makes the world go round. I absolutely love being different and not walking the same path as everyone else. The last racist comment I received was after I was named a National Hispanic Scholar. My assailant said in a mocking tone, "I wish I could be a smart Mexican." Feeling sorry for his cultural ignorance, I smiled and replied, "Yeah, I bet you do."

Christina Mendoza attends Yale University.

56

COMING TO AMERICA

As a Pakistani coming to boarding school in the United States, author Alamdar Murtaza can justifiably speak of flying on his own version of the *Mayflower*. Alamdar has a talent for intriguing analogies, as when he plays on the significance of Jerusalem in the Christian, Jewish, and Muslim faiths, while comparing the city to his dorm room. His reference to Whitman's YAWP sounding "over and above the 'quiet please' sign" is a master stroke that shows his skill as a writer and his literary knowledge (the YAWP being a reference to Whitman's "Song of Myself"). Alamdar's essay superbly combines passion and scholarship.

Essay by Alamdar Murtaza

I had sailed on the *Mayflower*. Fall had settled in its transitional air, slowly parting with the warmth of day. The air of the land was as untouched and virgin as it was to the first pilgrim to set foot on the soil of the New World. My *Mayflower* read "Continental Airlines 011."

I was in America.

The "City Upon a Hill" had been erected long before my arrival, but I carried the message. The endless possibilities a new day brought were now mine. The land had an immense power ingrained deep in its history and I would drink from the soul of the continent, its expressions of freedom and equality. I would have my belly filled by the fruit of justice.

My Alma Mater, of which I have become a Templar, breathed new life into my lungs. Blood ran through my veins. Guidance from inspiring teachers focused my energies in different areas of study. Letters and numbers equated to more than grammar and mundane algorithms. With surgical dexterity incisions were made to explore the depths of each literary text, mathematical proof, and work of art.

Collecting additional anecdotal information from the remains of the day I would return to a room I shared with a Jewish boy. Such a match could only exist in nature, for all the world seemed baffled at this bond of brotherhood. Along with our other friends of Christian faith and my own Islamic heritage, we rivaled the beliefs of the world and the frantic state of its current health. If there was ever a Jerusalem where the realms of faith merged, it was "Room 103, Potter South." The same God could be worshipped without the wedge of disunion. We fought the same demons hidden under a tentacle of ambivalent doubt; the Bible, Torah, and Quran revealed to me that we all read from the same scriptures, and learned from the fundamental teachings of a common ancestor. When I spoke with friends in Pakistan, I realized I had seen something different that had changed me forever, and they were excited and intrigued by it. There was a new message spreading out of what we created sitting in the space between our desks and beds, installing a vision of peace. But such a message can lose its meaning as it carries three thousand miles across the Atlantic. It was hard for me to articulate and express a love like this to those who were already too adult and wise in their ways. I needed to speak it to them simply and I searched for the right words with the right meanings.

> **The resonance of Whitman's YAWP had been sounded over and above the "quiet please" sign.**

Still I was incomplete. I had only scratched the surface of an oasis whose sands shifted much too quickly. Under the ground, from wells of wisdom came whispers. I heard Thoreau, Douglas, Emerson, and Hawthorne speak to me of a life natural and simplistic. The springs of this oasis were in the lower level of the Annenberg library, where Byron and Neruda sat in dusty aphrodisia well worn from a lifetime of curious fingers. The resonance of Whitman's YAWP had been sounded over and above the "quiet please" sign. Ms. Plath's mirroring lake opened up in the middle of the floor as Poe and Hawthorne made way with their intrusive first-person.

Here were men and women of words, who have shown me America.

Alamdar Murtaza attends Kenyon College.

57

FINDING INSPIRATION IN FAMILY

There is nothing fancy about the following essay—it is simple, honest, and works beautifully. The anecdote that opens the story is an experience everyone has had: blackening the ethnicity oval. The author goes on to describe the lives of her mother and grandparents, and why their experience continues to inspire and motivate her. In writing about the IB program, she highlights her drive to excel and gives strong evidence that she can thrive in a highly competitive college. Says Danielle, "I had so many ideas all at once that it was way over five hundred words. I asked my mom to help me edit it and cut it down, and got guidance from my college counselor on how to make it more fluid."

Essay by Danielle Marie Needles

In the beginning of third grade, I took my first standardized test where I had to fill out my full name, address, my birthday, and to shade in the corresponding ovals. My teacher then said to fill in the oval that represents our ethnicity. One of the choices was "Hispanic/Latino." I paused for a moment. I knew that I was Mexican American; my grandparents emigrated from Mexico to El Paso, Texas, where my mom and her ten brothers and sisters grew up. However, when I came across this question about my ethnicity, I never fully realized what it meant to me. I filled in the oval labeled "Hispanic/Latino" and then smiled, for it was the first time that I could remember where it was going to be recognized that I was, in fact, Mexican.

Growing up in a middle class family, I never experienced the hardships that my grandparents (the Navarros) and my mom had to go through in their daily lives. My great-grandparents never went to school; my grandmother never received an education past third grade, while my grandfather never exceeded fouth grade, in their home in Chihuahua, Mexico. They emigrated to El Paso after they married, where my grandparents had to teach themselves English.

My mom and her siblings went to a predominantly white high school, where the only Mexicans she knew of were her extended family. My mom was very studious, always breaking the boundaries and exceeding expectations about how a Mexican girl in high school should be. Her counselors would tell her she should be taking homemaking classes which would help her out of high school, but she stuck with the most rigorous math courses and took four years of Russian. After she graduated, her dreams led her to a place outside of El Paso; my grandmother helped her secretly leave El Paso to Miami, Florida, for the hope of a better future. My mom ended up working at a law office and took night classes at Miami-Dade Community College. Her job gave her the chance to help her family financially, but it consumed all her time, leaving her studies behind. My mom became a very prominent and well-respected real estate settlement manager for twenty-five years at the firm, but to this day her only regret is not to have completed her education. For me the way to keep this story alive is through a strong education and by surpassing all stereotypes and keeping my faith.

> **I filled in the oval labeled "Hispanic/Latino" and then smiled.**

In my high school, 35 percent of the students are Hispanic. Since I've entered Washington-Lee, I've always been in the most advanced classes. During freshmen year, I knew a lot of people with various ethnic backgrounds. At the end of my sophomore year, it was time to declare if one was to become an International Baccalaureate (IB) candidate. The majority of students who declared themselves as IB candidates were white, while a small minority were from various ethic groups.

During the end of my junior year and the beginning of my senior year, more ethnic students dropped out of the IB Program. Today, there are only a handful of students of ethnic backgrounds. The main reason why I've been pursing the IB diploma was to challenge myself and that although I am Mexican, I am capable of beating the odds and trying to accomplish a task my mom's family was not given the opportunity to. In a way, I'm pursuing this diploma for my entire Navarro family, especially my mom.

I am thankful everyday for all that I have: a wonderful supportive family, the drive to pursue an IB diploma, and to be surrounded by a strong, dedicated group of friends. I know that the history and struggle of my mom and her family runs through my veins; although I don't have stories of personal experiences of growing up in poverty, or struggling through a time of racism, the best I can do is to tell my family's story by keeping it alive, it gives me hope and confidence to exceed through the boundaries by graduating high school and attending college—a task neither my mom, *mis tios*, or my grandparents achieved. As a third-generation Mexican in my mom's family, what being Mexican American means to me is to embrace my past and to excel in the future.

Since that test in third grade, whenever I fill out my ethnicity on a standardized test, I fill in the "Hispanic/Latino" oval and I smile as I remember who I am and that I am proud to be Mexican American.

Danielle Marie Needles attends the University of Virginia.

58

COUNTRY GIRL, PRIVATE SCHOOL

The two worlds of author Jessica Lynn Parr come together in this engaging essay. She uses the first part to tell about the most exotic of the two, her tiny home town of Elgin, Texas. Images of small town life—from the local hardware store to the annual hay harvest—offer a sharp contrast to the more affluent culture of Jessica's private school. Another key to the essay is her ability to tell about both worlds without being judgmental of either, in the process demonstrating the sort of flexibility that is necessary to thrive in a new environment such as college.

Essay by Jessica Lynn Parr

"A time for warm hearts and hot guts." This is the slogan of the annual Hogeye Festival in the Hot Sausage Capital of the World: my hometown of Elgin, Texas. I have lived on Pistol Hill Ranch in Elgin, population c. 5000, for all but the first two of my seventeen years. I have grown up on small-town morals, values, and ways of life. Elgin is a place where parents still teach their children to say "yes, ma'am" and "no, sir." Wiry old cowboys with weathered leather for skin take their coffee black at the City Cafe, and most men have two pairs of cowboy boots: one for working, and one for Sunday church. I can count on running into at least a handful of people I know upon each trip to the local H-E-B grocery store or the Elgin Post Office. Employees at Main Street Pharmacy and Ace Hardware have known me since I was a little girl too small to see over the counter. A familiar sight as I drive down Main Street is of men in Wrangler jeans, western shirts, cowboy hats, boots, and shiny rodeo belt buckles, leaning on their 4x4 trucks as they discuss all the important issues of slow but friendly small town life.

My parents and I live on about 140 acres of land where we raise cattle and farm hay. For as long as I can remember, ranch work has been a way of life for my family. Many summer days spent working in the hay fields and barns last until midnight or even later. My mom taught me to drive my Granny's maroon 1983 Buick Regal when I was only nine years old, so that I could take fresh ice water and box lunches out to my dad and the other workers on the farm. My parents both hold full-time jobs and yet they still manage to keep up with our ranch in their scarce spare time. I learned my earnest and diligent work ethic from their tireless examples. I remember the looks I got as a middle-schooler from the teenage boys working as hired hands on our ranch when I hopped out of the truck with my own pair of work gloves to help load the sixty-five pound square bales of hay. I have even had farmer's tan lines from driving our John Deere 4020 tractor all day long cutting and raking hay. I know the feeling of aching muscles and itchy bits of hay from head to toe after a long day laboring in the hot sun. I have grown up as Daddy's little cowgirl and ranch hand, and have learned invaluable lessons about agriculture, livestock, and the workings of a close-knit small-town community.

On the flip side of the coin, I have attended private school in Austin, the "big city" nearest to Elgin, since second grade. Top priority for my parents has always been that I obtain the best possible education, and thus they chose to place me in private school despite the daily hardship of commuting. My high school is at the complete opposite end of the socioeconomic spectrum from Elgin. Many of my peers at St. Andrew's drive Mercedes-Benzs or BMWs instead of muddy 4x4 trucks and old rusted hand-me-down cars. I attend a school where 100 percent of our graduates enroll in four-year colleges, whereas in Elgin, a great many students work and attend a community college or trade school

> **I know the feeling of aching muscles and itchy bits of hay from head to toe after a long day laboring in the hot sun.**

part-time after receiving their high school diplomas. Granted, there are several exceptions to either rule, however my point is to demonstrate how different these two worlds really are. I realize how privileged I am to attend my high school, and thus have always completely dedicated myself to taking full advantage of every opportunity. I commute a full hour each way to and from school, but have nevertheless participated in a fitness conditioning class that required I be at school by 6:15 every morning, musical rehearsals that kept me at school until ten o'clock on some nights, and demanding varsity sports schedules. My high school has given me a first-class education with infinite opportunities, and my exceptional environment has made it impossible for me to ever take these privileges for granted.

I have always been a little bit different because of my circumstances. My friends at school never tire of joking about the fact that I live on a farm with real cows. In Elgin, my friends have often teased me about being "too good" for their public school, or given me a hard time about spending half my life thirty-eight miles away in Austin. However, both sets of friends know me well enough to understand my dedication to education, and respect me for my unusual circumstances. I am fortunate to have such a broadened perspective as a result of my dual experiences. I recognize that my experiences are extraordinary, and I cherish the fact that I am able to enjoy the best of both worlds. Thanks to my unique background, I have an ability to adapt easily to new social and cultural climates. I bring my own distinct perspective to a situation because I have thrived simultaneously in two very different environments.

Jessica Lynn Parr attends Southern Methodist University.

Politics and Religion

A side from athletics, this category of essays is probably the toughest to pull off. Political issues don't usually lend themselves to personal reflections, and religion is hard to make concrete. That's not to say that it is impossible to write an outstanding essay about politics or religion. Sometimes, as in Essay 61, the question helps dictate the subject. Essays 59 and 63 succeed because the authors make the topic personal, while in Essay 61, the author describes a change in his personal views.

59

NO "CLARK KENT FEMINIST" HERE

This killer essay didn't even start out as a college essay. "I actually just wrote it for fun," says author Aviva Ariel. She takes a risk in writing about feminism, but rather than lapsing into generic political commentary, she sticks to talking about her own life. The result is a masterful essay that illustrates the power of vivid detail—for humor and simply for lively storytelling. "I don't think the topic is as important as the tone of the essay," says Aviva. "Two people can say the same thing, but you'll be attracted to the person whose personality shines through even when they say a simple 'hello.'"

Essay by Aviva Ariel

Sometime between waking up at the crack of dawn and fourth period I became a teenage werewolf. No, wait, I mean feminist.

It's as if I didn't know until someone pointed it out to me in English class, but it was more like an "Ooh, dude, I think you just stepped in some feminist," or a "Damn! You smell like feminist," or maybe even an "I think you spilled some feminism on your shirt, and it stains…"

I've been labeled many things throughout my life in Cleveland, Ohio, from preppy (but don't ever expect to see me in a collared shirt and khakis) to punk (maybe my new lip piercing and occasional green eyeliner add to this, but even for Cleveland, I'm about as punk as Marcia Brady) to slightly insane (a mix between MTV's hidden camera show *Punk'd* and starlet Nicole Richie)—I've even been told that I'm unique looking (why am I so sure it's not a compliment?) and maybe labeling me makes it easier to figure out who I am (hell—I don't even know!), but recently my whole class seems to have decided that I'm a bra-burning, men-hating Feminazi.

My English teacher, a minority-equalizing, feminist-loving, all around pro-everything-liberal kind of man, said that if a guy were to ever hold the door open for me, I would "punch his lights out."

I pictured myself through his eyes, toned and fuming hatred, simultaneously liberating the oppressed and crushing lanky teenage boys with my bare hands, their awkward limbs flinging in the air as I fought in honor of my fellow womyn.

Would I? I wondered. Maybe I would just thank him and walk through the door. Teenage boys displaying chivalry is not something I see every day, so I might pause. I might wonder, why this gesture of civility, right here, right now? But punch his lights out? I'm barely five feet tall—I aspire to meet the height requirements for amusement park rides, not to dominate all who cross my path.

But I should have seen it coming. After sharing with the group several weeks earlier that being whistled at in the hallways or told that I have a fine ass (or some other creative come-on) was about as flattering to me as being compared to Santa Claus (jolly, red, and round), it is only fitting—they finally discovered that I am the monster within their midst. It's as if I was biding my time at school until I could become a trophy wife for some successful businessman or an exotic dancer with breasts filled with more than my brain, and suddenly I've crushed their dreams by becoming this, this, this breathing, thinking, independent young woman!

I am not about to apologize for wanting to be seen as the lovechild of Mary Wollstonecraft and Justin Timberlake (smart, sexy, and awesome on the dance floor). And even if it angers them to hear I think so, my guess is I will be more financially and personally successful than most of the boys I know.

I know I'm a feminist, but I am also just a teenage girl trying to survive junior year (because everyone knows being in high school is almost as enjoyable as four years of paper cuts). I could be a Clark Kent feminist—you know the ones; coy and giggly when the boys are around, fierce all-grrrl when she's alone with her posse. I could be the kind who keeps *Ms.* hidden inside a copy of *Seventeen* on the bedside table, or I could go all-out old-school in ripped jeans and combat boots—but that's not me, either. I want to be who I am, big or small, editor-in-chief or head cheerleader, point guard or math geek, and I want to make it so that when *my* daughter goes to high school and says she's a feminist, everyone in the school, from the kids smoking in the parking lot to the principal, just yawns and says, yeah, who isn't?

> I am not about to apologize for wanting to be seen as the lovechild of Mary Wollstonecraft and Justin Timberlake.

Aviva Ariel attends Skidmore College.

60

WRITING ABOUT RELIGION

There are many pitfalls to essays about religious faith. Since faith is in the mind (and therefore abstract), the challenge is to make faith come alive with concrete stories and anecdotes. The following essay begins as a story about singing and being on stage. Only in paragraph four does the author, Rachel Dubois, begin to explain why singing in her temple has special meaning. By the end, she is talking about *tikkun olam,* "healing the world," in a much more convincing way than she could have by beginning the essay with a testament to her faith. Says Rachel, "Writing about my religious/cultural background was the easiest topic I could have chosen because it was something that was inherently me."

Essay by Rachel Dubois

As I step up to the pulpit, I feel a familiar sense of calm come over me, the calm I always experience before singing to my congregation. Scanning the audience, I look out at the parents and grandparents, making eye contact with those I recognize and those I do not. I begin to sing with my youth choir behind me, and take a deep breath in preparation for my solo. I can feel the eyes of the congregation locked onto me, waiting, and then my voice soars out over the expectant faces.

When I finish singing, I see rapt expressions and tears. Even though I know they would be touched regardless of how I sound, every time I sing at a service, I am overwhelmed by the amount of warmth that meets my participation.

"Beautiful. Absolutely beautiful." I turn to see my cantor beaming at me, and I smile back. As I walk out of my synagogue, I am stopped repeatedly by wrinkly little women who grin unabashedly at me and well-wishers who say how much it means to them to see and hear young people at their Friday night service. The amount of praise I receive is almost embarrassing and feels somewhat undeserved, but it gives me joy and gratification that I can't find anywhere but here. Where else could you get a sticky, lipstick-smeared kiss from a complete stranger, and feel like it was the most heartfelt gesture in the world?

I have spent countless hours singing and performing, but there is a tangible difference between performing in a concert with my school choir and singing for my temple community. Whenever I contribute to my synagogue, I know that people appreciate my effort, whatever the results. To be able to participate without being judged gives me full rein to enjoy the experience. For this reason, belonging to a close-knit Jewish community has always been a vital part of my life. Over the years, I became more involved, moving from attending Sunday school classes to teaching younger students and helping to found my temple youth group. I joined the temple choir, chanted Torah on major holidays, and wrote for the temple bulletin. The more I undertook, the more I wanted to be active in my community. Gradually, my religion turned into a force that has grounded me and kept me centered throughout high school. An anchor point in my life, it has provided me with a rare sense of connection to my own identity and to the needs of those around me.

The summer I turned fifteen, I attended Kutz, a Jewish leadership camp, and was exposed to a vibrant and energetic group of teenagers. The passion that permeated the camp was infectious, and that summer, I realized that I wanted to devote my life to leading and nurturing a Jewish community. Abandoning my plans to become a doctor, which I had formed in kindergarten, I decided to pursue the goal of becoming a cantor. A cantor, similar to a rabbi, is a member of the Jewish clergy who leads a large portion of the song and prayer during a service. In pursuit of this ambition, I became the Religious and Cultural Vice President of my temple youth group, writing and leading services for teens at every youth event.

I truly feel like I am participating in *tikkun olam*, or healing the world.

This past summer, I journeyed to Israel on NFTY's L'Dor v'Dor program to examine my roots and solidify my goal of becoming a cantor. Seeing my ancestral homeland was the final step; I felt a visceral connection to all aspects of Judaism.

What my community has offered me, I want to give to others. To be able to bond with a diverse congregation, create a spiritual moment for those many years my senior or my peers, and inspire all of them through song and prayer is an incomparable sensation. I truly feel like I am participating in *tikkun olam*, or healing the world. Not many people have had their career planned out since age fifteen, but to me, being a cantor was the only path that combined my passions with my identity. I know that nothing else in life could give me the spiritual joy and fulfillment that I crave, while having a positive effect on others.

Leaving the temple parking lot, I am perfectly content. Just as on every other Friday night, I smile an inward smile and think to myself, "Yeah, this really is what I want to do with my life. Good choice."

The only choice.

Rachel Dubois attends Yale University.

61

WHO SAYS THE MAJORITY IS ALWAYS RIGHT?

Some of the toughest questions are those that ask you to examine issues or beliefs. The best response, often, is to tell a story from personal experience that you can apply to the issue. The author begins this essay with an unexpected proposition, that the rule of the majority may not be so great after all, and then sets out to prove it with reasoning and experiences from his life. Tocqueville and *Federalist No. 10* come from the author's reading; C-SPAN and the Michigan ballot initiatives are examples from his life. The essay shows the author to be well-read, politically aware, and willing to challenge a principle that others take for granted.

Essay by Alex Houser

Discuss an issue that you once thought you understood but have since learned to question.

I once believed in the power of the majority to make acceptable decisions. Now I realize that that viewpoint was flawed. What I learned about American government came from prescribed classes and from watching C-SPAN. The classes taught me about "the system" and how it should work. C-SPAN showed me various viewpoints, teaching me to see through political rhetoric. The blind worship of democracy is reinforced through every aspect of American life; school, radio, news coverage, and sports programs pay homage to "Democracy." Despite this brainwashing the last election brought into my awareness the intrinsic weakness in our democratic system, the desire of the majority to expand upon its own power.

The American system of government has, as one of its founding tenets, the belief that the majority is incapable of good governance. The founding fathers were aware of the problems of majoritarian rule. *Federalist no. 10* and Mr. Tocqueville expounded on the problems that democracy would face. Yet, through referendum the majority has successfully granted itself far greater power than the fathers intended.

The Constitution says that all men are created equal, the philosophical implication being that all men are entitled to the same rights. Yet if these protections were removed, the majority would steal away the rights of all others and grant power all to themselves. To illustrate this I would speak on two tragedies that have befallen the state of Michigan, entitled Proposals I and II.

Proposal I is an attempt to transfer control of the state lottery to the voters. It forbids the lottery commission from developing new programs without submitting them to popular referendum. The proposal passed by a 10 percent majority despite extensive campaigning against it by the governor. The disturbing aspect of Proposal I was its theme of "let the voters decide." The concept that voters don't trust their representatives to make decisions is deeply disturbing.

Proposal II draws upon the prejudice of the majority to deprive the gay community of equality by banning civil unions. Civil unions hurt no one, yet a ban would de-legitimize the gay community's right to equal treatment before the law. The majority does not even benefit by taking away spousal rights/privileges. It simply deprives those it finds loathsome of their equality.

I don't think there's an easy solution to human greed, but I enjoy watching it. I want to study economics. Not to change the world…there are already enough economists to do that. I would like to have the tools to predict the near future. How are we changing? Where will we be? I don't think there is any other study that will teach this kind of insight, besides augury. Perhaps it is the joy of the gambler: to make a prediction and wake up the next day to find out if you are right.

> **I don't think there's an easy solution to human greed, but I enjoy watching it.**

Alex Houser attends the College of Wooster.

62

TACKLING A TABOO SUBJECT

Religion and politics are topics to be avoided at cocktail parties, and the same generally applies to college essays. Everybody has an opinion about politics, and few other topics make it so easy for you to offend your reader. But author Will Marks shows that it is possible to write a good political essay, so long as you stick to emphasizing personal growth and your own life experiences. "I worried about writing about politics, and I actually still don't really like this essay," says Will. We think he should give himself a bit more credit.

Essay by William Thomas Marks

Al Franken's book *Lies and the Lying Liars Who Tell Them* led me to a recent dive into the world of politics that has made me examine my own values and reevaluate how I see the world. My parents are very politically active people. My mom, a social worker, has always been a strong Democrat. My stepdad is a Lebanese American citizen who sees the world through an immigrant's eyes. My dad was more politically active in his younger days, but his Vietnam veteran roots show through when you start talking to him about the government.

I had decided around three years ago that I was a Republican. I may have not agreed with certain stances on moral issues, but overall I felt that the GOP represented my views and interests better than the Democratic Party. When President Bush decided to go to war in Iraq, I strongly supported his decision. I never realized how little I questioned my own beliefs until the war started to go wrong. At this time, I decided that I was going to get to know both sides of the argument and really figure out where I stood. First, I decided to make sure I kept up with the news. I became an avid CNN watcher and read CNN.com everyday. Then I started reading. I had a firm grip on what the Republicans stood for, so I decided to go for Democratic literature.

As I read Al Franken's book, I started to question my support for the Republican Party. The whole point of this book was to expose the lies of Right Wing politicians and journalists. I read the book skeptically, wondering if Al Franken was really somebody I could trust. When I looked through the footnotes and appendices, I realized that almost everything he has talked about was backed up by a study or poll by some major, non-partisan organization. Reading this book had a profound impact on me. It made me want to learn more about politics and government, so I continued to read.

I next read *Bush at War* and then read *Plan of Attack*, both by Bob Woodward. Once the election came closer, I bought John Kerry's book *A Call to Service*. I came to realize that, in truth, I sided with the Democrats on almost every issue. I completely changed whom I sided with and became an avid supporter of the Democrats. But this change was not the biggest thing that changed in my life.

These readings set in motion a major change in my thinking. I feel that reading these books and questioning my own values really matured me as a person. I was forced, page by page, to think about where I really stood on the issues. I decided that I had to make my own mind up on things. I really learned to think about our country and how our government worked. I also came to believe that it was very important to protect those in poverty in our society and to make sure that we strive to achieve equality in all settings in our country. Reading these books really sparked my life to move in a different direction. I started to realize how important it was for me to fight for what I felt was right on these issues, any way I could. These studies have changed the way I view the world, made me realize what my own values were, and have steered me into the direction of a life of public service.

> When President Bush decided to go to war in Iraq, I strongly supported his decision.

William Thomas Marks attends Georgetown University.

63

WHEN YOU CARE ABOUT THE WORLD

Essays about international affairs can be dicey, but the rare student who genuinely cares about what happens in, say, Sudan, can pull it off. Madelyn Sullivan does so by connecting her first voting experience, which happened within weeks of when she wrote, with an article she read about human-rights atrocities in Sudan. The essay works because of her powerful idealism. At the polling place, her "heart beat slightly fast" and her hands "shook unsteadily." The article about the Sudan violence left her "brimming with tears." When Madelyn writes that she herself hopes to prevent tomorrow's Holocaust, most readers will believe her.

Essay by Madelyn Sullivan

I voted on November 2nd. As an eighteen-year-old woman in America, I am legally allowed to exercise my right to vote. Although my heart beat slightly fast, and my hands shook unsteadily at the polling booth, upon arriving home from my first voting experience, I was filled with a sense of accomplishment and relief. I sat on the couch that night, when I picked up a *TIME* magazine and began to read an article on Sudan by Massimo Calabresi.

The vast nation of Sudan is divided by both religion and culture, but mainly ethnicity: Arabs and Africans. While all citizens of Sudan are African, the nomadic tribes of Sudan are referred to as Arabs, while the sedentary tribes are called Africans.

The images I saw of the battling Arabs and Africans were stark and the stories I read were more horrific. The Janjaweed, "devils on horseback," is an Arabic group of local tribes funded by the Sudanese government to crush the radical Sudan Liberation Army. The group began attacking civilians, claiming that they were aiding insurgents. Janjaweed ride or fly into African villages, firing guns on men and children alike. They rape the women, leave most children, and kill all the men. These are of course, very loose rules. One woman described a Janjaweed rampage: "A fighter unwrapped a swaddling cloth and rolled a newborn baby onto the dirt. The baby was a girl, so they left her. Then the Janjaweed spotted a one-year-old boy and decided he was a future enemy. In front of a group of onlookers, a man tossed the boy into the air as another took aim and shot him dead."

Suddenly voting didn't seem as important as it had fifteen minutes earlier. Suddenly I didn't want to go to school the next day, but fly to Africa and give all my hot lunches to a starving family at a refugee camp. What surprised me the most, however, was a common theme throughout the article about the lack of world response. We cannot let another Rwanda or Holocaust occur while we are alive. Genocide is supposed to be a thing of the past. It is a story we read about in books or a special we watch on the history channel. Let Sudan be the one time that the world learned and said "never again" and meant it.

As I sat on the couch, brimming with tears and watching the muted images of election results, I felt a desperate sense of despair. I had to remind myself that I am able to affect what happens in my life.

> A fighter unwrapped a swaddling cloth and rolled a newborn baby onto the dirt. The baby was a girl, so they left her.

I voted on Tuesday. I am a woman. I am eighteen. And I had a choice. I am lucky, and I have the obligation to help people without my same rights. On Tuesday, what I voted for will not only affect my local and national community, but also the world. I am indebted to the citizens of countries like Sudan to vote for them, to give a voice to the people who cannot speak above the gunfire and violence that reigns in their country.

I realized then that my trip to the ballot box was perhaps not so futile and that I would indeed attend school the next day, no matter how great my desire to flee the country and save the world as a self-proclaimed knight-errant. I reminded myself that although I am an adult with adult responsibilities, I am still a senior in high school with plans to go to college. I can only hope that the best possible use of my time right now is to attend school to better educate myself. I can only hope that what I learn today will give me the courage and knowledge to stop tomorrow's Holocaust.

Madelyn Sullivan attends Bowdoin College.

A Significant Experience

W e've warned you about trying too hard to find one of these. Even for the person who really did have an earth-shaking experience—in the form of her house burning down (Essay 66)—what comes afterward is the meat of her essay. Two of our student authors, in Essays 67 and 69, write about outdoor experiences that boosted their self-confidence. Essay 65 offers another variation; it describes a life lived in the aftermath of divorce, but events immediately surrounding the divorce are never discussed. The cardinal rule is not to let description of the facts crowd out your reflections on the significance of those facts.

64

THE FACES OF ALUMNAE HALL

If you've had any Latin, you'll remember that "alumnae" is a feminine plural form. If you're really smart, you'll deduce that CSG (Columbus

School for Girls) is an all-female institution, and that it is the faces of the graduates that have transfixed author Maria Dixon. The essay is at its strongest when she is studying their expressions, wondering at how photography can capture a moment in time, and what the young women in the pictures must have been thinking. The middle paragraph describes an anecdote; think about why it is so powerful.

Essay by Marla Dixon

Among the constant sea of plaid and enormous initial-embroidered Northface book bags which make up the campus of CSG, a student must find her place of security. She must safeguard herself from examinations, college gossip, and the long night ahead of writing papers and studying which rests cozily in the back of her mind weighing down any hope of an early bed time. I have found my safe haven to be a simple passage-way entitled "Alumnae Hall." With golden block letters, the name towers over even the tallest twelfth formers. To the students, the hallway serves merely as a path of travel. To guests, the pictures receive a quick glimpse which leaves an impression of the history and tradition of the institution. But to me, this gallery of antiquity reminds me of a lesson my Latin teacher instilled in each of her Latin IV scholars on a cloudy Wednesday morning.

"Field trip, girls," Mrs. White declared as she motioned towards the door with her delicately manicured hands adorned with rings detailed with ancient Roman inscriptions. It was the second week of school and the novelty of senior year was wearing off at the same pace homework was being assigned. In between yawns and "Good mornings," twelve of us sluggishly crawled out of the cluttered class-room and followed our instructor around the bend to Alumnae Hall. We came to an abrupt stop before a glass frame encasing pictures of nine graduated classes. "This is my daughter's class," she expressed with maternal pride of her only daughter. Our gaze followed her finger until it landed on a petite girl dressed in a formal white gown with ballooned ruffles over her shoulders and a fairy tale spirit of design. Her daughter Shannon was to be married in just weeks, and Mrs. White had been filling us in on all the major details of this extravagant event. "This is Shannon's best friend and her maid of honor, and this would have been her second bridesmaid," she muttered with a melancholy expression glowing in her tearful eyes. Her sudden somberness snatched our attention from the alumnae and onto the teacher's face. She continued by explaining how the girl's life was so drastically lost in a fatal car accident her first year of college. At this point, tears filled each student's empathetic eyes as we listened. "This story is not to upset you, but rather to teach you a lesson." The phrase that followed this sentence was said with passion and meaning, and took the simple infamous Latin words to a level of purpose. "Carpe Diem. This girl would have done anything to have the opportunities that Shannon has had, and the vast possibilities of your future. You never know when it all will end." With that, we walked in silence back to the classroom, and the study of Latin resumed.

Recently, I found myself escaping to my place of refuge where my rational mind melts away with my worries, and the faces in the photographs enlighten and ground me on the importance of reality. I inspect each year's class, allowing my imagination to soar through their facial expressions discerning what they may have been thinking as a camera snatched that moment in history. They range from the serious grins of the school's founding class, consisting of two women graduating the following year to continue their education at Wellesley College, to the giggly smiles of 1954. So much success, laughter, and strength encompass the yellowed photographs of the women who have gone before me. Not only the solemn picture of Mrs. White's story, but the women in every picture encourage me to not let a single moment pass by without a thankful heart and a willingness to appreciate each moment. I have taken this lesson to my service sites where I support and give confidence to those I am helping, to the classroom where, without hesitance, I speak up and express an opinion, and to my daily life in general. At times I just have to step back and realize how special any given situation is, and imprint that feeling at that exact moment in my heart to always be remembered. The

> **At this point, tears filled each student's empathetic eyes as we listened.**

legacy staring each girl in the face as she walks down the hallway has taught me that in any situation all you can do is seize it for all it is worth. The women of Alumnae Hall have taught me that each moment is truly priceless.

Marla Dixon attends Trinity College (CT).

65

A SHORT WALK, A SPECTACULAR ESSAY

One stroke of genius is all that author Juliette Mandel needed to make this essay sparkle. The walk, punctuated by the **256 steps**, becomes the occasion for reminiscing about her life. Each new milestone, marked by a specific number of steps, brings her back to the fact that she is walking between her parents' homes. Brilliant. Of course, the other part of the equation is that she poignantly renders the conflict, pain, and disorientation that come with divorce. The 256 steps are both a physical and metaphorical distance that separate Juliette's two worlds.

"256 Steps" by Juliette Mandel

It's 256 steps from my front door to my front door; a journey I make every other day that sparks reveries of reminiscing over the days when my parents were one. So close are the two houses that shelter me and yet so far apart are my two parents.

Twelve steps up the road, I see the crack in the pavement and I remember the first time I rode a tricycle—a hot pink contraption with a white wicker basket. My mom helped me up on to the seat while my dad adjusted the pedals. Slowly, I began to pedal, faster and faster. Soon I was riding without the security of my parents. Yet within seconds I reached a bumpy part of the road and was propelled into the air. I distinctly remember the way my parents ran towards me, together, and when they reached me… I felt safe. My mom carried me while my dad made funny jokes to hush my crying. I laughed so hard I couldn't even feel the stinging pain in my knee. All I could think about was how happy I was with my parents.

Ninety-eight steps and as I round the corner, a car comes speeding past me blasting loud music. I dive into another memory, as the voice of Evanescence transforms into the voice of Cyndi Lauper. 2350 Broadway, apartment 716, my dad and Cyndi were in the midst of a "recording session." I ran around the room, playing with my airplane wagon while my mom sat separately, busy in conversation on the telephone. Mom told me to be serious for a moment while Dad and I continued to jump up and down, mimicking a "famous rock star" for Cyndi. Something had changed. My parents stopped kissing in public. They spent less time together. My parents had always been on the same wavelength, but because I had what my grandmother called an "old soul," I sensed intuitively that they were drifting apart. I was a stranger inside my own home—I was confused: my parents no longer seemed inseparable. In fact, they seemed so far apart, I could hardly remember when they'd ever been together.

After 187 steps, I feel tired and alone. I see a couple bickering in their yard, and I can't help but sink into my past. The fighting seems all too familiar. The screaming, the slamming doors, the vulgar language all envelop me. I had to change. I had to adapt to my new situation. My parents were fighting again, the word separation floated throughout the house, drifting in and out of every room stinging my ears. I became a chameleon, morphing from one parent to the next. I celebrated Christmas with my mom, Chanukah with my dad. I ate pasta with tomato sauce with my mom and mac and cheese with my dad. DIVORCE.

> I see a couple bickering in their yard, and I can't help but sink into my past.

They decided to go to court—the question of custody made me nervous. Monday: dad. Tuesday: mom. Wednesday: dad until 9, then mom. Thursday and Friday: mom. Weekends: even more confusing. And holidays: alternate depending on even or odd year. My body split in two, mitosis rendered me into two completely different people. Two houses, two rooms, two beds, two pillows, two ME's.

237 steps, I'm almost there. It's time to think of an opening to put him in a good mood. I'm forty-five minutes late, I know. It was because Mom needed me. Think positive, what can I say to distract his attention from infuriation? How about his girlfriend, or maybe a compliment regarding the house. Hundreds of opening lines whirl around inside my head. A whirlpool of words; I try to organize my thoughts so that they flow like the words in a sweet song. Time to switch into "Dad Mode." No mentioning of Mom, no asking for

money to buy shampoo or conditioner, no acting "rude," no complaining about the food served for dinner—I can do this.

256 steps, I've reached my front door and the transformation is complete. I'm ready. A five minute walk has sent me wandering through my past, zipping by the good times and the bad. I know they both love me, they just love different ME's. In only fifty-five hours and fifteen minutes, the short weekend will be over and I'll begin my journey back to my front door.

Juliette Mandel attends McGill University.

66

RISING FROM THE ASHES

A dramatic experience is not necessary for a good essay, but if you've had one, there is no reason not to write about it. Author Daria Taback didn't need to look far to find an engaging anecdote. Her house burned down less than a year before she wrote her essay, and the drama of that experience guarantees that the reader will be drawn in. But after the opening, then what? This essay shines because of Daria's heartfelt description of acts of kindness from friends, neighbors, and strangers. Most stories about a personal transformation sound phony, but this one is believable because of the circumstances and Daria's concrete descriptions.

Essay by Daria Taback

On May 30, 2004, I woke up to bloodcurdling screaming that I'd only heard in horror movies. The haziness of the deep sleep from which I emerged was still fading when I realized that the piercing cries were coming from my mother. I rubbed my eyes as she stood over me, frantically sputtering that I needed to get up, that there was a fire. We ran down the stairs in the dark, because the lights were no longer working. I opened the front door, grabbed my old, senile dog by the collar, and ran across the street to my neighbor's house. As I stood, facing my home, I saw for the first time the fire in its full blazing glory. The black night lit up with hot, menacing flames that were eating away my room, my journals, my sketchbooks, my stories, my watercolor paintings, my music, my piano, and my home.

As I stood watching in a daze, my parents went to wake up our neighbors because the fire was raging and their lives were in danger. Meanwhile, I was motionless, unaware of my surroundings, utterly numb and disbelieving. Twenty minutes later, the fire department came. By then, most of the house was in ruins. After a couple of hours, the last of the flames and billowing smoke was out. The verdict was that nothing was salvageable.

Neighbors across the street, who had woken to the sound of the fire trucks, gave us chairs to sit in, sweaters and blankets. They comforted us immeasurably. Strangers showed us their compassion and goodwill by going around the neighborhood and collecting clothes for us to wear, since we no longer had any. One family let us stay in their house for three weeks. Another couple went to buy us our medications, while others gave us toiletries and other supplies. These were mostly individuals whom we had never seen or spoken to before in our lives.

This experience was a turning point in my life. I have always been a bit of a critic and skeptical of human nature, but this experience gave me a new perspective on the capacity for human generosity. When I felt most vulnerable and scared, the friendly smile of a passing neighbor, the strong hug of a family friend, the warmth of nourishing food brought endlessly to sustain us by parents of my mother's school was a lifeline to recovery.

> **Neighbors across the street, who had woken to the sound of the fire trucks, gave us chairs to sit in, sweaters and blankets.**

I don't know if a person ever completely recovers from an experience like this. But, ironically, I do feel that the fire has given me several remarkable gifts. I feel a deep connection to my community and a great need to give to others the help and caring that I experienced. Interacting with many new people has helped me grow from a more timid, self-involved person, to a more mature individual who cares deeply about the needs of others. Most of all, I have gained a vivid appreciation of life, flames and all.

Daria Taback attends Oberlin College.

67

A FRESH TAKE ON CAMPING

Many essays begin with an air of mystery that lasts for a sentence or two, but this one prolongs the uncertainty through a five-sentence first paragraph. Author Megan Topolewski drops a clue for each of the five senses, but only in the second paragraph does she spill the beans that her subject is a camping trip. Note as well that in cataloging what she "learns," Megan starts with the small stuff: how to pack ziplock bags, and the joys of eating off the ground. Starting with the mundane makes her more credible when she moves on to the big lessons.

Essay by Megan Topolewski

Please write, in some detail, about an experience, an achievement, a person, or a matter of particular significance to you.

Last year I got to taste life; the lukewarm water of revival flowing down my throat. I got to feel it, in the pumping of my heart, the layers of dry dust encrusted on my hands. I got to smell it; the magnified aroma of my body fused on my clothes. I got to hear it too; the melody of zippers. And I got to see it; the orange mountains and cliffs, and sand that I thought I was used to. But this time I didn't just drive by them or admire them from a pool side.

I went shopping for hiking boots and pants that made me look like a miniature version of the tent I would be sleeping in for that week. We call it "Project Term" at my school, where we get to pick one of several trips to go on. I picked the most difficult, the one with the warning attached. The one without the bathrooms, the mirrors, the showers. I went into it so scared that I could not imagine a "me" that could have survived it. My big goal for myself was to do just that; to get through it. But I came out of it, indeed, as no one who I could have foreseen. I came back with clothes that needed to be washed twice, hair that had wildly regressed back into its natural curl, and the notion that the suburbs would no longer pass as satisfactory. I learned to eat spilled pasta off the ground, that it was fun and tasted just fine. I learned that there are more stars in the sky than I thought. I learned how to package my clothes air-tight, into zip-lock bags. I woke each morning with every muscle muttering in complaint, but hiked a mountain that day anyway. I treasured my bruises and the new holes in my clothing. I felt what it was like to hold myself, dangling in front of a waterfall. I learned that my mountain bike at home has no idea of its luck in escaping the torturous trails out west. I know that it's best to take small baby steps to walk up a steep hill. I'm also learning that these things can be metaphors for life. The most important thing I came back with was a new belief in myself, where I had previously harbored doubts. I came back with ambition to learn about the world. Life, I'm ready for you.

> **I learned to eat spilled pasta off the ground, that it was fun and tasted just fine.**

Megan Topolewski attends the University of Wisconsin at Madison.

BOOT CAMP 101

The following essay is jolting because it begins with images that are alien to American high school students—a commander, an M-16, and a hand grenade. The interjections of Hebrew tell the reader that the author is probably an American in Israel, but not until the second paragraph does Danielle Weinberg pause to fill in the details of why she is there. Good dialogue and the harshness of army life sustain reader interest. To conclude, Danielle pulls off an extended analogy between the Sabra cactus and Israeli society, which further shows her creativity, her ability to think abstractly, and her skills as a writer.

Essay by Danielle Weinberg

I trudged onward at the exhausting pace set by my commander. The stripes of mud on my face mixed with the sweat of the desert, running into my tired eyes. I was not allowed to roll up my pants or long sleeves—the enemy might see my white arms or legs. The M-16 grew heavier as I carried it hour after hour. "*Azar!*" yelled my commander. I ran as fast as I could, counting in Hebrew, "*Esrim v'echad!* Twenty-two! Twenty-three!" On twenty-four, I flung myself to the ground, covered my head, and crossed my ankles. That was when the *rimon*, the hand grenade, exploded.

"If you had been any slower, you would have been dead!" my *mefakedet*, commander, yelled. That was field day, the day I spent emulating Israeli soldiers as part of Gadna, a week-long program that Israeli high school teens attend before entering *Tzahal*, the Israeli Defense Forces. This experience was just one of the eleven weeks I spent last fall at the Alexander Muss High School in Israel. The course emphasized the reality of life as an Israeli. At first, I relished the novelty of it, but soon I truly came to understand the harsh reality of life in Israel.

Throughout Gadna, I watched the majority of Israelis mock their commanders, ignoring them as if they were simply reveling in a seaside Tel-Aviv café. I was shocked by their behavior and couldn't understand their motives, but as the week wore on, I stumbled upon the true meaning. For an American tourist (for that was what I was), Gadna was exactly what it is, a simulation of the army. For Israelis, it, too, was just a game, but because they knew that soon the game would end and they would become real soldiers, they relished all the free time they had left.

Often, as I trained in the Israeli wilderness, I would see (or feel) the Sabra cactus, a prickly, green cactus that bears sweet red fruits. I would watch these tough kids rolling over the cacti without a grimace and yet,

I ran as fast as I could, counting in Hebrew, "*Esrim v'echad!* Twenty-two! Twenty-three!"

later that day, I would see them eating the sweet, fleshy fruit with a laidback smile on their faces. Thus, I inevitably stumbled across the true mold of Israelis, the secret success of their society—the sabra. Like the sabra, the harsh environment Israelis have been subjected to for so long forced them to evolve the tough, thorny skin of sabras that is evident on the street, at the cafes, and in the army. The rough, outer layer, compelled to absorb the cruelty of life in the Middle East, gives way to a sweet, juicy heart, full of love and the will to live amidst a war of terrorism. Because of this, so many Israelis lay down their schoolbooks, hoes, or guitars for an M-16 and fight, simply to exist.

Danielle Weinberg attends the University of Michigan.

69

IN THE HIGH MOUNTAINS

If you're going to write about an experience away from home, there is one simple rule: give details. The trip offers a ready source of fodder: the sights, the sounds, the smells, but most of all, the people. For Harden Wisebram, it was the experience of being trusted by thirty-five classmates to cook breakfast, or lead a mountain hike, that ultimately led her to develop such a strong sense of place at the High Mountain Institute. The essay works because she is able to speak convincingly about how her experiences fostered her personal growth.

"Winter's First Snow" by Harden Wisebram

On November 1, 2003, halfway through my four-month stay in Leadville, Colorado, the winter's first snow fell from the sky. My peers beamed with excitement; ski season was upon them. I, however, stood staring in awe at the gentle, white flakes floating to the ground. The green and blue world that I was accustomed to faded to shades of grey and white. I came from Georgia to attend the High Mountain Institute for a semester, and this was my first experience living in a world at peace with the snow.

Quickly, I learned that unlike the icy snow that occasionally fell from the Southern sky, Western snow stuck around, and I was going to have to deal with it. Rather than hibernating inside my house, gas fireplace burning, heater running, I awoke at two in the morning in order to re-stoke the fire in my cabin's wood-burning stove and add another layer of Carmex to my cracking lips. Rather than receiving an anticipated snow-day off from school, I still had breakfast cooking duty, and no matter how many times I slipped and fell on the freshly snow-blanketed path that was just shoveled yesterday, I had to prepare the meal. For the first time in my life, if I did not take care of my communal responsibilities, no one else would, and consequently, I would disappoint thirty-five of my closest friends.

During those four months, my fear of surviving in the cold was not the only obstacle I overcame. There were other things such as having to face conflict because of the inevitable intimacy of nineteen girls sharing one bathroom, or the monotony of wearing the same red snow bibs with a green patch over the right knee for three days straight because laundry was Saturday. More importantly, there were the mountains to climb: Mt. Elbert's 14, 443 feet of new self-confidence and Mt. Massive's 14, 313 feet of intellectual awakening.

Seven days into our first backpacking expedition, it was my turn to be leader for the day: it was my responsibility to plan the route, check the maps, and guide the group to our next campsite on Mt. Elbert. I presented the day's RAD—route and description—plan to the group and stood shocked when no one second-guessed my words. In my own mind I had been listing my imperfections, but they trusted me, they believed that I could successfully lead them through the day. That night after camp was set, I realized just how many opportunities I wasted by doubting myself in the past. I could be a leader, and I could trust myself.

Having allowed self-confidence back into my life, I knew that no longer could I just go through the motions of life. On our second backpacking trip, through the woods of Mt. Massive, I discovered a passion for living and learning. As I sat in history class, snuggled among trees with snow leaves and eight hot chocolate-drinking friends, my least favorite subject in the world transformed to more than words on a page. Since that day, I have not slugged through masses of pages in a McGraw-Hill textbook hoping to make an A, but rather embraced the opportunity to learn and let the words become images and thoughts in my mind.

> **On our second backpacking trip, through the woods of Mt. Massive, I discovered a passion for living and learning.**

One day after the Mt. Massive trip, I sat on the front steps of my cabin listening to individual snowflakes come to rest upon the white blanket that covered the ground. Aware of the new thoughts and emotions evoked within me, I worried that upon my return home those gifts would fade away. But now, a year later, as I sit looking across my backyard in Georgia, I see Leadville and its two majestic mountains with snowcapped peaks. I know that the passion, curiosity, and self-worth instilled in me by living with those thirty-five people in harmony with the world will never leave.

Sleeping bag is warm,
Hot and sunny like summer.
It is ten below.

Harden Wisebram attends Oberlin College.

Humor

The world is full of people who laugh at their own jokes. Making other people laugh is harder. The best humor essays are spectacular; the ones that fail are embarrassing. Since being funny on paper is much more difficult than cracking a joke with your friends, only excellent writers should make the attempt. Be aware that there is often a humor generation gap, and get an adult to make sure that what is funny to you will also be funny to the older person who reads your application. The essays in this section show various approaches, from sustained parody on a single theme to free-floating, hit-and-run mockery of various subjects.

70
ESSAY AS MONOLOGUE

Says author Laura Cobb, "It all just hit me really quickly one Saturday. I had gotten my National Merit application, and the question about what set me apart had been rolling around in my head for a few days. A light bulb went off in my head; I repeated the line a few times, and then I sprinted as fast as I could to my computer." From there, it was less than an hour before Laura had completed most of her essay. For anyone with aspirations of being funny, the best way is often to get on a roll like Laura does in this essay. The key is to make them laugh while doing a stream of consciousness that highlights interesting and important things about yourself.

Essay by Laura Cobb

In your own words, describe your personal characteristics, accomplishments, primary interests, plans, and goals. What sets you apart?

I won my school's Pickleball tournament in tenth grade. How many National Merit Semi-Finalists can say that?

What? That's not enough to set me apart in the massive pile of applications? Well, maybe I hold the world record for most snow cones eaten in the summer of 2004, or the record for most piggy back rides given as a camp counselor. I'll have to double check on those. Academically, I'm valedictorian of my class. My sixth grade graduating class, that is. I gave a speech and everything.

Well, perhaps my work with autistic children would set me apart. Has anyone else mentioned being stabbed in the eye with a plastic zebra? (Fear not, my eyesight fully recovered a few minutes later.) Aside from that incident, the experience I had volunteering in a special education classroom has motivated me to pursue autism studies at a graduate and post-graduate level. I want to solve autism's puzzles. I want to research, to discover, and to cure. I want to make my mark in one of science's most fascinating and mysterious fields.

I only failed my driving test once.

I've won awards for placing seventh nationally in the Grand Concours National French Exam, but I'm also building my Spanish vocabulary by watching soap operas on Telemundo. *"¿Como puedes llegarme, Consuelo?"* See? That's academic initiative.

How about wanting to change the world? I've been active in my school's chapter of Amnesty International, I petitioned local government to support amendment of the Fair Labor Standards Act to protect youth workers, and my peers know never to challenge me in a debate over gay rights.

Also, two of my best friends have webbed toes. I don't know whether or not that means I get along best with people who are part duck, but it's an interesting coincidence.

Maybe, in order to stand out, I should focus on awards and other honors. I won the Brown University Book Award, and I also won the "Streaker" award for a particularly unattractive tan line at a recent camp. Plus, I was inducted into the National Honor Society around the time someone titled me the "least aggravating person in the world."

In the end, I could describe dozens of things that would suggest unique motivation, interests, or personality traits. However, I think the best representation of

Has anyone else mentioned being stabbed in the eye with a plastic zebra?

myself cannot be restricted to five hundred typed words. Perhaps I've scribbled in more correct bubbles on my standardized tests than some, but I think my biggest accomplishment is the confidence I've built in my entire person. I haven't spent my entire life trying to be a student at an elite university, I've spent it trying to be the best, most well-rounded person I can be. I hope, in the long run, that this is what will truly set me apart.

Laura Cobb attends Washington University in St. Louis.

71

THE APPLICANT HAS NO CLOTHES

For the few applicants who can be consistently funny in an essay, the following one will offer plenty of ideas. Author Daniel Fredrick is an actor who shows that he is also a pretty fair writer. He turns the application/audition process into a parody, and in the process shows unusual self-awareness. Was the admission process frightening enough to drive him into the college of business? Not hardly, but it obviously gave him plenty of material to consider for a different career: stand-up comedy.

Essay by Daniel Fredrick

Do you ever have those dreams where you've arrived at school and suddenly realize you've forgotten to wear pants? Well, for most high school seniors that dream becomes a reality, at least figuratively. We must bare our souls, not to best friends, or family, but to complete strangers who may not even want to hear about it and may even flat-out reject us. What twisted institution would ever subject young adults in the formative stages of emotional growth to this experience? Oh, right. College.

During the sixth, seventh, and eighth grade, my family lived in New York City, where public high school is not the best option for a serious secondary school education. This means that students must apply to high schools all over the city, in much the same way they will proceed four years later in the college search. At the time, I considered how fortunate I was to be able to get some experience in this realm before I had to do it "for real." I had no idea how wrong I was and how ill prepared I would feel. I eased into the college process with a nonchalance belying the gravity of the situation. I figured that I would never actually *go to college*. This was all just an elaborate joke. I'd stay suspended in high school in perpetuity. Isn't that what the *Happy Days* kids did?

After views to the contrary were repeated enough times by teachers, parents, and friends, it dawned on me that maybe I really would have to go to college. And so it began. As a student who plans to pursue a degree in acting, not only did I have to write essays, visit colleges, and participate in interviews designed to yank out the weeds, I

> **I figured that I would never actually *go to college*. This was all just an elaborate joke.**

also had to audition. It is disconcerting enough to be told by a college that they don't feel you are right for them, but to also be told that you just aren't talented enough? It is a prospect frightening enough to drive me into the school of business (well, maybe not quite). So I dutifully prepared my two contrasting monologues, one contemporary and one classical, totaling no more than two minutes in length each, and prepared to go to school with no pants.

As of this moment, I've auditioned for two of my four prospective schools and although I've been accepted to three, the decision of each theatre department will be the deciding factor. Writing this essay has suddenly made me realize the gross unfairness of the college process, and inspired me to try to balance out the issue. From now on, every college rep, department head, and theatre professor I meet, I'll simply request that in the interest of fairness, they remove their pants.

Daniel Fredrick attends Texas Christian University.

72

EMILY DICKINSON, JIMMY BUFFET, AND A CHEAP BOTTLE OF SHAMPOO

Multifaceted people sometimes write multifaceted essays. Though there is always danger in having a blurry focus, an essay that encompasses a number of topics can work if the purpose is to show the various sides of an author's personality. Alysa Hannon's essay, below, is packed with details. She says that her personality includes "an accumulation of quirks and nuances," and the same can be said for her essay. As is so often the case, the proof is in the details, which reveal her wide-ranging knowledge. Says Hannon, "I don't think it matters whether you write about your trip to Uganda or your first comic book: just so long as what is written is a glimpse into what it would be like to sit in a room with you."

Essay by Alysa Hannon

Contrary to what you may think, buying a bottle of shampoo is a complex and tedious process. First, I chose the five most outwardly appealing bottles, conscious that my seventeen-year-old female mind is being manipulated by blatantly false phrases like "made with real herbs so your hair will stay shiny for up to eight and a half hours." After repeatedly inhaling the essentially same fragrance from each bottle, mulling over which label and aroma has won my four dollars and seventeen cents, the Marxist impulse within me, instilled by my unfathomably cheap father, compels my reluctant hand to pick up the sixth, cheapest bottle which was eliminated in round one. I've described this process so that, to some small degree, you may understand how difficult it is for such an indecisive, meticulous person like me to choose a topic for what has been unconsciously labeled by my teachers, advisors, parents, and friends as the most important essay I will ever write. In my quest for the perfect subject, I have realized that my three-faced personality does not ameliorate the situation. (I'm relatively sure that both illuminating my indecision and disclosing my undiagnosed multiple personality disorder did not rank high on my college advisor's "Tips for Writing Your College Essay.") To speak bluntly, I assume three personas no one is less truthful than the others and each has a parallel essay topic with which I toyed.

The most visible facet of me is Ms. "I have a 4.27 GPA." She is a perpetually working student, a basketball starter, and a good Catholic schoolgirl at heart. Those who see me as my résumé consider my quest for a perfect paper topic asinine. From their perspectives, my subject was strategically chosen when I submitted my down payment for my community service trip to Africa last spring break. Despite the indelible mark my Malawian excursion left upon my perceptions, I have an intrinsic, unexplainable aversion to turning that experience into a Hallmark postcard.

Having discarded my African journey as a viable essay topic, I was persuaded by a small but disproportionately influential constituency to narrate the convoluted soap opera, melodrama also called my life. Because I am a relatively private person, I have disclosed my story to only a few travelers I have encountered along my way. My family and I have mastered the art of duality. As a child, I could emerge from a household teeming with turmoil and tension and saunter into my first period class with a ribbon in my hair and a gentle smile sketched across my face. Despite how important my college admission is to me, I don't think it appropriate, helpful or wholly insightful to recount the

> **It is my instinctive compulsion to say a silent Hail Mary upon hearing the drone of sirens.**

convoluted, unorthodox string of events that have taken place from second grade to the present. I continue to be shaped by my upbringing; however, I have made certain that I am much more than a familial sob story.

The final facet of my character is the most vague but most dynamic and to me, most telling. It is simply the accumulation of the quirks and nuances of who I have become over the course of seventeen years. It is I, the Bruce Springsteen admirer, the Jimmy

Buffet parrothead, and the eternal hummer of those skillfully written hymns I can never seem to remove from my subconscious all day Sunday. It is my instinctive compulsion to say a silent Hail Mary upon hearing the drone of sirens and a quiet "God Bless You" after even the most remote sneeze. It is the way in which the words of Emily Dickinson can transport me into a realm of thought and reflection after an interminable day of tests and deadlines. It is the spine-chilling anticipation with which I long for November when I can start playing Nat King Cole's "Chestnuts Roasting on an Open Fire," and the eternal ability of a star-studded sky to leave me awestricken and contentedly trivial. It is I, the last girl to leave the locker room after every basketball game, intentionally taking a little extra time so that she can walk through the now dimly lit, empty gym, which always seems sacred. And the topic that sprung from the most basic instinct of this girl was a very simple story, one that seems to evoke suppressed chuckles when told. Two nights ago after returning from a field trip to the Metropolitan Museum of Art, I sat at my desk at around 10:30 p.m., in an attempt to shorten the seemingly unending list of tasks I had to complete by the next morning. An experienced studier, I could easily envision the order in which my assignments should have been undertaken: AP European History test, college applications, Bible reading quiz, math homework, etc. At the very end of the list remained an optional assignment for my AP Art History class, which entailed writing a poem after visiting the Egyptian temple of Dendur earlier that day. Despite the tests I would inevitably take the next morning or the applications due the next afternoon, I sat for thirty minutes and let my hand poetically glide across the blank sheet of paper before me, completely aware of my inefficient use of time, but unable to feign concern. To a stranger, my decision to narrate the manner in which I approached my homework may seem ludicrous; however, to me it is a fable of freedom. Two years ago, even two weeks ago, I would have felt the innate urge to write a poem instead of studying for an imminent test; but being the responsible student I am, I would have suppressed that Thoreauvian compulsion as I memorized the six wives of Henry the eighth.

In forty years, I suppose that my laundry list of credentials will have been many times amended and my collection of stories to tell, tragedies and comedies, will be gorged. But I hope, given the opportunity, I will always choose to write the poem.

Alysa Hannon attends Georgetown University.

73

IF *THE NEW YORKER* CALLS, SHE'LL BE READY

Most essays are tightly focused around one theme—the tighter, the better. But it is also possible to write an excellent essay that meanders, as long as the meandering is artful and intentional. Author Leah Jordan's essay flows like a stream of consciousness, from her love of reading to a more general love of learning, then to Judaism, her ambition to write the great American novel, and her love of *The New Yorker* magazine. The free-flowing quality of the essay makes for a human portrait, with the last paragraph accentuating its quirky charm.

Essay by Leah Jordan

The first thing anyone must know about me is that I love to read. I devour books. If I could, I would eat my favorite books. I would. You laugh, but it's true. This love of reading, which began in earnest when I fell in love with *The Hobbit* in third grade, naturally led me to all sorts of things. The most important of these is one for which I am ever grateful—a love of learning. I am fascinated by history and, though I almost collapsed under the weight of my European History class, I survived because I loved the subject itself. I also enjoy sociology and psychology and their studies of human behavior and interaction.

I love language. I have been taking French since freshman year and started Spanish last year. I can pronounce and read Hebrew fluently, though half the time I don't know what I'm saying. Because of this, I plan to spend a year in Israel in the near future. This is perhaps my greatest goal at the moment. I would like to be part of a specific, post-high school program. It's based out of a poor neighborhood in Jerusalem, and I would spend the mornings in a four-hour Hebrew immersion course and divide my time in the afternoons between community service (teaching English to Israeli high schoolers) and other academic classes.

My fierce love of Judaism fills my life in many ways. I visited Israel for five weeks this past summer as part of the Bronfman Youth Fellowship in Israel, a merit-based, all-expense-paid program that takes twenty-six North American Jewish teens each summer to Israel—to learn about Jewish people, Israel, and, more specifically, the Arab/Israeli conflict. In eighth grade, I became a Hebrew teaching assistant, and for the past four years I have spent two hours each week teaching Hebrew to classes of elementary school students at my synagogue.

I would love to become a rabbi one day. If not a rabbi, then a professional academic, so I can continue to eat books all the time. I also wouldn't object to traveling the world bohemian-style for as many years as I can still move, writing novels, and discussing politics, art, and love with absolutely everyone. But I found out recently that it drives me crazy to live out of a suitcase, so perhaps that idea's a flop. Ah, and quite seriously, my secret ambition, one that I sometimes suspect many people entertain, is to write the next great American novel. It will go something like this: "One of the first things I was aware of in life was that my parents had loved other people before me." And it will be a thin novel, subtle and crisp—or maybe sweeping and imprecise, Whitmanesque, but everyone will love it because, as people do, they will sense how much love I poured into it, and they will smile.

I would also saw my left arm off, never the right, to work for *The New Yorker*. God, how I love that magazine, even if their movie reviews are the most elitist, blind exercises in pretentiousness I have ever seen. *I'm* pretentious. It could work.

Leah Jordan attends the University of Kansas.

74

SHE'S A PERRIER DRINKER, AND PROUD OF IT

If the whole college-essay thing seems a little contrived, feel free to make a joke out of it. Just make sure you have the writing skills to do the job. Author Angèle Larroque delivers a wicked parody by using her taste for Perrier to showcase her off-beat sense of humor. She invents screwball reasons why she loves Perrier, creates tongue-in-cheek categories of Perrier drinkers, and suggests that her devotion to Perrier shows her ambition. But is her love of Perrier enough to get Angèle into college? Read on and see for yourself.

"The Beverage That Changed My Life" by Angèle Larroque

I love Perrier water with the depths of my soul. I cannot get enough of the cool, fizzy bubbles rolling on my tongue. The crisp taste is pure bliss for the palate. The bitter aftertaste is the best part of the Perrier experience.

Maybe I love Perrier because I am French to the core. I have a complicated name that is difficult to pronounce, the metabolism of a hummingbird, and I own quite a few black clothes. I also drink bitter coffee and eat baguettes and I am sometimes rude to strangers. Je suis francaise, hence, I have inherited the Perrier gene. Perrier is not just a beverage; it is a way of life.

There are two kinds of Perrier drinkers. There are those who are snobby and sophisticated who take small snooty sips from a glass while at a swanky café, and there are the free-spirited drinkers. I am the latter. I am one of the c'est la vie, I-have-class-but-appreciate-chaos, fine-art-loving, passionate drinkers. We drink Perrier with almost every meal and carry it around in small bottles during the school day. Unlike the snooty Perrier drinkers, you cannot pretend to be one of us. Either you are born with the Perrier gene or you are not. I hate to admit the fact that when I was young, I hated the taste of Perrier. But what set me apart from other preteen Perrier haters was that I wanted to love Perrier and inevitably would one day. I then subjected myself to years of

I am one of the c'est la vie, I-have-class-but-appreciate-chaos, fine-art-loving, passionate drinkers.

training the palate in order to love the taste. This shows that I am ambitious. I saw something I wanted and with hard work and dedication, I drank so much Perrier that I developed a love for it. I am a Perrier lover and can never escape it!

As I was writing this essay, my table companion and classmate told me something amusing.

"You know what you're going to be when you're older?" he asked. "You're going to be one of those skinny French girls in a Parisian café, chain smoking and laughing at all the American tourists!"

I can't wait.

Angèle Larroque is a graduate of Parsons School of Design.

75

DO YOU BITE YOUR NAILS? WANT TO WRITE ABOUT IT?

For a topic that literally everybody can write about, all you need to do is look at your hands. That's what Samantha Levy asked readers to do when she wrote the following essay. Samantha bites her nails—a fact that she is not proud of—but nail-biting gave her all the fodder she needed for a terrific essay. Nail-biting? An unconventional topic to say the least, but she pulls it off. The essay shows, among other things, her attention to detail, her ability to confront her insecurities, and her aspirations for the future.

Essay by Samantha Levy

Take a moment and look at your hands: their shape, texture, size, and delicacy. These parts of your body are one of the most important creations. They are the scribes of every document; the builders of homes, offices, and shelters; and what comforts many during a frightening experience. But, for me, my hands have yet to display any external similarities to the role they were created to fulfill.

One of the functions our hands are supposed to perform is a firm handshake. It shows character, attention—qualities that represent a good person. My handshake, although firm, embarrassingly reveals the pitiful remnants of my fingernails, outwardly signaling a nervous habit. And, at the end of each day, I must look in the mirror and recognize that I am a nail biter, an occupation I'm certainly ready to retire.

Unfortunately, and trust me I've searched, there are no official support groups for nail biters. All nail biters are left in seclusion to nibble away at what remains of their fingernails and their self-esteem. During these isolated moments, as I bite my nails or cuticles, I think of individuals with aesthetically pleasing nails in fear that they will look down upon me for the way I torture my fingers.

Likewise, I oftentimes find myself observing other peoples' hands. For instance, when dining at Greensboro's local Chinese buffet, Panda Inn, I continually notice that most of the female employers take great care maintaining their nails: they ensure that they never reach far beyond the fingertips, nor do they paint them a strange color. I've also found that these same qualities are present with the cashiers at the grocery store, and even most of my peers.

It would seem that all I desire is to give up nail biting. However, in my heart, what I'd really like to do is find happiness in the accomplishments my hands achieve rather than focus on their appearance.

For even my hands possess beauty. They have delivered muffins to elderly in the hospital, typed continuously to finish newspaper articles within a deadline, and were very useful in pointing out each syllable while teaching my younger brother to read. Though superficially they are unappealing, my hands have led me to success throughout my life. Undoubtedly, I do wish that I had long, French manicured nails. But hopefully, I will grow to regard such physical features as simply superficial.

All nail biters are left in seclusion to nibble away at what remains of their fingernails and their self-esteem.

I am certain that the university I attend will help me strengthen my education and nurture my character and confidence to the degree that I would no longer perceive myself according to the physical condition of my nails. Instead, I will present myself to the world as Samantha Levy, a young woman who learned among the brightest, explored with the courageous, and took on the world hands first.

Samantha Levy attends the University of North Carolina at Chapel Hill.

76

WRITING ABOUT UNDERWEAR

If you want to write your essay about underwear—or a similarly inane topic—be our guest. Just be sure you know where you're going. Author Briana Mahoney uses underwear to set up a flight of fancy that showcases her skill as a writer. Why does Colgate ask a question like this? Not because they care about what you would bring, but because they want to know what you can embroider from musings about what will be (in most cases) an ordinary item. Briana uses the underwear to get to her madcap story, then loops back to explain that, yes, the story really did have to do with underwear and Colgate.

Essay by Briana Mahoney

What is one thing you would bring with you to Colgate and why?

Underwear. Say it to a kindergarten class, and they'll giggle endlessly. Write it in a college essay and… well, I guess I'll find out. But specifically I'm talking about long underwear; cozy, toasty, stretchy long underwear. I've never been much of a cold weather person, but give me a pair of long underwear and I'm "good to go."

I've only been skiing once in my life, but I remember it as one of my most exhilarating experiences. My first run down the mountain, my knees felt a bit weak and I was having trouble steering myself from side to side. With my family watching, I desperately tried to stay upright. Suddenly, I was blazing down the slope with my skis perfectly parallel as parents urgently tried to shuffle their children out of my way. With snow flying out in a wake behind me, my eyes locked in on the lodge dead ahead. Fearing for my life, and for those of the people carelessly milling about in front of the lodge doors, I finally caught on to proper skiing technique—in one direction, at least. With arms and ski poles flailing, I careened to my left, zooming past the horrified faces of the seasoned professionals waiting for the ski lift. Now completely off the slope and still flying across the level ground, I knew the end was near...then I spotted it—the fence. During my last moments of dignity (if any such moments had existed on this trip), I closed my eyes, braced myself, and slammed into the wood. As I recovered from the shock, I burst into giggles and thought to myself, "Let's do that again!"

Now, the important thing to remember here is not that I have virtually no skills on the slopes or that I might endanger the safety of your children. No, the thing to remember is that I was wearing, at that glorious moment, a pair of

> **As I recovered from the shock, I burst into giggles and thought to myself, "Let's do that again!"**

long underwear. And so, you see, if I'm accepted to and attend Colgate, the first item I'll throw into my turquoise duffel will be my long underwear. Because if my run on the slopes comes anywhere near the thrills and chills of Colgate, I'm going to need a little warmth and some extra padding.

Briana Mahoney attends Furman University.

77

WHY DOGS ARE BETTER THAN CHILDREN

Animals are a fertile subject for tongue-in-cheek essays, and author Emily Perryman gets on a roll talking about the difference between a screaming toddler and an adorable puppy. There is no over-arching theme or meaning in the essay, but the ability to show a wry sense of humor and a flair for writing is more than good enough. When you're an admissions officer gazing at applications piled up to your navel, a little comic relief is much appreciated.

Essay by Emily Perryman

It's odd how a random thought can pop into your head and completely change the way you view something. Well, I realized today that I do not want children. This revelation came to me while walking into the grocery store. An exasperated young mother was trying to comfort her child. The little girl was throwing the ultimate temper tantrum, one worthy of an Academy award. She was stubbornly sitting on the ground, flailing her arms, kicking her feet, and was screaming at such a high pitch that it made me cringe. As I passed this sight, the mother looked at me, gave me a faint smile, and muttered, "kids…." under her breath. She then proceeded to carry her child to the car, kicking and screaming the whole way. I laughed and didn't think about it for very long.

When I was leaving the store, I was half expecting to see the mother still trying to get her child situated in the car seat, but I was denied that privilege. Instead, my attention was focused on an adorable Labrador puppy that was entertaining its owner while his wife was inside. It was doing such a great job of entertaining his owner that several other shoppers had stopped to enjoy the show, too. Well, this puppy was the epitome of an unproportional animal. Its lanky legs and huge paws were no match for the puppy's "pleasantly plump" body. It kept tripping over its feet while trying to catch its tail, even though its tail was not much more than a stub. When it would fall down, its belly would cushion the fall, but if the dog tried to roll over, his stomach prevented him from rolling all the way over. The puppy's owner would then pick it up and the whole cycle would start again.

That's when it hit me. Why in the world would anyone want a screaming, fussy child that grows up to be a screaming, fussy teenager when you can have a cute, playful dog that grows up to be your cute, playful best friend? As I proceeded to think about this on my drive home, I mentally compared and contrasted the two. Dogs don't complain if they are taken somewhere they don't like. In fact, dogs feel more than honored to get in the car even if it's just to the store on the corner. Children complain if they don't want to go somewhere and if it conflicts with their favorite TV show. Dogs are more than happy to eat *anything* you cook even if it's just flat out bad. Children say that their food is too spicy, too hot, too cold, not sweet enough, not pizza, too healthy, and too boring since homemade meals don't normally come with a prize. Dogs think that you are perfect, no matter how many times you might accidentally leave them outside. Children think that parents are weird and are anything but cool or perfect. The final thing was the one that sold me: the fact that the cost to raise children is on the rise since the education, housing, and medical costs are becoming more expensive, whereas the cost to have a dog remains constant.

> **Why in the world would anyone want a screaming, fussy child that grows up to be a screaming, fussy teenager?**

In the end, having a dog seems to be the better investment. They don't scream, kick, throw temper tantrums, and definitely don't complain about the cooking. Besides, when the dog turns eighteen, he's not calculating just how quickly he can get out of the house. He's just thinking about how much he wants to curl in bed with you to get his nightly belly rub.

Emily Perryman attends Southern Methodist University.

78

A NEW VERSION OF *SURVIVOR*

Author Carolyn Silveira wrote the following essay in response to one of University of Chicago's esoteric essay questions. In the process, she illustrates how doing a summer program at a particular institution can pay dividends in the admissions process. Carolyn already knows the place backwards and forwards, and has plenty of anecdotes about actually having been there. It helps that she is a clever writer. Says Carolyn, "I think my essay worked because I wrote about something I loved—without having to pretend that some extracurricular activity was my life calling—and was given permission to not be serious."

Essay by Carolyn Silveira

Use your imagination to create your own version of "Chicago Survivor."

...We interrupt our regularly scheduled admissions process for a special report brought to us by a member of the fantastic action-adventure series, *Chicago Survivor: Summer 2001....*

Unbeknownst to the common Angeleno high school student, a strange and wonderful game for the strong of heart is held annually and inconspicuously at the University of Chicago; unbeknownst to the common man, I *am* the Chicago survivor. Under the guise of an innocent summer study program for teenagers, Chicago lures promising, robust students to volunteer a precious month of their young lives to eat, sleep, work, and survive in conditions modeled after a typical college world: there would be dorms, strange classmates, late nights, peculiar professors, questionable food, and countless trials that would be neither planned nor trivial. Though I signed myself up completely unaware of the strange world I was about to enter, I did not and do not complain. I have conquered the system. I have survived. I have been to the edge of Hyde Park and back. My tale is one of trial and triumph.

To the untrained eye, the typical college dorm seems a pleasant place of coziness, community, and cookies. It is. But do not be fooled! Acquiring such a level of comfort and security requires a certain savvy, a finesse, a level of sophistication. My arduous task begins the instant I pay my taxi driver an obscene amount of money and pass through the doors to the Woodward Court Building. The desk lady looks hungry and impatient, but knowing that she holds the key to my lair, I approach the lion's den…. Having secured a key to room 1407, I wheel my embarrassingly bulky suitcase down the hall, only to be ambushed by a snappy, sarcastic, and—dare I say unhinged—blonde R.A. named Colleen. In the following week, I learn to catch fireflies, walk down Kimbark to 57th to get Gracie's Apple Pie at Medici, to wrestle open my little mailbox, and to take showers at 2:00 a.m., when the hot water is all mine, and I can harmonize to popular music without my friend in the adjoining stall. Special missions completed: surviving treacherous Midnight Soccer against screaming banshee boys and sports-bra sporting girls, making my way to the Bursar's to cash travelers checks (a task which actually involves several trips back and forth if you forget to bring your ID), and deducing the exact positioning of two standing fans to get the maximum cooling possible in our hot-box, fourth-floor, corner room. Tasks yet to be completed: getting to know my ghost of a roommate, figuring out what makes "RIBS-kids" (science students) tick, and tolerating those unsettlingly long silences when our brilliant, lovable professor fades into his own reverie. **[Points earned: 500]**

By the end of the second week, we make our alliances known. We call ourselves the Food Club (for reasons visible at the time), and we, in our solidarity and perseverance, represent Los Angeles, Philadelphia, Houston, Brooklyn, Minneapolis, Champaign, and lesser-known parts of Jersey and Rhode Island. Our only means of survival are the paltry funds of starving college students, ten rides apiece on our Metra passes, and a basic knowledge of map reading. We have already proven ourselves adept at splitting checks, writing papers to the sound of sirens and nightlife, and making Mac'n'Cheese in Tupperware. I can sort my own laundry and work the lights in the library stacks. By now we have even undergone the panic of nearly losing a teammate: Minnesota was indefinitely stuck in an elevator with nothing to comfort her but the sweet songs of Colleen. Only three challenges remain. **[Points: for resourcefulness, 300; for surviving, 500; for letting Colleen sing, -50]**

First, we must prove ourselves street-smart enough to walk through Hyde Park at night in a group of no more than five brave souls. We stake out a movie theater, watch crummy cinema until we can stand it no more, and venture into the night to find our beloved base, Woodward Court. As we meander, we come upon a raggedy-looking woman who stops to compliment a particular tie-dyed shirt one of the alliance is wearing. But before we thank her and move on, she immediately demands that we hand it over! Never! "Run!" cries Brooklyn, and run we do. Frantic and winded, we run faster as we hear her lumbering steps behind us, her shrill voice piercing the night with "Gimme that shirt!" Ducking into the nearest McDonald's, we call a taxi and huddle over McNuggets until the cab arrives. We never look back. **[Points: 75: did not walk three blocks before needing rescue]**

> **First, we must prove ourselves street-smart enough to walk through Hyde Park at night.**

Second, we have to demonstrate the ability to coordinate fun activities for ourselves (to preserve morale, of course). Desperate, we secure four tickets to see Jon Bon Jovi, live in concert. In our excitement to taste such elements of Midwestern American culture as "Living on a Prayer," we tragically jump the gun and board the Metra three measly minutes too soon—heading in the direction dead opposite of the concert. We hop off as soon as we realize our mistake, only to find ourselves stranded at the railroad tracks in a none-too-pretty part of town. Once again we call our trusty friends at Checker Cabs. About an hour later, as we watch the sun droop down toward dingy buildings and junkyards, we give up and head homeward, having lost all hope of ever seeing the great Bon Jovi. Ten dollars and twenty ounces of junk food later, we feel slightly redeemed. **[Points: 30, for bravery in the face of the unknown...and pity]**

Our final and most revealing challenge hits us with an unpredicted force. It is to learn to let go of our team, our world, our game. At the end of one fleeting month, we know that, despite all our spilt milk, we should only smile. After all, we did it. It was all us, all the time. The secrets, the laughs, the fights, the terrors, the finger cramps and paper cuts—all are ours to keep forever. At our beloved Medici, I eat my last BLT and know that without doubt I am leaving stronger, brighter, wiser, and more independent than when I had arrived. We missed our concert, but the entire month has been a show… an intimate portrayal of how much one gains from a single friend, let alone a whole new group. It was drama depicting that whatever the final score of one's first game, winning is inherent in playing. I am the ultimate Chicago Survivor. Learning and playing at Chicago was the ultimate reward, but I am hungry still: games are no substitute for reality. So I am waiting, two thousand miles away, for the Grand Prize—the chance of a lifetime—the sequel.

Carolyn Silveira attends the University of Chicago.

Family and Relationships

The usual problem with writing about a person you admire is that the essay becomes about the person you admire—and not about you. The following essays all succeed in describing a teacher, friend, or family member(s) while also saying plenty about the author. As a group, the student authors show keen powers of observation—of how their relationships have evolved, and of what those relationships have meant to them. Particularly inventive is Essay 79, which begins with the aroma of French perfume in a sock drawer.

79

A WHIFF OF FRENCH PERFUME

Scents can leave a lasting imprint on our minds—a fact that Dori Chandler uses to her advantage in the essay below. She doesn't waste her breath telling about the importance that memories of a foreign visitor hold for her. The memory of French perfume in her sock drawer says it all. At only 261 words, this essay will put a smile on the face of any admission officer staring at a pile of applications on a cold winter's night. The bookend reference to the perfume in the last sentence helps the essay end with a flourish.

Essay by Dori Chandler

I identify Laetitia by the tights scented with French perfume in my sock drawer, her ten-pound black boots, which still live in my closet, and her beautiful laugh I hear over the phone every so often. Laetitia lived with us as an exchange student in 1994, the year my youngest sister was born. She was the first and only big sister I have ever had. Laetitia got my room and I moved in with my sister. From my eight-year-old perspective, she towered over me; she was tall and beautiful, a French masterpiece. Laetitia taught me so much over the year she lived with us and has continued to do so till today. During Chanukah, as we lit the Menorah she began to cry—remembering her father who had recently passed away. She was the first "adult" I saw cry. Laetitia taught me what a baguette, chocolate mousse, and crepes were, and how amazing it was to listen to her converse in French over the phone. When Laetitia left, I moved back into my old room but there was a void; my family felt it too. So, four years later we visited Laetitia in France. Her family was so welcoming and generous, even if we didn't always understand each other. In 2000, we went again for her wedding, a French Jewish Sephardic wedding. Her culture and language may be vastly different from my own, yet the love and care we have for each other is the same. I believe her scent in my top sock drawer will linger forever.

> **When Laetitia left, I moved back into my old room but there was a void; my family felt it too.**

Dori Chandler attends the University of North Carolina at Chapel Hill.

80
FAMILY LIFE AS ESSAY FODDER

Tufts University does not cut anybody a break with this difficult question. Rather than addressing the more generic issue of how your environment has shaped you, this question wants to know how your environment has shaped your goals. One possibility would be to talk about career interests, but for liberal arts students, the primary option is to reflect on how you want to live. This essay is a textbook illustration of how concrete detail—from the weedy garden to the jilted women—can create a vivid and interesting story. The idealism at the end has credibility largely because of the thoroughness of the description in the beginning and middle.

Essay by Marie Crowder

Describe the environment in which you grew up and how it has shaped your personal goals.

I grew up in a brick house on Nottingham Drive, a place with old furniture and young faces, with small rooms that never seemed to be empty. I grew up with my pointy nose buried in books, wearing stretch pants and bows and listening to my father's new songs on the guitar. I sat at a dinner table as girlish voices made fun of that pointy nose along with my big ears, and I finally learned to laugh about them. I grew up with a big-nosed father who always had a joke on his tongue and a mother who always had an answer. I heard that as long as I worked hard enough, I could do anything.

> I heard stories from the adults' fold-out table, of women abandoned by the men whom they had depended on.

I grew up eating fresh tomatoes from my grandpa's garden and later saw that same garden overrun with weeds. I grew up during summers at the lake, with cousins who couldn't read until fourth grade and could break every object in sight. I watched at a distance as relatives struggled through life, searching for paths to independence. I heard stories from the adults' fold-out table, of women abandoned by the men whom they had depended on. Somewhere amongst those stories, I made up my mind not to make their same mistakes.

I grew up with a determination to make something of myself, to stand apart from the crowd. I listened to seemingly endless stories about the Depression and wars and old friends. I wondered if I would ever get a chance to tell my stories. I wondered what type of stories I would have to tell.

I began to understand that I have a choice. I can choose the stories that I want to tell. I can choose whether or not I repeat others' mistakes. And I can choose what I make of myself. As to how I make these choices, I'm sure that all I have to do is remember the stories from when I grew up.

Marie Crowder attends the University of North Carolina at Chapel Hill.

81

A RED-HAIRED, RED-BEARDED, RED-FACED MAN

The impulse to write about a favorite teacher is relatively common—and often a recipe for a mediocre essay. The problem, as we have noted elsewhere, is that the essay turns out to be about the teacher, not about you. The following essay shows how you can avoid that fate. It has plenty of vivid description of Mr. Matthews, but even more about how the author thinks and feels. The author has a strong grasp of how Mr. M. shaped her as a student, and also a well-developed sense of her own motivation. As the essay ends, she shows awareness that she is still learning and growing—just the sort of awareness that colleges love to see.

Essay by Amy Hollinger

I should not have dressed up. Apparently, no other fifth grader had felt driven to celebrate the first day of school via fancy clothing, and so I stood out not just as a newcomer, but as an awkwardly dressed one. Scratching at grainy black tights with the toe of my sneaker, I paused uncertainly in the doorway of the Writing room.

Pausing uncertainly, however, was not the way of the world of Mr. Matthews. This red-haired, red-bearded, red-faced man beckoned wildly at me to enter. I scuttled over to a seat, and in three minutes of casual observation was convinced that I had never known an adult like him. He laughed from his belly, wiggled his ears on request, and then blushed an embarrassed shade redder. His students loved him; it was evident from the way they greeted him to the way they relaxed when they entered his room.

On the contrary, I was not relaxed. I was nervous, I was in a room full of strangers, and I was, at best, apathetic towards writing. My only previous writing experience had been in cloth-covered books with more room for illustrations than print. I had no idea what to expect from a class that was just called "Writing," but I was certain I wasn't going to like it.

Yet Mr. M spent that first class entertaining us. He told stories, cracked jokes, and then dismissed us early for recess. Our assignment to write about the best part of summer seemed almost an afterthought for him.

Nevertheless, I was seized by an unprecedented and inexplicable desire to do my homework. It wasn't anything specific he had said in class that day, but the way he had acted. I wanted this crazy, charismatic, exuberant man to like and approve of me, and the quickest way to earn this was through my writing.

Tricky.

That night, despite having dealt with a word processor all of twice in my life, despite spending more time on this single homework assignment than any other night's combined, and despite an embarrassingly trite roller-coaster-ride topic, I wrote with fiery passion. Triumphantly handing it in the next morning, I was sure it was the best thing I'd ever written.

For the rest of the year, I worked to relive, again and again, that feeling of accomplishment. I challenged myself to write well, as much for myself as for Mr. M. This one-man audience inspired me to constantly strive to improve and impress, and in the process I discovered that I, shockingly, liked to write. The aforementioned, overdressed fifth grader would never have guessed that, six years later, writing would become a voluntary, daily activity, flowing from journals to emails to poetry workshops to newspapers.

> I wanted this crazy, charismatic, exuberant man to like and approve of me.

Mr. M left our school at the end of that year. At his goodbye party, he thumped me on the shoulder and said, "You've got a good head on your shoulders, kid. Use it well." It was only in looking back that I realized this was the moment I had been waiting for all year.

Over time, Mr. M.'s approval and guidance has grown with me; it is my mantra to push myself further, to think before acting. He believed in me as a writer, and in some ways as a person, before I did, and these high expectations have carried me further than anything else could have. Today, I am still curious about what he saw in me, and I think I am still growing into the person he might have predicted. But I also still am, and always will be, striving to surprise him by becoming even more.

Amy Hollinger attends Princeton University.

82

GUESS WHO'S COMING TO DINNER

If your family offers a cast of characters as vivid as those described by author Charlie Leeper, you'd be crazy not to write an essay about them. Charlie portrays his relatives in loving detail, skillfully using dialogue and description to evoke their unique personalities. Note his vivid rendering of the chaotic conversation in paragraph two, especially the thread of the story that Kit tells. Says Charlie, "I wrote the Greek essay in one long evening and night. I like to write essays in one sitting, if possible. I find that with each new day, I am in a different mood, and my writing reflects it."

"My Greek Family" by Charles Dimitri Leeper

A range of academic interests, personal perspectives, and life experiences adds much to the educational mix. Given your personal background, describe an experience that illustrates what you would bring to the diversity in a college community, or an encounter that demonstrated the importance of diversity to you.

Today's lesson was almost over. Our topic was the alphabet, and my grandmother was intent on expanding my limited knowledge of alpha, lambda, and pi that I had gained from my school science classes. I called her Yaiy, from the Greek word for grandmother. "The Americans, they stole our language," Yaiy would say confidently, "You see this word, psychiatrist? It's is actually 'psychiatros.' You see?" I would nod dutifully and continue writing. Yaiy would choose random phrases, and I would write them in Greek, slowly rotating the page to show her when I was finished. When I became confused over the three different letters that all sounded like "e" or the absence of a letter "d," she would laugh and remind me that the British made their own superfluous additions when they "borrowed our language." We continued until a telephone ring broke the silence, and Yaiy answered beginning in English and then jumping into Greek after recognizing my mother's voice. I could smell the pastachio cooking in the oven as I heard Yaiy say that dinner would be ready at seven o'clock.

After three impatient doorbell tones, my aunt Kit bumbled in, worn out after a long day of work. She is an optometrist at Eyestyles, her optical practice. Her loud entrance was followed by the arrival of another aunt, two uncles, my mother, father—who is not Greek, but feels right at home—and a cousin from England. As we gathered around the table for dinner, the air was filled with the familiar banter of family. "I had this patient who just wouldn't stop laughing, whatever I did!" Kit said. "I got a little self-conscious because I wasn't sure if there was something on my face..." Her voice trailed off as my uncle Pete interrupted with a vivid description of his day. My uncle Phil expressed his frustration with a computer program he had written. I could hear Kit's voice competing for attention, "...I finally asked her if something was funny." I just listened to the cacophony. Such chaos was commonplace.

Everyone was silenced as Yaiy presented the first course. It was phakess, or lentil soup, and it met with murmurs of satisfaction. With the room now quiet, Yaiy began recalling her aunt's "world famous" lentil soup. Her incredible exaggerations added a bit of comedy to an otherwise unexciting tale. She is an expert storyteller, like all my relatives. They can turn the most boring events into animated epics that last for hours. A delicious appetizer is the only way to truncate these potentially long narratives.

My family has a respect for language and communication that makes each day exciting. Whether it is my grandmother's sporadic Greek lessons or the verbal mayhem around the dinner table, my relatives have always demonstrated an appreciation for both grammar and creativity. The Greek culture that is characterized by food, music, and dance is complemented by the colorful descriptions used to share it. I have inherited their gift, and it is an asset in writing as well as a tool for self-expression. My preference for engineering is enhanced by my love of language; I

> **Her incredible exaggerations added a bit of comedy to an otherwise unexciting tale.**

have recognized that technical writing requires just as much creativity as any other composition. My family has sparked my interest in the sciences because they all work in scientific fields. I will not abandon language by choosing engineering; I will actually enjoy the best of both worlds. The gifts of my Greek family will be put to good use.

Charles Dimitri Leeper attends Cornell University (NY).

83

A SISTER WITH DOWN SYNDROME

Though its title includes her sister's name, author Claire Wyatt's essay is really about her perception of her sister and how it changes. She uses the first paragraph to describe the evolving relationship in exceptionally concrete terms. The two sisters have become somewhat distant, at least in Claire's mind, until an interesting and slightly mysterious moment when their roles reverse. The last six lines are noteworthy both for what they reveal, and for what they leave for the reader to deduce.

"A Lesson from Katie" by Claire Wyatt

I was never really upset about it. I never resented my parents for it. I didn't ever feel unlucky because of it. My sister had Down Syndrome, and that was that. Sure, I found it a little odd that while most of my friends' big sisters secretly applied lipstick on the walk to school, mine collected worms, which she would make into jewelry. But except for the occasionally painful quarrel (one of which left a bite mark on my right shoulder) my sister and I got along. The only problem was, after a while it became difficult for me to think of Katie as my sister, a person whose flesh and blood were identical to mine. There were just too many things that separated us, and soon I became the older sister, the leader and decision maker. In grade school, I noticed that the gap between us was growing larger. I outgrew monkey bars, but Katie didn't. I stopped climbing trees, but Katie wouldn't. I learned to write poetry, but Katie couldn't. I stopped roller-skating and began diving; I stopped trick-or-treating and began dieting. I'm not sure if Katie ever understood why, and to be honest, I'm not sure if I understood either. By high school the gap between us had gotten huge, and I remember feeling more like Katie's parent than her sister. But then, one strange and snowy night, something beautiful happened.

It was the winter of my junior year. The sky was black and empty, and its breath ached inside warm lungs. Life, it seemed, had either burrowed itself underground for warmth or had gone south for the winter like my Uncle Sherman, who can't stand the cold. The trees were bare and lonely, and every once in a while they would point to a dimly lit, second-story window where my silhouette lay motionless on a bed. I was in one of those moods, those strange moods, where the world suddenly appears to be under water. Its sights and sounds majestically blur together, like some sort of half-dream. I felt uneasy and unfamiliar with myself and with everything around me. It's one of those states that comes occasionally in adolescence probably because of hormones, anxiety, and greasy foods all reacting with each other inside of our bodies. All I could do was lie on my bed. After I had counted something like three hundred of the tiny little dots on my ceiling, my sister entered my room. "What now, Katie?" I barked at her in my head, unable to make words come out of my mouth. I was anticipating her to begin her nightly ritual of describing, in exact detail, the events of her day: the food she's eaten, the friends she's talked to, the boys she might marry. But I stayed silent. I glanced in her direction to see if she was still there, and she was. She approached the foot of my bed and gently adjusted my feet to make room for herself. She sat down and stared at me for what must have been a long time. And then, as if she was aware of my inability to form words at that moment, she began to talk to me in sign language. (She had been learning it at school as part of some enrichment program.) I remembered only a few gestures that I had learned in elementary school, so she began teaching me. "School." "Mom." "Boy." "Bathroom." "Stupid." "Sister." "I love you." All of a sudden I realized that for the first time in nearly a decade, Katie was the older sister again. For the first time since we were kids, *she* was teaching *me*. And just like that, the gap disappeared. Just like that, we were sisters again. My emotionally masochistic fog quickly lifted and the world seemed clear to me

> By high school the gap between us had gotten huge, and I remember feeling more like Katie's parent than her sister.

again—clear but not perfect; not perfect, but adequate. I realized then what I should have known all along: that my sister and I, despite significant differences, will always be sisters; that she's taught me much more than I have ever given her credit for. And I'll always be grateful to her for the night when she taught me to say, "Sister, I love you," in the only language that I could comprehend.

Claire Wyatt attends the University of Kansas.

A Moral Dilemma

T read lightly when describing how you handled a moral dilemma. It is easy to come off sounding smug when you describe "Why I Did the Right Thing." The best of these essays describe a real dilemma that requires a real choice and which may not have come to a tidy conclusion. Essay 84 is a particularly effective example of how to take a moral position without sounding moralistic. All four essays in this section reveal the author as a person who genuinely cares about doing the right thing.

84

AFTER EIGHTY YEARS, RIGHTING A WRONG

Author Alex Milne's essay sparkles partly because the reader doesn't know where it is going. Winnie the Pooh sounds sweet and innocuous, but before we know it, she is talking about her grandfather's racist views and why he changed the pronunciation of the family name. The juxtaposition of her typical high school life with the unfortunate origin of the "Milney" (formerly "Miln") pronunciation leads to an obvious question: does it really make a difference to a teenager living eighty years after the fact? The answer for Alex is a resounding yes, and her thoughtfulness in confronting the issue shows her intelligence and idealism.

Essay by Alexandra Milne

"I love Winnie the Pooh! Are you related to A. A. Milne?" I can't even count on two hands the number of times I have been asked that question. "No I'm not; our last names are different. Well sort of… Well, there's a story… It's complicated."

I arrived at my new school in second grade. Another small private school, but here no one knew me. No one knew my family, where I'd come from, what I was like, and no one knew my name. I'd introduce myself; "Hi, my name is Alex Milne, I'm new." I've been at the same school ever since, and the same people have been calling me the same thing, Alex Milne (pronounced Milney). The invisible "y" never bothered me until I learned about the family history of it. Originally, my family pronounced our name as "Miln," one syllable. There aren't supposed to be two ways to pronounce my name. My grandfather, George Milne, was born in 1907, and, like many of his peers, he was a racist until the day he died. When he entered the military, he met a man in his unit with the same name: George Milne. However, much to my grandfather's displeasure this man was black. My grandfather, under no circumstances, would have the same name as a black man, so he immediately changed the pronunciation of his family name from "Miln" to "Milney," and that is the way it has been pronounced in my family ever since. I have always been known as Alex "Milney"; that is the way it is pronounced not only by my family but also by my friends and teachers. Many people just call me "Milney"—a nickname to distinguish between the four Alexes in my grade alone. When people call me by my last name, the emphasis on the change is magnified; I can't help but think of my grandfather. Sometimes the people in my school community, even teachers, whom I have known nearly my entire life, will ask which way it is pronounced. To avoid confusion, or having to retell the story for the millionth time, I tell them that it doesn't matter. I can do this because I can accommodate both mindsets, a sort of cognitive dissonance: I can accept the family name while I internally disagree with the origins behind it.

Now I realize the severity of my grandfather's decision. The fact that he would take the extreme step of changing his given name to avoid comparison to another person he deemed inferior seems to me not only childish and foolish and trivial, but also immensely offensive. This change that he made really has had a large impact on me, enough so that I toy with whether or not to affirmatively revert my name back to the original pronunciation. It's hard to do, but I think it is worth the effort to be able to express my opinions. I understand that family history, especially family history I'd rather not own up to, is not unique to my family. Whether good or bad, every person has family history, and the hard part is dealing with the weight of it. However, in confronting our history we are allowed to build our own beliefs and create our own. My grandfather had personal values that left intangible marks on my family history, but I, Alex Milne, whether pronounced with a hard "E" or a silent "E," have taken the responsibility to forge my own beliefs and write a new history—one that includes George Milne—much to my grandfather's dismay.

> **Whether good or bad, every person has family history, and the hard part is dealing with the weight of it.**

Alexandra Milne attends Vassar College.

85

PAGE 217 OF YOUR AUTOBIOGRAPHY?

Penn's notorious "Page 217" question has struck fear in the heart of many an applicant. Students are often befuddled because they aren't sure whether to write about something in the future (on the theory that page 217 would come when they are forty or fifty) or about a topic in the present. In truth, this question offers the flexibility to write about almost anything. Author David Onuscheck's essay is noteworthy for its superb structure. The first sentence describes a dramatic moment, the second sentence explains the moment, the balance of the first paragraph gives necessary background information, and the second paragraph goes back to the dramatic moment and begins the story.

Essay By David Onuscheck Jr.

You have just completed your 300-page autobiography. Please submit page 217.

I remember feeling my stomach do a flip turn as I watched who entered the room. A friend of mine was sitting in front of the Honor Council. At my high school, the Honor Council is an elected group of six students including four faculty advisors, which hears cases of students who have broken the school's honor code: "I pledge on my honor not to lie, cheat, steal, plagiarize, or vandalize." I was elected at the end of my sophomore year to the position and had promised my peers to hear cases with an unbiased ear and to speak for all of them in the panel's discussions. It was not until I was hearing the case of a friend that I knew how difficult that promise was going to be.

As the meeting started, I quickly learned that she was the person who had been stealing money from lockers. The most troubling aspect of the case was that we had been friends since the third grade and had shared a number of special moments; I had never expected her to be the culprit. I remembered her dethroning me as champion in a multiplication game in Lower School and more recently joking about one of the funnier names in our AP US History book, Terrence Powderly. These thoughts echoed as she began her testimony.

She stated that she merely found herself stealing money one day, and then the problem grew into a destructive habit. She asked for our forgiveness. After she left, the council discussed proper punishments, which included expulsion, for nearly an hour and a half. I weighed our friendship and my knowledge that she was a kind person versus her serious, knowing transgression. When the time for the vote finally came, I felt physically and emotionally drained, but I had reached a decision. I raised my hand in favor of expulsion. I knew that my convictions for upholding the honor code were too strong to not vote for her removal. Her violations had been clear and unequivocal, and although she was my friend, I did not feel that she could remain at our school. The final decision rested on the head of school.

I learned a few days later that my friend had indeed been expelled, and that part of what influenced the head of school's decision was the Honor Council's unanimous vote favoring expulsion. I was extremely disappointed to see a friend leave the school, but I knew that her blatant disregard for the values of the community made her unfit to attend. I was proud that I had assembled the courage to vote for expulsion, especially when my fellow junior on the council abstained from voting. I believe that deciding whether to favor the expulsion of a fellow student and friend was one of the most difficult decisions of my life. It was only after I had seen the school's secretary clean out my friend's locker that I realized how much courage I had mustered to make such an emotional decision.

I felt physically and emotionally drained, but I had reached a decision. I raised my hand in favor of expulsion.

David Onuscheck Jr. attends the University of Notre Dame.

86

LYING AWAKE, REHASHING AN ARGUMENT

If you've ever laid awake at night replaying an argument in your head, we have an idea: write your college essay about it. That's what author Austin C. Pate did after staying up all night thinking about a tiff over race and political correctness. The essay is long, 881 words, and its success hinges on Austin's ability to let his thoughts unfold as he is telling the story. As he describes wrestling with what happened, he thinks it through with the reader at his shoulder. His reasoning ability makes for interesting twists and turns. The length of the essay is in sync with the topic; Austin is clearly a thoughtful young man who will follow the truth wherever it may lead.

Essay by Austin C. Pate

The aim of argument, or of discussion, should not be victory, but progress. —Joseph Joubert

Much of what we learn, and most of our best thinking, is not because of what is spoon-fed to us, but rather as a result of interactions with other people, including active questioning of our surroundings, beliefs, and ideas. Sometimes the best of these opportunities go unexplored. During rehearsal for an American Conservatory Theater production I was in this fall, a fellow cast member offered to tell a joke, which she warned, might offend some people. After her disclaimer, and to the horror of the rest of the politically correct and socially aware cast, she recited what turned out to be a racially provocative quip. The result was a moment of disgusted silence, followed by a barrage of angry remarks. Embarrassed, but still defending her claim that she did not retell the joke out of prejudice or malice, I watched as she was verbally beaten down. Though it was initially hard for me to justify, I could see both the humor and the reasoning behind the joke. This caused me both shame and concern, but I still felt inclined to play devil's advocate among the group. The attempt was not as fruitful as I had hoped. The topic was too immense to argue on nerves alone, so after my quick questioning of the opinion we collectively had reached, I left it alone.

Unable to sleep that night, I ran over the argument again and again in my head, each time altering how I should have responded. Lying in bed I stumbled upon a painfully obvious and yet completely ignored parallel between our conversation and the context of the play we were all proudly performing. *School Girl Figure* is a dark comedy by author Wendy McCloud about the horrors of anorexia and the society that perpetuates such a disorder. Does the play not serve the same function as the joke told? What we—as a cast—were doing was taking a very serious topic and making light of it in an over-the-top, surreal manner. This made me realize that, contrary to how it may appear, politically incorrect jokes or storylines may not be created in order to ridicule the subject, but rather as social commentary. There are two sides to humor: it can be destructive when used at another's expense, or it can be constructive by bringing controversial humor to an otherwise ignored or taboo subject.

"It is different if you are making fun of yourself," others yelled at her. "But *you* are not allowed to joke." If someone suffering from anorexia were to come see our play, it may be painful or offensive; however, in a different crowd the words might have an eye-opening impact. Is it necessary for me to suffer from anorexia in order to comment about it and society's roll in its proliferation? When I laugh at an offensive joke, I am not doing so because I accept the generalization that is being made; I am laughing because of the ridiculousness of the existence of such a stereotype. People cope in vastly different ways. Some people choose to deal with heavy topics through serious conversation, and cannot see how

> "It is different if you are making fun of yourself," others yelled at her.

it could possibly be made light of. Others deal even with tragedy through humor. Both are completely legitimate ways of coping. I don't think it is right to judge why one person might see humor in a given situation, or why another does not. To determine that all material that could be offensive to anyone cannot be joked about is dangerous. Censoring humor limits the tools that we as a society have to understand and examine our faults and shortcomings, and without it as our filter, we risk misunderstanding and handicap our possibility for change.

"Stereotypes just perpetuate ignorance," shouted one of the disgruntled cast members. I found it hard to disagree with this assessment. Under the wrong circumstances, in the wrong context, to the wrong person, the potential awareness that controversial comedy can create is nullified by inappropriate employment. I came to the conclusion that common sense trumps any good intentions, and while we cannot be responsible for our own feelings, we must try to be responsible for the feelings we invoke in others. Nevertheless, there is a clear danger in labeling a particular way of communicating as "wrong."

As the sun was turning the sky from pitch black to a deep blue, I realized two things: first, I had to forget about trying to get any sleep; and, second, I had been thinking, and the cast had been arguing, not just about the joke that had been told, but also about political correctness in general—specifically, the underlying tension we were all experiencing because of the nature of our play.

When we question our initial reactions, though our opinions may not change, we may better clarify our own feelings and gain insight into those of others. Had I not been bothered enough, I would not have lingered on the subject at all, and any subsequent thinking I did would not have occurred. Education is not only the acquisition of facts, but also the constant questioning and dialogue that brings us closer to some sort of understanding. School is just one catalyst; conversations, art, or arguments are all potential lessons that we sometimes neglect to utilize.

Austin C. Pate attends California Institute of the Arts.

87

OFFERED A FREE CAR, HE SAYS, "NO THANKS"

Author Charlie Shrader has a moral dilemma over an issue that most people would not give a second thought. Should he accept the gift of a car from the father of a friend? Charlie is able to write a 547-word essay about his uncertainty because he develops all the layers of the issue: his longstanding love of cars, his father's mixed feelings, his surge of euphoria upon receiving the car, and the ambivalence that he begins to feel after receiving the car. In one of his best lines, Charlie notes that the gift "caused both my mind and my driveway to become a little too crowded."

Essay by Charles Crichton Shrader

"So, you want this car or not?" Dr. Matt Petrilla asked again, in his simultaneously pushy yet polite manner.

This smart, stocky man, a medical doctor and the father of a friend, had thrown me into a sudden state of blissful surprise: less than a minute before, he had offered me a free car. We set a time for me to test-drive the car, and then he left me astonished and dazed.

Since my early childhood, when I begged my father to let me drive the golf cart at every opportunity, and when I developed a certain fascination with bumper cars, driving has always ranked high on my short list of life's great pleasures. Most of all, it affords the extreme satisfaction of independence, that glorious freedom for which the adolescent heart traditionally yearns. The idea of having my own car floored me.

That night, I told my father about the car. Until then, he had provided me with a car for regular use but not one I could call my own. "That just doesn't happen!" he exclaimed disbelievingly. He spoke in total favor of accepting the car, since he loathes denying what he calls his "thrifty Scottish side"; his mannerisms, however, were not entirely in synch with his words. In my overriding excitement, I did not see what exactly had disheartened him.

A few days later, Dr. Matt handed me the key to my new car: a forest green, 1993 Mazda 626 sedan, fitted with the most comfortable beige leather and a brand-new CD player. Dr. Matt, who thrives on rebuilding wrecked cars and giving them to kids in the community out of sheer generosity, also proved his genius by converting it from automatic to manual transmission, since he knew how much I enjoyed the stick shift. On the way home, I quickly popped in my new CD of Respighi's *Pines of Rome* and trembled in ecstasy as my car's powerful speakers pummeled my senses with the grand final movement, "The Pines of the Via Appia." I was in love.

Over the next three weeks however, despite my great contentment with the car itself, conflicting emotions beset me. Guilt bothered me most: "Why do I deserve this car? Shouldn't I give this car to someone who needs it more?" I often asked myself. I also felt guilt concerning my father's feelings, for now I understood his initial distress: he had worked diligently to provide an extra car for his family, and he knew how much it meant to me to be able to drive; I felt that I was almost disrespectful of my father by accepting this gift, though he would never mention it. The now-burdensome car caused both my mind and my driveway to become a little too crowded.

> **Guilt bothered me most: "Why do I deserve this car? Shouldn't I give this car to someone who needs it more?"**

I agonized over what to do, since returning such a stunning gift bordered on the unthinkable, but in the end I found clarity. I returned the car to Dr. Matt, who completely understood my dilemma. No decision had ever so thoroughly freed me. Dr. Matt now could give the car to another thrilled kid, and again I could appreciate my father's gift. Never in my life did I think I would turn down a free car, but in this case, nothing could have made better sense.

Charles Crichton Shrader attends Brown University.

Personal Growth

It isn't easy to take your own measure, to honestly evaluate where you have come from and where you are heading. Perhaps you have had a brush with peer pressure (Essay 88), or have begun to confront your fears of leaving home (Essay 91). One of our authors uses Western history as a metaphor for his life (Essay 93); another offers a more whimsical view of growing up (Essay 89). The best essays about personal growth succeed in showing a real transformation toward a more mature perspective on the world.

88

WHO NEEDS NINJA TURTLES WHEN YOU'VE GOT CARE BEARS?

Growing up in the Ninja Turtle generation, author Adam Baumgarten was into Care Bears toys—which was emblematic of what he says was a "gloriously eccentric" childhood. Adam uses this and other quirky facts to paint a vivid picture of his slightly off-center family. Truth be told, any family is slightly off-center if you know it from the inside—the trick is to be able to describe it as well as Adam does. As for the rest of the essay, suffice it to say that Adam has a sudden revelation while listening to a Limp Bizkit CD, and lives happily ever after.

Essay by Adam Baumgarten

The pursuit of being an "original" has widely dictated the actions of my young adult life. From an early age I harbored a zealous fixation for anything different or offbeat. Perhaps I should clarify; you know that clichéd box everyone refers to? Well, I'm not talking simply thinking outside of it. I'm talking looting, plundering, pillaging, strangling, and ultimately killing that box. Regardless of how I render that box, it is clear that unconventional is my conventional.

Considering my bohemian, post-hippie mother, my shrewdly independent father, and my gloriously eccentric childhood, this trait is hardly surprising. My parents constantly stressed the importance of originality in my upbringing, and as the middle child in a family oozing with personalities, competing for attention became a daily ritual. Therefore, the quirkier, the better, as if peculiarities were some sort of Darwinist advantage in my house ensuring prolonged attention.

My first signs of individuality were predominantly unintentional; rather they were inherited. For example, at Adat Shalom Kindergarten "Ninja Turtles" action figures were all the rage. However, my parents were vehemently opposed to any toy advocating violence, even if said violence was perpetuated by teenage mutant ninja turtles. Therefore, the less aggressive "Care Bears" became my play toy of choice, a decision wholeheartedly supported by my family. After a brief lamenting period, I overcame this petty obstacle and began identifying with my "dolls," forgetting all about my lack of "action figures" (a vast difference in five-year-old nomenclature, mind you). Within my group of kindergarten colleagues, I became the kid without a Rafael, Donatello, Michelangelo, or a Leonardo—the first benchmark in my illustrious career as an individualist.

Beginning with my days as the turtle-less kindergartner I held a certain reverence for individuality. However, my entrance into high school introduced me to my greatest foe yet, fitting in. For the first time in my life, I became susceptible to the pressures of popularity, as I practiced conformity with feverish intent. I needed that new MP3 player, that pair of baggy jeans, that Donatello action figure.

This new and significantly less improved version of me continued throughout most of freshman year. My epiphany and reentry into unwavering quirkiness came in the form of a new CD, and a bad one at that. For weeks I had been begging my mother to buy me the new Limp Bizkit CD (undoubtedly the worst, most repulsive band name ever). All my friends had owned it for weeks, and I was slipping behind the coolness curve. Finally my mother met my demands and purchased the disc. Within seconds of my listening, I had a revelation; *Wow, I hate this music. This isn't me!!* Soon thereafter, I decided that baggy jeans weren't exactly cutting it either. They felt like diapers, causing me to waddle rather than walk.

After my brief fall from grace, I triumphantly returned to peak form; listening to and wearing only what I liked, practicing an impressive neglect for anything hip, trendy, and not me. Essentially, I defined my own cool. While I remain close with the same group of friends, my refusal to surrender my character for the sake of fitting in has ultimately strengthened our bonds. Recently, I wore a toga to school, claiming I misinterpreted "Geek Dress up Day" for "Greek Dress up Day," a boldly eccentric move celebrated by my friends.

> **The less aggressive "Care Bears" became my play toy of choice, a decision wholeheartedly supported by my family.**

My sudden encounter with conformity was utterly unrewarding, resulting in a transitory loss of self. And in exchange for this muddled self-identity I experienced that whole teenage angst thing, an unfair trade if you ask me. So, I don't have "Ninja Turtles." Who cares? I got "Care Bears" and much better music.

Adam Baumgarten attends the University of California at Los Angeles.

89

WHEN YOU'VE LOST YOUR MARBLES

Childhood memories can make for an endearing story, as long as you don't try to wring too much significance out of them. Author Juliana DuTremble tells a story about her childhood curiosity with flair and telling detail. The essay doesn't describe a life-changing transformation, but it is much better than most that strain for one. It ends with a light-hearted reference to the admission process that simultaneously makes the point that Juliana wants to get in, but that she isn't so uptight that she can't poke a little fun at herself.

Essay by Juliana DuTremble

It was my fifth birthday. Imagine the joy that must pulse through the veins of a hungry homeless person who just happens to find a winning lottery ticket laying in the gutter. The look on that person's face would be much like the one I wore when tearing apart my present to reveal nothing more than a bag of marbles. The marbles fascinated me. They weren't just pretty pieces of painted glass smoothed into a nice round sparkling ball. There were worlds, whole universes even, contained within the intricate weavings within them. It made my little mind wander through uncharted mind quests, thinking that perhaps my house, my town, my world, was also contained within a marble cherished by another little girl.

One by one, my beloved marbles were swept under the carpets, consumed by the vacuum cleaner, or lost on the playground, until one day I had one marble left. It was a hot, humid day in the middle of June and my mother was outside making some new additions to her perennial flower bed. I'd been observing her work over the past few months and noticed a fairly simple pattern: she would dig a small hole, put in a tiny round object, and a few weeks later there would sprout a beautiful flower. Well, my naive brilliant self had a far better plan, and I at once set forth upon planting my glass ball in hopes of growing a "bed of marbles."

Ten years passed, and the marble garden had been long forgotten. Then one day, my mother was carrying out her annual gardening ritual, when suddenly a shimmering blue-green marble surfaced in the dirt. She hastily called me to her side, placed it in my hand, and instantly the flashback of my childhood endeavor played through my mind. Naturally, I kept the marble in a safe place—the safe place being a zippered pocket in my purse. It was as if I'd suddenly been showered in good fortune from the good-luck gods. At the time, I attributed much of my luck in making it to the county-wide spelling bee to my marble, as well as actually being admitted into the Maine School of Science and Math.

It is with great regret that I report the mysterious disappearance of this marble which I have cherished most of my life, as silly as it may be. I would love to finally discover where exactly my marble

> **It was as if I'd suddenly been showered in good fortune from the good-luck gods.**

vanished to. It is a deep shade of indigo, and when you hold it up to the sun it shimmers in an iridescent green that will take your breath away. If you happen to discover my marble laying on a park bench, or upon a table at a yard sale, please, call my toll-free hotline at I-MISS-MY-MRBL. If at all possible, try to make it before I receive my decision letter from Cornell College—I might need a little luck.

Thanks.

Juliana DuTremble attends Cornell College (IA).

90

DOLPHINS, THE PRESIDENT, AND A SPUNKY SIX-YEAR-OLD

The following essay is more than merely a tale superbly told. At the beginning, author Anne Erickson is a six-year-old who sees the world in black and white; by the end, she is a sophisticated thinker who sees the world in shades of gray. The essay flows so well because of the follow-up information that gives texture to the stages of her life. As a six-year-old, she was pleased and then disillusioned, while as an older person she lived her ideals in Albuquerque. Says Anne, "Sitting down knowing that you're writing a big, scary college essay can make you sound wooden and formulaic. Instead, have fun writing about yourself. Later, you can work on all that college-essay-checklist stuff."

Essay by Anne Erickson

Potential to Contribute: Tell us about a talent, experience, contribution, or personal quality you will bring to the University of California.

In my six-year-old mind I see the president, sitting at his plush desk chair in a navy blue suit. He's examining an important document. Or better yet, he's in the middle of a crucial meeting with leaders from all over the world. His secretary enters. She looks worried. "We've received a letter of some importance," she says. His brow furrows as she hands him a small envelope addressed in sparkly pink pen. "Anne Erickson, age six, Oakland, California," he muses, examining the careful writing. He rips open the envelope to read my note. "My God, Louise, it's regarding dolphin-safe tuna. Call out the National Guard!" Louise would head over to that red telephone, dial a few numbers, and the powers of the U.S. government would be unleashed for the sake of my carefully articulated plea for the dolphins.

It was lucky that I learned to write just as my emerging sense of justice took hold—my letters gave me an outlet for my worries about the world. I remember the feeling of satisfaction it gave me to stick those letters in the mailbox. I was, after all, imparting crucial information: someday, when they were old and retired, the politicians would all thank me. "If it hadn't been for that little girl," they would say, "I'd never have known about those dolphins."

I was thrilled when I received my first presidential envelope in the mail, but soon became indignant to discover that the president sent me the same photocopy in response to each of my painstakingly crafted letters. I didn't give up, however. I simply broadened my target audience, pursuing my dream of a planet safe for animals through posters, clubs, subscriptions to Greenpeace newsletters, and the sheltering of a variety of odd creatures. The Norwegian ambassador renewed my faith in humanity when he sent me a handwritten note in response to my concerns about whaling.

As I've grown, so has my perspective on environmental issues. I still feel just as passionately about the need to save the dolphins, the whales, and all manner of animals, but my passion has been complicated by my slow realization that everything needs "saving"—even humans. A trip to South Africa when I was fourteen left me addicted to international travel, and I came away just as intrigued by that country's people and politics as by its monkeys and lions. Volunteer work in Panama and Honduras has shown me first-hand how difficult it is to strike a balance between human survival and environmental preservation: I'm still angry when I hear about "slash-and-burn" deforestation on TV, yet in the Panamanian village that was my home for two months, burning trees meant farmland, survival, and a way of life for my host family.

My loyalties and passions have expanded as I learn more about the world. In both Panama and Honduras, I worked in schools with kids I adored, and learned to discuss politics and history in Spanish. This fall, I used that Spanish in Albuquerque, New Mexico, where I became an Election Day volunteer, getting my first taste of political action and becoming acquainted with volunteers from across the nation, not to mention the unforgettable residents of Albuquerque precincts 67 and 73.

I am no longer the little girl with the one-track mind who wrote letters to the president. Each time I discover something new about myself—my interest in politics, in public health, in teaching—life certainly becomes more frustrating and complex. But my passion for new experiences, and my tenacity and commitment to working for true justice in the world, has never wavered: it will follow me into college and beyond.

Anne Erickson attends Stanford University.

91

NO PLACE LIKE HOME

The typical high school student moans about wanting to get the heck out of high school, a proud few are not ashamed to say that they like it and will hate to leave. Great idea for an essay. There is no better essay topic than an affectionate description of your world. Admissions officers know that students who are successful in one place are likely to be successful in the next. In this essay, author Jennifer Gaffney offers an honest and vivid description of a slice of her school's life, showing how she was transformed from a shy girl to a confident (if slightly wistful) young woman. Her essay reveals her as a sure bet to do the same in college.

Essay by Jennifer Gaffney

"You know that time in your life when you realize the house you live in isn't really your home anymore? That idea of home is gone. Maybe that's all family really is. A group of people who miss the same imaginary place."

—*Garden State*, Andrew Largeman

My greatest fear is leaving home. Reaching a place where I do not know that there are exactly six minutes and forty-two seconds left until math is over. It is a place where I cannot talk about the Red Sox game with the dean of students or play hangman with my college advisor. My greatest fear lies in a place where my teacher's voice does not escalate with excitement because I ask a question. It is a place without student artwork hanging on the walls or "Johnny B. Goode" blasting through a radio in the corner of the English room at eight in the morning. My greatest fear is knowing that even though my knuckles are white from trying to hang on to this place for a few more laughs, I will have to let go and walk away. My greatest fear is reaching the day when "that idea of home is gone."

The first morning of my sophomore year I walked onto the St. Andrew's campus wearing wrinkled khakis and a white T-shirt. My stomach collapsed when I realized that everyone else was dressed in their best outfits, carefully picked out for the first day of school. As I searched for a sign that said, "lost and confused new students," I caught the eye of an extremely hairy man who stood just short of 9'9".

"Are you looking for your locker? Whose advisory are you in? Do you know where you need to be?" He's like a machine gun, I thought as I stared at him with my mouth open. Having trouble making sense of what he was saying due to the violent, nervous thumps in my stomach, I mumbled something and hustled away.

Trying my best to get as far away from him as I could, I noticed a group of students clumped together near the flagpole. They seemed to have a bubble around them and I could not figure out how to pop it. I stood there in my rumpled clothing, watching them throw their heads back with laughter as one rehashed a story. The discomfort was similar to that of a wool sweater in July. I gazed with envy at the group, feeling my stomach sink lower into my intestinal tract. As the nagging voice in the back of my head whispered to forget about friends, a recognizable sound drifted into my ear.

"Jen!" someone yelled. I peeped my head out of the puddle of self-pity I was sitting in to see where it came from.

"Jen, what are you doing? Come over here!" The voice came from a blonde girl who I recognized from the week before. She was standing in the group near the flagpole so I scuffed towards them hesitantly, trying to remember her name. As I walked with my head down, horrible images flashed through my mind. I imagined them spitting scowls and the grunts, repelling me away from the perfectly crafted pyramid of people that seemed to have taken years to construct. I was instantly ashamed when the looming faces I dreaded wore gentle, warm expressions.

"Hey! So you're from Connecticut? How do you like Texas so far?" a slender black-eyed girl asked with bouncing enthusiasm. As I opened

> He's like a machine gun, I thought as I stared at him with my mouth open.

my mouth to answer, a stout girl standing closest to the flagpole interrupted with, "Yeah, is it different? Do you miss the cold?" It was like that for the next fifteen minutes. As they pelted me with questions, the knot that sat in the pit of my stomach began to loosen. A smile eventually cracked my sullen face, leaving me completely vulnerable to the friendships I had resisted only moments before.

This was the first of many wet-bathing-suit-in-a-cold-movie-theatre-like experiences I found myself in. They were the kind of problems that every awkward adolescent confronts, not only in the beginning of the high school adventure, but through the entirety of their four years as an overgrown child and an undergrown adult.

The oddity of my situation, however, lies in the people who have allowed me to convert that discomfort into drive. The ape-man I met on the first day came to be my physics teacher. After a trimester of brutally painful work and emaciated grades, I yelled, "This is impossible!" He replied calmly, "Nothing's impossible. Just difficult," and proceeded to transform my frustration into an appreciation for a subject I saw no hope in. The seemingly simple blonde girl I had boxed up in a stereotype blew the walls of the box away and opened my eyes to the potential people have to change you. These people have become my family and helped me to understand that there is no limit to what you can discover by allowing momentary pain to pass. They have made St. Andrew's my home.

This place will be gone in eight months. It will slip away quietly even if I dig my fingernails into whatever I can hold onto for a few more moments. However, I have learned that fear and discomfort make up the first knot at the bottom of the rope you climb in gym class. Once you have hoisted yourself over it, you realize that there is an amazing height to be reached. You are able to see a beautiful world of crisscrossing rafters and filtered patterns of light that wait for you at the top. As you lean forward to ring the little bell, you catch a glimpse of how high up you are and realize that even though you have found a new world, you have a perfect view of what you have left behind.

Jennifer Gaffney attends Rhodes College.

92

NINJA TURTLES TO THE RESCUE

The author of the following essay shows a storyteller's eye for a terrific anecdote. From deep in his memory banks, Jacob Levy-Pollans recalls a long-ago incident in which the Ninja Turtles intersected with one of his most important current interests, politics. The result is a clever segue to discussing his involvement in politics, from his contribution to a successful ballot initiative to his work on a losing political campaign. Says Jake, "I originally got the idea for this topic in a writing class my junior year with an assignment about 'a strong childhood memory.' As I was writing it, I realized that it had college essay possibilities."

Essay by Jacob Levy-Pollans

When I was four I adored the Ninja Turtles. I owned all the action figures, T-shirts, and straight-to-video movies that there were to possess of the Ninja Turtles. Every Saturday morning I would wake up with plenty of time for the nine o'clock start of my favorite half-hour of the week. By the tender age of four my parents (and my dog Tovah) had learned not to bother me during that time.

On one particular Saturday I flipped on the television, and began to sing, "Heroes in a half-shell turtle power!" The television, alas, did not sing back. Instead, my television was displaying an overhead shot of old, bald, white men, in suits. It did not take long for the crying tantrum to begin. My dad tried to console me. He tried to explain, but I did not understand. I did not care.

Two years ago, with that morning seared into my memory, I decided to ask my father if he remembered that solemn day twelve years ago. Surprisingly he said yes. He explained that that was the morning of one of the sessions for Clarence Thomas's confirmation hearing, and that the men in suits were United States senators.

A lot has changed in thirteen years. My interest in politics has evolved from my worry over the future of the Ninja Turtles to a part of my identity. That morning was my first significant experience with politics. Since then my young adult life has been filled with a wealth of different political experiences. These experiences have been at times rewarding, and at times depressing. I have celebrated the victory of an Open Space ballot proposal at a local brewpub. I had seen that proposal grow from an idea in the mind of Ann Arbor's mayor, to a hard fought campaign, to an overwhelming victory. I sat in the same brewpub as the returns of a congressional primary showed that the woman I had donated my summer to was going to lose by double digits.

From the tantrum over a confirmation hearing to the joys of victory, my political experiences have taught me much more than just political lessons. They have taught me life lessons, in a way my parents were never quite able to do. My early childhood experience taught me a simple lesson: you do not always get what you want. That lesson helped carry me through the political losses I would face in the future. During that day thirteen years ago, I could not understand why someone would want to take away my happiness. I learned a simple lesson: what is best for me may not be what is best for everyone around me. This was a lesson that helped form my political ideology, and determine which candidates and proposals I would campaign for. In light of issues like terrorism and our fluctuating economy, the Ninja Turtles are a bad reason to be interested in politics. However, I do have a good story to tell when someone asks me, "So why did you get interested in politics in the first place?"

> **On one particular Saturday, I flipped on the television and began to sing, "Heroes in a half-shell turtle power!"**

Jacob Levy-Pollans attends Macalester College.

93

"BEAUTIES WHICH PIERCE LIKE SWORDS"

Lack of a grandiose topic was no problem for Sean O'Keefe, who penned this essay to describe little more than the fact that he went into intellectual slump in middle school. He compares his life to the course of Western civilization, telling his story with on-target references to Plato, St. Paul, C. S. Lewis, Dante, J. R. R. Tolkien, filmmaker Peter Jackson, and Malcolm X. The essay speaks eloquently about both the breadth of his reading and his mastery of the themes therein.

"How Reading Changed My Life" by Sean O'Keefe

One overpowering image appears whenever I remember my middle school years: the Dark Ages in Europe. Was I suffering through isolation, oppression, or misery? Fortunately not, yet I was, as Plato would put it, in the gloom of my cave, bereft of the light of intellectual illumination.

I liken my early childhood, a time of radiant learning, to Greek and Roman antiquity. Whenever a particular topic (like dinosaurs, wildlife, or astronomy) seized my interest, I would read every wisp of related information I could find. In Classical Greek and Roman fashion, I laid the foundations of my future through my love of reading in my childhood. I stopped reading for pleasure, however, when I reached adolescence and became consumed with athletics. Like the Europeans after the fall of the Roman Empire, I vaguely sensed that something great still existed, dormant but waiting to be reborn.

As Dante's *The Divine Comedy* ignited the Italian Renaissance, J. R. R. Tolkien's *The Lord of the Rings* rekindled my dormant love of reading and ignited my life's Renaissance. Seeing Peter Jackson's first "*LOTR*" movie in ninth grade inspired me to tackle the book itself. Immediately, I was swept off into Tolkien's heroic tale. I discovered a story, inspired by the ancient world's greatest legends and myths, with profound relevance to the modern world though its timeless themes of friendship, courage, corruption, good and evil, war and peace, victory and defeat, love and hate, and hope and despair. I was moved by, as C. S. Lewis put it, "Beauties which pierce like swords." I felt like St. Paul when the Lord knocked him off his horse on the road to Damascus. For the first time, I realized that literature helps us discover how we want to live and where we want to go in the future.

During the seventeenth and eighteenth centuries, the philosophers of the Enlightenment brought about remarkable progress by re-evaluating Europe's previously accepted doctrines and traditions. Reading *The Autobiography of Malcolm X* incited my Enlightenment. The book demonstrated how personal growth comes from having honesty, compassion, and a capacity for sincere introspection. Malcolm X's story gave me, for the first time in my life, an open mind. I recognized how everyone, including me, will instinctively clutch onto preconceived beliefs and prejudices. Additionally, Malcolm X's remarkable regard for history taught me that without an understanding of the past, there is no wisdom to guide us in the future.

The future is uncertain. We will face many great challenges in the twenty-first century: achieving peace and stability in the Middle East, defeating the ideology of Islamic Jihadism, and harnessing

> **I felt like St. Paul when the Lord knocked him off his horse on the road to Damascus.**

the energy of globalization to improve the human condition. Difficult choices must be made to meet these challenges, and I want to help make those decisions. My favorite stories have armed me with a love of reading and the sense of history and faith I need to face the future with enthusiasm. That is why I'm so excited to discover what the future will hold.

Sean O'Keefe attends the University of Chicago.

94

DOLLY PARTON, THEN AND NOW

It takes creativity to handle essay questions such as the following one from the University of Pennsylvania. The trick: don't spend too much time worrying about whether your preferred topic fits the question. What do they mean by a "first experience"? Author Allison Rapoport gives one answer with an inventive essay about seeing the world with a more mature eye. Says Allison, "An applicant should steer the essay to a topic about which they are passionate, and s/he should not be afraid to take some risks in doing so. It is not productive to spend time anticipating what the admissions staff 'wants' to see."

Essay by Allison Rapoport

First experiences can be defining. Cite a first experience that you have had and explain its impact on you.

I first became aware of the transformative power of music in the winter of 1992 when I attended my first live concert. This was my first weeknight excursion with my father, the culmination of many episodes of desperate begging and pleading. *Dolly Parton.* The sound of her name alone was enough to get my pulse racing, my feet tapping. I knew every chord, every lyric, of every song. However, if Dolly had walked past me on the street I would not have recognized her. Up until this concert I had only experienced music through my 1960s era Realistic™ radio. It was neither an attractive nor a reliable piece of equipment: paint-splattered, with a broken antenna and a faulty speaker which gave way to a gritty, faltering sound. I had never been disappointed by it. This night would leave my expectations forever changed.

In person, Dolly's singing was crisp, processed, easier to digest, and presented with an intensity that my radio had somehow filtered out. I was captivated, absorbing every word and every visual cue from this highly engaging and amusing speaker. I grinned, and danced. I stood on my seat in my effort to hear better, to get a better view of the stage. I marveled at how lucky I was to be in the presence of such a beautiful and talented woman, whose sequins and smiles lit up the theatre in rapid succession.

I left the concert feeling utterly elated. I had discovered a new context in which to set my musical appreciation. This revelation would set me on a search for more moments where I could be similarly elevated, a search that continues to this day. With these memories in mind I once again sought out a Dolly Parton show this past October. My hope was to rekindle the emotions this experience had stirred in me as a child. What I saw in this revisit, however, was a complete reversal. From this vantage point I could see that the idol of my childhood was lip-syncing every word. She merely pretended to play the instruments set before her, and the onstage banter that had once titillated me now seemed crude and unsophisticated. I did not dance, and I rarely smiled. As I began to second-guess my memory of my first concert, my attention drifted away from the stage. Then I spotted her—a younger girl standing in the front row. Eyes widened, she stood motionless, mesmerized by the scene before her. We experienced the same concert, but while she longed to be pulled in, I could not help but pull away.

My first concert instilled in me a wonderful sense of what the visual components of a live show can yield—a magical and enlightening experience that entertains without detracting from the music. I found myself unable to recreate the feelings it stirred in me. However, I do not regret my attempt to discover them anew, as I realized something important about the moments I inhabit. Even

> **I could see that the idol of my childhood was lip-syncing every word.**

if I were given the opportunity to return to the exact place and time of the first Dolly Parton performance, I would still not feel completely the same as I once did. Experiences are shaped not only by the circumstances that surround them, but also by the perspectives that we bring. Perceptions change and evolve inevitably as the mind matures. This is a process that should not be lamented, but rather, embraced. It is what fueled my search for Dolly's music in the first place, and it motivates me to search for the next music, the next transformative experience that will resonate with my present state of mind. My first concert showed me that the search is worthwhile. My revisit demonstrated to me that the search will never end, nor should it.

Allison Rapoport attends the University of Pennsylvania.

Anyone who wants to write about a trip should keep in mind that thousands of other applicants are doing the same. Avoid the travelogue essay, which ploddingly recalls every place you saw and everything you did. Better to write about sitting still and listening, as did the author of Essay 95, or to write about how going abroad changed the way you see yourself (Essay 97). Write about misadventures with family if you like (Essay 98), or use a piece of literature as an ongoing metaphor for what you experienced (Essay 99). The main thing is to use the description of your travels as a jumping off place for reflection rather than as an end in itself.

95

ON A BAR STOOL IN
THE VILLAGE OF HESSEN

Plenty of high school students take trips abroad, but not many are as savvy or adventuresome in learning about their new surroundings as author Walter Brummund. The essay has two highlights: the description of how he overcame resistance from the guidance counselor and others, and the interlude on the bar stool which shows his curiosity. The latter makes the generalities in the last paragraph much more believable. Walter also shows that it is possible to write a fine essay without a flashy opening paragraph.

Essay by Walter Brummund III

Evaluate a significant experience, achievement, risk you have taken, or ethical dilemma you have faced and its impact on you.

My junior year abroad in Germany was a very significant experience for me. At the beginning of my sophomore year of high school my family decided to take in a Japanese exchange student. Over the course of the year, Satoru became a part of our family and a dear friend. I had been thinking about going abroad even before we decided to host Sato, but by observing what a great experience his exchange year was for him, I was given the courage to go ahead and apply for a place in the Youth for Understanding year abroad program in Germany.

I faced some criticism for my decision to pursue a year abroad. My high school guidance counselor was worried that I would not be able to take the PSAT and try for a National Merit Scholarship. My parents did not want me to go because they did not want to lose one of my last years of living at home. I was discouraged by many people who thought a year abroad was something outside the norm that would jeopardize my academic career.

> I was discouraged by many people who thought a year abroad was something outside the norm.

By going I decided to take that risk and am better off for it. Not only did I improve my German and live in a different culture, I was able to meet all kinds of people. During our Easter vacation my host family took me on a family retreat to a small village in Hessen. The first night was so beautiful and clear that I decided to take a walk around the village. I lived in a larger city in Germany, and wanted to experience what life was like for the inhabitants of the village. While walking around I stumbled across a small hotel. I went inside and took a seat at the bar. It was a Sunday night and there were only a few people there. I ordered something and just sat at the bar, looking through a magazine and listening to the conversation the middle-aged men sitting near me were having. They were discussing the politics of the local men's soccer club and the feasibility of organizing a competitive team. They talked for hours about it quite animatedly. By listening to this one conversation, I was able to capture the spirit of life in that village and felt that I could understand the people there. Moments such as these were the high points of my year.

My year in Germany forced me to look at things in a different way as I was confronted with a different culture with different ideas. By experiencing new perspectives I was able to contrast my views with the views of others, and thus understand myself better. I got a better understanding of what is important to me and what defines my life. The most important thing I learned during my year abroad was that there is a lot to learn from your environment if you take the time to appreciate the perspectives of others.

Walter Brummund III attends the University of Wisconsin at Madison.

96

A TRIP TO FRANCE, AND AN ESSAY ABOUT GETTING THERE

The following essay has two parts: a description of author Catherine Davis and her tendency to be "part of a minority," and Catherine's quest to pay for a trip to France. The strand that holds it together: Catherine's determination to follow her own interests rather than those of others. The balance of the essay is serious, but she does a good job of showing her ironic sensibility. In the first clause of the last sentence, she skillfully echoes the opening of the essay by returning to the accomplishments of her brothers and sisters as a foil for her own.

Essay by Catherine Davis

I'm somewhat used to being a part of the minority. I've always been considered the "different" child of the family, the one not quite like the others. My three older brothers and sisters were all quiet, athletic, highly motivated scholars, excelling in subjects like math and science and being awarded MVP of the team. I was different.

I've never been a very shy person. Math has never been my best subject, I don't always do what I'm told, and I've never been named MVP of any sport.

In seventh grade, I became a part of another minority: the French class. Most of my friends decided to take Spanish, because it would "be more useful in the long run." I didn't care about the long run at that point; all I knew was French sounded beautiful and fluid and promising.

I wanted to learn the language flawlessly and be as creative with it as I could be with English. I continued French as I entered high school—year after year, word after word, grammar rule after rule. It was my top class, the one in which I felt most comfortable expressing myself.

Finally, last year, I received the chance for which I had been waiting. Our French teacher, Mrs. Besserer, had contacted an English teacher in Pau, France, and set up a foreign exchange program for that spring break. A small group of French students in the high school were invited to go to France for ten days in March. I was completely euphoric, until I heard the news that it would cost over $2,000.00. For others, the money meant nothing, but my parents could not afford to pay for my trip. They advised me to forget what seemed to them a luxury.

I wanted to go to France more than anything, and I knew that I couldn't let this chance pass me by. So I decided not to play my favorite sport that winter. With the help of my French teacher and the dean of students, I secured two jobs tutoring fourteen- and sixteen-year-old students in French, biology, English, and science. I also took a job at a resale shop slaving long hours under the stern eye of Mrs. Collins, who taught me what indentured servitude must have been like.

By about a week before the trip, I had collected enough money to go, and my excitement was unsurpassable. In mid-March, Mrs. Besserer, three other students, and I flew eight hours straight to Paris.

I will never forget that experience. Not only did I see the Louvre and the Cathedrale of Notre Dame, but I was submerged into a culture completely unlike my own and completely fascinating. When we flew to Pau for the second half of the trip, I went to live with a girl named Emmanuelle, to whom I grew very close. She took me to her high school, where I gave an English talk about America to the students in her English class. We went shopping together, and we visited the famous Chateau of Pau.

> I don't always do what I'm told, and I've never been named MVP of any sport.

I may not ever be the star of the basketball team like my sisters and brothers, but I've found my own little niche in this vast wall of opportunities, and I intend to dig even deeper into it for every year that passes.

Catherine Davis attends the University of Notre Dame.

97

IN COSTA RICA, SHE FINDS A NEW SELF-IMAGE

Author Abby Fried provides a textbook example of how to write about community service or foreign travel. It isn't about the helping, or the sight-seeing, but rather what you learn about yourself. For Abby, the revelation comes from being "physically content" in a place where physical appearances don't seem to matter as much. Her writing process is a model of how to approach the essay: "I sat down and wrote the entire thing in one sitting. Then I left it alone for about a week. Then every day I went back and made changes. My first draft was twice as long as it should have been, so I did a lot of editing."

Essay by Abigail Fried

The upbeat rhythm of merengue music electrified the air. My unaccustomed feet quickly adapted to the practiced steps of my dance partner. As the tempo of the music increased, my partner swept me across the floor in a rush of quick movements that I carried out with little skill, but with all my heart. As the song came to an end, I breathlessly thanked my partner and tried to explain what a fun time I had in my slightly broken Spanish. I noticed the seventeen other Americans, with whom I had traveled from the United States to Costa Rica, sitting together on one side of the room. A month earlier, seventeen Americans from all over the United States had anxiously pulled up next to this hall in Santa María, Costa Rica. We would be living in the town for a month, helping the "ticos" build a gymnasium, paint buildings, and do other jobs around the town. We were a group of teenagers, some more eager than others to start work the next day. I was among the more eager ones. I had participated in many community service projects at home and I looked forward to the work in Costa Rica, yet nothing could have prepared me for the fabulous jolt that would send me head-first into a new culture and a new life.

On the first day some of the men and boys engaged us in a soccer game. They quickly separated us into teams, although I realized they were a little confused as to which positions the four girls should play. They were simply not used to female athletes. However, once the game began, I recognized that we were a pleasant surprise. Having just recovered from an injury, I was far from being in great shape, but there was something about the atmosphere around me that was wonderfully energizing. Even as the rain started to fall, we continued, slipping and sliding through the mud. I, completely delighted, finished the game brown from head to foot. The men had accepted us into their community.

As the weeks progressed I won further respect with the females as well as the males in the community for my dedicated work and enthusiasm. My appearance mattered little; all they seemed to care about was getting to know me. This discovery was shocking. As a teenage girl, who for the past few years had been trying to fit her naturally athletic build to waif-like model ideals, I was accustomed to being assessed physically before any inquiry was made into my personality. I learned how differently these people think. During work hours they would often work with me, sweat dripping down our faces, cement crusted to our clothes, paint staining our skin, and having a great time. Evenings we danced, played games, and talked. I learned more from them about myself and what it means to be a person than I have ever learned elsewhere. I started to look at myself and see the aspects I liked instead of those I wanted to change. Being physically content left me free to concentrate on who I was. I found myself to be more expressive and energetic than I had ever been.

> **Even as the rain started to fall, we continued, slipping and sliding through the mud.**

Santa María, for me, was a turning point in my life. The people there accepted me immediately. I didn't have to be anything. I just had to be myself. Now at home and at school, I feel confident that I no longer have to present what I think people want. I only need to present me, and they can find what they like in me. As I danced with my tico partner, my American friends merely sat and watched, not suspecting my newfound revelation. My Costa Rican experience transformed me from a passive observer, mired in superficial appearances, to an active, self-confident young woman prepared for my adult life.

Abigail Fried attends Boston College.

98

TWO PARENTS, FIVE SIBLINGS, AND ONE VERY CROWDED CAR

Author Clare Malone hit pay dirt when she decided to write her essay about family vacations. She explains her choice this way: "I am only eighteen years old, I don't have any really unique life experiences, like living in a foreign county or traveling around the world in a sailboat, so I decided to write about my family." Good choice. Clare sets a light-hearted tone from the beginning with her tongue-in-cheek rhetorical question—"Sweatshop?"—in the second sentence. She uses a kids'-eye-view to gently mock her mother, always a good thing when done with affection. Anyone who ever got dragged along by mom or dad can relate to this fine essay.

Essay by Clare K. Malone

Sweltering heat, abhorrently close quarters, and short tempers. Sweatshop? No, such were the family vacations of my youth—countless hours in a poorly air-conditioned vehicle, seven traveling companions and a driver whose frustration often bordered on road rage. It has been said, however, that traumatic experiences forge strong relationships and teach us important life lessons. In fact, it is unavoidable not to learn a little bit about human nature when you are seated so close to another person that you can't tell where they end and you begin. Looking back, summer vacations have constituted some of the most vividly memorable times of my life. From my cramped place in the back seat, I developed a curiosity for knowledge, an appreciation for my lively family, and learned more card games than a career gambler.

My mother's ardent wish to immerse her children in the sights and history of the United States was the inspiration for our summer sojourns. She had the idea that we should visit all fifty states before she was through with us. Her ambition sucked the historical marrow right out of every possible tourist destination. We began with the thirteen original colonies and set out to embrace Americana. Along the way, each child was expected to keep a journal recounting his or her reflections of the trip. My mother was very gung-ho about these logs, and threatened that if we didn't write in our journal, we wouldn't be able to eat dinner. Consequentially, the majority of our writings dealt not with the sights we had seen, but instead discussed when we last ate, who got the window seat, and how many arguments had ensued. A large part of our sightseeing was spent on the road in our fire-engine red Suburban, a vehicle my mother lovingly refers to as her "seventh child." The hours in the car, though excruciating, taught me the importance of compromise and cooperation in human relations. Space was limited to say the least, and as the youngest, I had the smallest amount. I quickly learned that getting my way through means of force was not the answer, as everyone in my family had at least six inches and twenty pounds on me. In order to garner extra leg room or a pillow, I honed my powers of persuasion and came to realize the importance of a kind word or deed.

The first stop was Washington, D.C., an obvious destination for our inaugural trip. Countless exhibits at the Smithsonian, a visit to Ford's Theatre, and a tour of the White House were succinctly summed up in my journal: "It was a long day and I'm very sleepy now." D.C., of course, was only the beginning. While other kids did Disney World, we drove sixteen hours to Fort Ticonderoga to watch elderly men re-enact Revolutionary War battles. Then there was the period when my father, in a bizarre midlife crisis, decided that his calling was to commune with the whales of the Northeast. So, for a couple of Augusts we drove to Maine and Massachusetts in order to whale-watch in the icy waters of the north Atlantic. It was our family's answer to the traditional Caribbean cruise. Williamsburg, Virginia, was another favorite stop. Our family embraced the colonial feel of the town on varying levels. My parents were mesmerized by the process of eighteenth-century soap making, while, on the other hand, we kids headed straight for the gift shop. For the rest of the vacation, despite

During our first few journeys, sleeping at Knight's Inn was a novelty to say the least.

countless odd looks from strangers at rest stops, my sister refused to remove her treasured colonial coonskin cap from her head.

The best part of a trip always came at the end of the day when we got to rest. During our first few journeys, sleeping at Knight's Inn was a novelty to say the least. My mother recalls the first time my sister and I stayed in a motel; we literally screamed with excitement. Apparently the bathtub held a particular fascination for us. We insisted upon being photographed within it, as indoor plumbing was a new phenomenon. On later trips, my father found hotel costs for eight people to be overwhelming, and so we began camping as an alternative. Conquering the great outdoors with my family turned out to be quite the character-building activity, offering new, but not always pleasant experiences. One particular incident comes to mind that involved improper construction of a tent, a midsummer thunderstorm, and a rude awakening in the morning to find myself bathing face-down in rainwater. A few more fiascos convinced my parents we were not camping material, but I gathered a little more mettle and determination from our escapades (as well as an appreciation for hotel beds and maid service).

Our vacations have continued over many summers. We've seen the infamous Boston Harbor, tiny Rhode Island and her ocean views; Virginia's stately old plantation houses and have been charmed by the warmth of Carolina beaches. Though I have grown older, my excitement and enjoyment of our summer ritual has never waned. Each passing year gives me a greater appreciation for the living history I have witnessed, those who surround me, and fills me with anticipation for what lies beyond the next bend in the road.

Clare K. Malone attends Georgetown University.

99

IN STEP WITH GULLIVER, TRAVELING THE WORLD

Lots of essays use analogies, but only for a line or a paragraph. Author Casey Mank's entire essay is built on an extended analogy. After (conveniently) reading *Gulliver's Travels* en route to Europe and Africa, Casey tells the story of the trip as a rejoinder to the book, describing how her experiences parallel those of Gulliver. Along the way, she finds numerous points of comparison to maintain the analogy. Imaginary as they were, *Gulliver's Travels* were nothing if not exotic. Casey's own exotic details, such as being chased by crowds of children screaming "azungu," are necessary to put her own travels on par with those of Gulliver.

Essay by Casey Elizabeth Mank

I had never been outside the continental United States when I decided to travel to Africa. By the time I returned to school from my two-week-long sophomore spring break, I had landed in England, Kenya, Malawi, and South Africa. Maybe more people would have started smaller with, say, a tame vacation venture to Mexico or Hawaii, but since I had always planned on visiting everywhere eventually, I figured, why not? Why not make sure traveling abroad for the first time lived up to the high standard of excitement set by my vivid imagination. During the decidedly un-fascinating thirty-six hours of flight time required, I kept myself occupied with books. One of these was *Gulliver's Travels* by Jonathan Swift. Although he is a fictional, middle-aged British man, and I am a female high school student of the twenty-first century, I immediately recognized the similarities between Gulliver and me. With hypocrisy, egotism, and bitingly satiric outlook aside, I felt that Gulliver's perspective on his unbelievably exotic adventure could be no more full of surprise or curiosity than mine. We both found ourselves away from the home and culture we had always known, thrown into exciting and sometimes frightening situations which ultimately changed our comparatively sheltered perspectives and broadened our previously narrow horizons.

Gulliver's first unlikely destination, Lilliput, is home to a highly civilized but miniature society. My own first stop outside the country was Gulliver's homeland, England. The accents, the double-decker red buses, my first glimpse of Buckingham Palace (complete with impassive guards), and, of course, almost constant rain, made me feel as though I had stepped into a tourist pamphlet about London, rather than into the city itself. I admit to being a slight Anglophile, and during my brief time in London, I found it impossible to fully grasp that I was finally there. I imagine Gulliver felt the same disbelief in Lilliput, where every aspect of the land resembled a dollhouse. He took detailed notes about the appearance and customs of Mildendo, the Metropolis of Lilliput. As I scribbled in my diary on the red-eye flight out of Heathrow, I too tried to preserve every detail of Piccadilly Circus and the British Museum so that my friends and family back home would be able to see the city just as I had.

In Brobdingnag, Gulliver encounters giants, and escapes several near-death experiences. While I must admit that Gulliver's second stop was more dramatic than mine, I did have the first frightening experience of my journey at our second landing; Nairobi, Kenya. At the Nairobi airport, we were not permitted to leave the plane. Security officers came onboard and searched under our seats and in our bags. Armed guards were assembled on the ground around our plane, their weapons clearly visible from the window. I realized that, movies not included, I had never actually seen, let alone been

> **Armed guards were assembled on the ground around our plane, their weapons clearly visible from the window.**

close to, real people holding real guns and looking very ready to use them. Gulliver and I were both surrounded by unfamiliar and threatening forces that we had no way to control. Fortunately, in Swift's imaginary world, an eagle snatches Gulliver's box from the ground and flies away from the hostile country of Brobdingnag. As my plane took off, I felt only relief to be ending that particular brief and nerve-wracking episode in my adventure.

Even Gulliver's first experiences on the floating island of Laputa couldn't have been more astonishing than my own initial impressions of Africa. When I stepped off the plane in Malawi I was hit by a wall of humidity very different from the chilly March weather back home in Pennsylvania. We drove for hours on bumpy dirt roads, passing countless thatched huts and women on the roadside carrying water or firewood. I felt as if I had fallen into *National Geographic!* Everywhere I looked was something I had never seen before. As Gulliver expressed it, "The reader can hardly conceive my astonishment."

Africa became even more surprising as my trip went on, but I quickly learned to expect and look forward to cultural surprises and strange sights rather than facing them with apprehension. In less than two weeks there, I had danced with a witch doctor, seen a wild bull elephant, and been only a few feet from an irritated pod of hippos. I had been chased, on a daily basis, by crowds of children screaming "azungu," which means "white person." Suddenly I was the minority! I was just as much a mystery to them as they were to me. I had braces at the time, which was a constant source of fascination and amusement to our hosts. Small children would laugh and point, tugging on my clothes and pointing emphatically back and forth between my face and some nearby metallic object. When someone finally translated for me, I discovered that they had decided that my braces were earrings put in my teeth as a sign of wealth. Like Gulliver, I tried to learn as much of the language and culture as I could in such a short time, which resulted, just as it had for him, in many memorable confusions, and a few almost-conversations.

> I had been chased, on a daily basis, by crowds of children screaming "azungu," which means "white person."

Gulliver's last and most important journey takes him to a rational, peaceful utopia governed by talking horses. In this country, men have been reduced to a wild state and are used as beasts of burden. Faced with such a revolutionary social reality, Gulliver is forced to re-examine his own society and question the lifestyle he has always known. The aspect of my trip to Malawi which most deeply affected me was the volunteer work our group did during our stay.

We were exposed to people who had lived through hardships never experienced in the United States. We spent most of our time working with a temporary home for infants and toddlers orphaned by AIDS. We also painted, taught, and made donations at local schools. The gratitude of doctors receiving our boxes of latex gloves, for lack of which they had been forced to postpone many operations, was incredible to see.

The two weeks went by so quickly! When it was time to leave, I was torn between excitement and regret. Going out to dinner with my parents on the evening of my return was as much of a culture shock as my first meal in Africa had been! I was surprised by the price of my food, and ashamed not to finish it all. Two weeks in Africa had forced me to see the world differently. Like Gulliver, I began to question the aspects of my own culture that I had never even noticed before. I felt some of his disillusionment, but I had seen so many fantastic things on my trip! The hardest part about coming home was answering the ridiculous question, "How was Africa?" How could I explain to someone who had never been there? Every waking moment had been absolutely fascinating. Like Gulliver, I had carefully documented all of my experiences and adventures in far off lands, and my Africa journal is still some of my favorite reading.

Casey Elizabeth Mank attends Muhlenberg College.

100

BEATING THE MY-TRIP-TO-EUROPE BLAHS

You know the down side about trip essays—too much trite babble about learning from other cultures, not enough real insight. But how many travelers go off the beaten path in a country where they don't speak the language? Unlike ordinary travel essays, this one shows real passion. The author, Sarah Mitchell, demonstrates her eye for detail in her description of Rome, even as she makes the interesting point that in order to really appreciate travel, it is necessary to get out of your comfort zone. Sarah is impressive because she actively seeks such experiences.

Essay by Sarah Mitchell

I am most comfortable when I am lost. Deliberately getting lost fuels my drive for discovery. On a trip to Italy the summer after my sophomore year, I discovered the pleasure of using public transportation to get to know the city of Rome. This ancient city can intimidate and overwhelm a person, leaving her confused about how to process new information. You can easily forget that the city is alive because you become so absorbed in the ancient Roman ruins and the extravagant Baroque churches. The city becomes surreal. Escaping from a tourist's view of Rome enables one to appreciate Rome for the beauty of the ordinary in addition to the extraordinary.

By taking buses deep into the city, where few tourists venture, my friend Andrew and I attempted to discover the real city of Rome. Not knowing our destination or our surroundings we got "lost" within the city. Riding buses to the end of the line can lead to unexpected sights and adventures. Walking down unknown streets, we saw an old woman, hobbling along, weighed down by her bag of groceries and the weight of time, slowly making her way home. Yet the wise smile on her face clearly showed that she did not need my sympathy. Further along, young lovers stood bickering, screaming and gesticulating. However, minutes later, when their anger subsided, the lovers walked hand in hand out of the alley, covertly stealing a kiss when no one should have been looking. Tottering along, a young child took shaky steps, fell down, and cried. The mother swooped down, delivered kisses and soft, calming words, and picked her baby back up to try again. Images like these slip easily from one's notice when blinded by the tourist's dark glasses. These images broke down stereotypes and brought Italian culture to life in a completely new way.

My understanding of human nature increased greatly as a result of the discoveries that I made while "getting lost" in Italy. Vitality and passion for living are so apparent in all aspects of Italian culture. Every night during my week in Southern Italy, fireworks exploded and lit up the night sky for no apparent reason other than to celebrate for celebration's sake. I learned to live on my own time, rather than by the strict constraints of the time of watches and clocks. I could appreciate my surroundings so much more when I was not rushed and the fusion of the ordinary and the extraordinary filled me with a new sense of appreciation for life, human potential, and joy.

> **Riding buses to the end of the line can lead to unexpected sights and adventures.**

I believe that the ability to get lost separates the true traveler from the ordinary tourist. By being able to set aside my preconceived ideas, I truly experienced a new culture and did not just "visit" Italy. Although I hardly spoke a word of Italian, I was amazed by how much of a conversation I understood simply by observing body language and tone of voice. This experience really taught me about the similarities between human beings. As the culture became more real and more personal to me, I was able to see my own experiences reflected in the lives of the people around me. Whether you choose to be a traveler or a tourist goes much deeper than visiting far-off places. An individual can either choose to accept the view of the world presented to him or her, or be unafraid to seek the truth. I came to understand how much beauty the latter option holds, and how great a reward sacrificing comfort and letting go of fear can provide.

Sarah Mitchell attends Rice University.

101
THE MOST MEANINGFUL VACATION

We would hesitate to advise anyone to write a 934-word essay—like the one that follows—unless you have as much passion and skill as author Anne Ruleman. The length of this essay adds to the sense of wonder that Anne experiences in London and highlights the fact that she is in over-drive every minute. From her flight to London that finds her marveling "at the hugeness of the earth," to the flight back when she puts the finishing touches on her journal, she is intent on experiencing everything there is in London. Says Anne, "This essay describes one of the most significant events in my life, and writing it was an exploration of a portion of myself rather than a task."

Essay by Anne Ruleman

In June of this year, my parents and I took a weeklong trip to London. This trip was one my parents had been planning to take for years but had never had quite enough money before; it was to be our first real family vacation and my first time to go abroad. Such an event would, under normal circumstances, have inspired in us an unbearable level of excitement, but at the time the trip was scheduled, my grandmother was terminally ill with lung cancer and could die at any time. However, we decided to risk going anyway, and we took off from the Atlanta airport on a drizzly Monday afternoon, bemused and perhaps finding it hard to believe that it was really us, and that we were actually going to England. That night, with a quiet fascination, I watched the sun set over the Atlantic and rise again a few hours later, and I marveled at the hugeness of the earth.

When the plane touched down it was early in the morning, broad daylight. A haze of lines, shuttles, and buses took us from the Gatwick airport to our hotel in South Kensington, and a few hours after our arrival we stepped out onto the pavement to explore that area of the city.

I found that morning that I had entered a dreamland realized. I was a devoted Anglophile, and so London was the center of my world. From England's heart came nearly everything I held dear: the writers I loved and revered—Frances Hodgsen Burnett and Roald Dahl and J. K. Rowling, C. S. Lewis and J. R. R. Tolkien, Charles Dickens and Jane Austen—the great kings and queens of the past whose lives intrigued me so, the places I had no clear picture of but whose names, long ingrained in my mind, resounded with the quaint mystery and hidden power of an age-old melody—*Gloucester, Piccadilly, Charing Cross, Tottenham, Chancery, Blackfriars, Westminster*... I said them aloud to myself and felt something deep within me stir.

Over the course of the week, I explored what seemed like every part of London. I saw the White Tower left by the Normans and the little chapel under whose floor lay Anne Boleyn, her head in her arm, and Lady Jane Grey, Queen of England for nine days. I saw the crumbling fragments of the wall that surrounded Londinium, built by the Romans more than eleven hundred years earlier. I rode the Underground many times with an undying enthusiasm that only a small-town dweller could have for public transportation. I was moved almost to tears while wandering through Westminster Abbey, seeing the stained-glass windows that had been pieced back together with such courage and diligence after being smashed during the bombings of the Second World War. I walked across the Millennium Bridge and smelled the sweetly damp, faintly salty air of the River Thames. I strolled through Kensington Park, and the lush green of the grass and summer foliage was a thousand times more intense under the gray sky. I regarded with amazement the different people who inhabited the city—seldom had I seen in one place so many Indians, Muslims, Asians, and people whose ethnic origin was entirely lost to me, and I loved them all simply for their presence. I saw many, many beautiful things,

> **I saw the White Tower left by the Normans and the little chapel under whose floor lay Anne Boleyn.**

and I also saw imperfection—the filth, garbage, crime, poverty, and ugliness found in any city—but it did nothing to dim my idea of the magnificence of London. I had been afraid that the reality would be disappointing, since my expectations were so high, but it was not. Seeing the city's darker side made its lighter side all the more radiant.

But above all things, what I found the most surprising was how at home I felt in England. I was a foreigner in a country I had never visited before, and yet I had a stronger sense of belonging there than I had ever had before in my life. It was as if I had returned home after a long vacation. This feeling first struck me the morning we arrived, and it increased as the week wore on. Though I was certain everyone could tell I was American, the more time I spent there, the less I saw myself as an American, an outsider in someone else's land. I became aware that the world did not consist of "me" and "them," that the world was more enormous and grand than I had ever before understood it to be, and that I was very much a part of it. This at-homeness with the world—the world that, in spite of its divisions, seemed to come together in that ancient city—moved me perhaps more deeply than anything I had ever felt before.

I kept a journal that week, from the time we left Atlanta to the time we left London. As we took off from Gatwick I watched the city pass beneath the plane, then the misty rolling fields that looked like a green patchwork quilt. I was writing about what I saw and thought when I suddenly recalled a particular phrase from a poem I had read in *The New Yorker* a couple of months previous—"There is another world/ And it is this world." The poem's title was "The Visiting," and the poet was Franz Wright. I remember reciting the poem to myself and looking out the window of the plane, just before finishing the journal. I quoted those lines from the poem and, in the last sentence, observed, "I never quite understood what it meant until now."

Anne Ruleman attends Earlham College.

102

A PUMA WHO GOT A LITTLE TOO PLAYFUL

Author Laurel Janeen Smith finds herself in a jam as she opens her essay. It begins as she is traveling with an older sister in Argentina. After sightseeing for several weeks, the two of them have stopped to volunteer at a wildlife refuge. (Her sister had previously worked there.) To make a long story short, Laurel gets up close and personal with Sonko the puma and, well, we'll let Laurel tell the rest. Says Laurel, "I never thought my life was in danger, just my face."

Essay by Laurel Janeen Smith

His teeth clenched over my delicate skull, and I felt hot blood drip down my cheeks as his claws slashed at my face. My legs crumbled beneath his heavy weight as both of us came crashing down the rocky hillside. I fought to thrust myself from beneath him, remembering the mangled stuffed animals surrounding his cage. Finally I managed to get to my feet, but unable to pry my head out of the puma's mouth, I calmly called up to my partner. "Victoria, could you please help me?" After a minute or two she reached us and looked down at Sonko batting me around like a new toy. She cursed at the familiar sight and helped free me from Sonko's grasp. Trying to regain some composure, I wiped the blood from my face with my mud-and-sweat-soaked shirt. I readily passed Sonko's cord to Victoria and cautiously walked in front of the puma. I continued, deeper into the jungle, with nothing but an empty water bottle, a chocolate bar, and a cucumber in hand.

Everyone has gone to the zoo and seen these gorgeous creatures. Their golden fur flows like water and their black eyes pierce through the distance. Behind bars they look almost surreal in their cages where the adoring public views them at their leisure. Every time I walked past an animal at the zoo I never thought twice about the life beyond the bars.

The daily routines that have caged my life for eleven years had started to wear on me. That's one of the stronger reasons I found myself in South America last summer at a wild animal refuge.

I fell in love with the place when I found a "chuchi-chuchi" (a wild teddy bear with a tail) sleeping on my straw mattress as I entered the hostel. I started working in the monkey park rehabilitating monkeys. After having monkeys climb on me, pull my hair, spit, puke, and pee on me all day, every day, for nearly a month, the idea of spending a day in the tranquil jungle with a puma sounded more than inviting. Victoria approached me in the early morning frantically questioning me whether or not the monkey park could spare anyone to walk Sonko, one of the more "playful" pumas. I quickly volunteered, and laughter flew from Victoria's mouth as she imagined me walking a puma twice my size. Finally though, she led me to the puma's cage with much gratitude.

The morning sun glimmered through the thick jungle trees. Every time I turned around and saw the eyes of the huge cat following my every move, I became filled with a new excitement. Victoria passed me the cord after a few hours and walked up ahead. Sonko followed. Walking a puma in the jungle seemed oddly natural, and I enjoyed listening to the dirt rustle beneath his huge paws, his smooth flowing stride astounded me. I reached for rocks and branches as I climbed the rough, steep trail.

> I enjoyed listening to the dirt rustle beneath his huge paws, his smooth flowing stride astounded me.

Suddenly Sonko stopped and looked down at me, then back towards Victoria. She was nowhere in sight. A menacing grin spread across his big pussycat face, and before I knew it, he had jumped on my head.

After being attacked by the puma, I continued my day normally. I had just been mauled by a huge animal and had no time to sit down, nothing to drink, hardly anything to eat, and was in the middle of the jungle. None of this seemed slightly absurd; although, I did wish I had a knife to peel my cucumber. The truth is a puma jumping on my head wasn't abnormal. If people knew how often

Sonko jumped on heads, they would probably laugh at my dramatic re-enactment. Nevertheless, I still enjoy telling about "the one time a puma jumped on my head."

Laurel Janeen Smith attends Ithaca College.

Why I Love First Choice U.

A t least once during your college search, you'll be called upon to declare undying devotion to a college or university. You don't need to tell them all that they're First Choice U., exactly, but if you make them think you want them, you'll increase the likelihood that they'll want you. Specifics are more important here than in any other essay. Cite particular programs, as do Essays 108 and 109, and don't cop out by saying that, for instance, you want to go to Columbia because of the excitement of New York City. (Join the cast of thousands.) You may ultimately decide to attend elsewhere, as did the author of Essay 103, but that doesn't mean you can't make it look good in your essay.

103
"A CALM, SOOTHING FEELING CAME OVER ME"

As hard as the colleges try to sell their academic excellence, most students make their decisions about college based on intangibles: the look of the campus, the friendliness of the students, the feeling they get when they visit. Author Diana Hawkins is no exception, as she eloquently testifies in the following essay. It starts with the physical beauty of the campus, the first thing she saw, but moves on to more substantive topics such as the willingness of Swarthmore students to speak out on the issues of the day. By the end, Diana has shown that she is an engineer who cares about a lot besides engineering.

"Why Swarthmore?" by Diana Hawkins

"Have you considered Swarthmore?"

Swath what? I remember thinking to myself as I sat there in my college counselor's office. We were discussing which colleges I would be visiting over the spring break of my junior year.

"Swarthmore, it's a small liberal arts school with a wonderful engineering program. It's just outside of Philadelphia. I think you'd like it."

Alright, I thought, I'm going to visit Carnegie Mellon University after I check out Cooper's Union so it would be on the way. Having never heard of the college before in my life, I decided that I would take a look but would not put Swarthmore on my official college list until I was sure that this was a school that offered everything I wanted in a college: strong academics, a friendly student body, and social opportunities, since I am not the stereotypical anti-social engineer.

When we arrived at Swarthmore, a calm soothing feeling came over me. Was this Swarthmore with its perfectly manicured lawns, gorgeous buildings, and seemingly laid back and yet intensely focused student body? When we drove past the Swarthmore sign, I was taken aback and immediately became intrigued with the school. Once we parked and got out of the car, we couldn't find the admissions building to save our lives so we stopped a nearby student and asked them for directions. Their friendliness and willingness to not only tell us where the building was, but physically take us there struck me as different. The students at most of the other schools I visited weren't half as friendly or eager to show me their college. I instantly fell in love with Swarthmore.

When I returned to Swarthmore for the Discovery Weekend program, I was lost once again.

"Are you a spec?"

"A what?" I asked.

"A spec, a prospective student. You look lost."

"Yes I am. Could you tell me how to get to Sharples?"

"Sure, it's over here."

Once again the friendliness of the college and the student's willingness to help pleasantly surprised me. I later went to the Swarthmore Winter Formal and loved the atmosphere at the party. It was a nonalcoholic party, and I liked the fact that Swatties didn't need alcohol to have a good time. I then went to a talent show and experienced firsthand how outspoken and talented the students were. Students read their poetry about the war in Iraq, racial prejudice, and various other pressing issues in

> **It was a nonalcoholic party and I liked the fact that Swatties didn't need alcohol to have a good time.**

the world today. Swarthmore's students were knowledgeable and concerned about the world around them and that impressed me.

I went to club meetings, attended classes, slept in the dorms, and ate the food over those three days of Discovery Weekend. I discovered a lot. I found out that Swarthmore was a liberal arts school that happened to have an engineering program and not the other way around. I also learned that Swarthmore would teach me how to learn, a skill set that I can see myself using the rest of my life. I was looking for a college that had a friendly, knowledgeable, social, and open student body and a stellar engineering program, and I believe that I have found that college in Swarthmore.

Diana Hawkins attends Harvey Mudd College.

104

A LITTLE HELP FROM DAVID LETTERMAN

If there is one kind of essay where a little overkill may be in order, it is the "why us?" essay. Even if they give you a tiny space, give them some meat. This essay does just that with a top-ten list. Along the way, author Rebecca Kastan shows her thorough research; she has visited the chamber of commerce website, knows about the football team's record, knows that cookies are served at the Schulman Center, etc. She also shows the second requisite quality: passion for the university.

Essay by Rebecca Kastan

Rebecca Kastan's Top Ten Reasons Why Vanderbilt Is Her #1 Choice (*David Letterman Style*):

10. Weather: I have lived in Columbus, Ohio, my whole life. Although it has been the best place to grow up, I have to admit that weather is not our forté. Weather can have an effect on people's mood and outlook. I checked out what the Nashville Chamber of Commerce says about weather, and it sure sounds good to me!

9. Football: In my house, knowing the game of football is not a luxury, it's a necessity. Not just because my dad is one of the biggest Buckeye fans you will ever know, but because my brother, Jake, is also the quarterback for his high school team. I have been his number one fan since day one, and if I didn't understand and love this game, I would not be able to participate in dinner conversations. While looking into the nuts and bolts of Vanderbilt football, I discovered an extremely challenging schedule. I also learned that the Commodores have won many awards for being the smartest bunch of guys in the conference. This team is improving each year, and I would love to be around to see them **win more games.**

8. Cookies at the Schulman Center: My Judaism is a significant aspect of my life. Given my priorities, I will be spending much time at Hillel. It's nice to know that while I'm there, I can enjoy a yummy cookie.

7. Size: Vanderbilt University is the perfect size with 6,146 undergraduates and 4,566 graduates and professional students. The university is not too big, yet there will always be new students and faculty to meet. I also appreciate how the administration has set a goal of diversifying the student body.

6. Nashville, the Music Capital: I am a fan of all music from hip-hop to country to jazz, and I learned on my visit to Nashville that it is the mecca of the music industry. During my college years at Vanderbilt University I know that the music culture will be something I would love to explore.

5. Field hockey and lacrosse: These sports have had an incredible impact on my life. I have played seven years of field hockey and served as captain of the Junior Varsity and Varsity teams (two varsity letters and the "Hustle Your Buns" award 2003). I have also played five years of lacrosse (two varsity letters and the "Most Improved Player" award 2004). Playing team sports has been one of the most enjoyable experiences of my life. I also believe in the value of exercise and staying in shape. While my coach is encouraging me to try to walk on the lacrosse team, I know that I can continue to always play club or intramural athletics at Vanderbilt.

> **It's nice to know that while I'm there, I can enjoy a yummy cookie.**

4. Fun: Whether it's school, sports, or social activities I know I'm going to enjoy and love this school. I have heard nothing but tremendous things about Vanderbilt from previous graduates and students who still attend, and I have really had a great time when visiting. The "fun factor" is pretty important when you are eighteen years old.

3. Extracurricular Learning Activities: Jewish tradition teaches that community responsibility is not an "extracurricular" activity—it is a requirement. In my family it is not a question of whether or not you do community service—it's just a question of where and how often. When I researched Vanderbilt's community service history there was a long list of different opportunities for me to get involved in as a student. I was excited to learn that Vanderbilt has a study abroad program at Hebrew University. If I were to study abroad, this might be a good match for me and my interests.

2. Academic Opportunities: I have worked hard in high school, and I want to go to a college that offers me great opportunities for academic excellence. I know that in the future, when I am looking at jobs or graduate school, having Vanderbilt on my resume would be a terrific asset. I believe *this* university is the place where I will be able to surpass everyone's expectations as well as the ones I have for myself.

1. Magic: Vanderbilt University just feels like the right place for me.

Rebecca Kastan attends Vanderbilt University.

105

THE JOYS OF FALLING IN LOVE (WITH A COLLEGE)

Colleges love enthusiasm, especially when that enthusiasm is directed toward them. Author Catriona Morrison begins with her hesitation to visit Sewanee (formally known as University of the South). But soon after she arrives on campus, the clouds part, the skies brighten, and she falls in love with it. Catriona immediately picks up the lingo of an insider—she refers to being "on the Mountain"—and from there extols all the reasons why Sewanee is perfect for her. Her paragraph on community service is particularly effective because it talks about how she plans to get involved after she enrolls.

Essay by Catriona Morrison

As we drove up the steep mountain road with rain streaming across the windows of our Hertz Rent-A-Car, my dad assured me that we weren't completely wasting our time: "Just keep an open mind," he said, "at least we can use what they tell us when we're in Nashville tomorrow." I was not amused. Having woken up very early in the morning in order to arrive at this remote campus on time, I was more worried about getting wet than I was about the day ahead of us. My dad and I were on our way to the Admission 101 Program, something we thought would be an excellent way to start what was promising to be a very tedious college search.

After sprinting to the admissions office, we were given umbrellas and asked to walk with the group over to our first lecture. It was during this walk that the sun started coming out and I suddenly realized what an amazing place I had just set foot in. Attempting to maneuver around the puddles that now lined University Avenue, I began taking mental notes of everything that surrounded me: not only the glistening trees and towering chapel, but the special feeling that seemed to be hovering over everything on the Mountain.

I left the University of the South that day knowing where I was going to college. The tour we had in Nashville the next day couldn't have gone by any slower, and before we reached the car, I was already explaining to my dad how it paled in comparison to the previous day's events. In the car and on the plane ride home, I went page by page through every pamphlet, letter, and campus map I had received in my Admission 101 packet—I was sold.

That weekend marked the first of the many encounters I was to have with Sewanee in my life. As I started my junior year and became more involved in the new youth program at my church, I began seeing little reminders of my weekend everywhere I turned. I remember first noticing the Sewanee bumper sticker on the back of our lovely white fifteen-passenger church van and was amazed to see that almost everyone over age twenty on the ski trip I went on that year sported their fashionable Sewanee outerwear every chance they got. I evidently wasn't the only one who had felt that special something on the Mountain.

Even more exciting than that initial visit was the realization that I had fallen in love with a school that fit my every need and would be able to cater to all of my passions. Having attended my current school since I was three years old, I knew I needed to find another small student body when I went to college. Not only did it need to be the right size, however; it also needed a dedicated staff and an encouraging and challenging academic and social environment— check. A liberal arts education was very important to me because I believe that this type of background is essential for communication with colleagues and clients in whatever career one chooses to pursue. As for my current career aspirations, I would love someday to be involved in the business side of the music industry, and nearby Nashville presents every opportunity for me to follow those dreams and make them a reality.

> I went two consecutive summers on medical mission trips to Honduras with a nearby Episcopal church.

During my high school years I have been very involved in community service. I went two consecutive summers on medical mission trips to Honduras with a nearby Episcopal church and it took a summer off (my last month at camp) for me to realize that, despite the long hours in the pharmacy, severely limited diet, various creepy crawlies, and violent illness that comprised a significant part of my experiences, I loved what we were able to do down there. This is just one example of the various activities I have been involved with, and it is really exciting to know that Sewanee places just as much importance on community service as I do. I would hope to gain a better understanding and compassion for human life through the community work I would participate in at Sewanee, and I know that these experiences would be important ones in shaping who I will be as a person long after I have graduated.

There is no doubt in my mind that I would receive the best education possible at Sewanee; however, it is important to remember that advanced calculus and term papers are only a small part of what a liberal arts education is all about. I will eventually be sent out into the world knowing how to read, write, and divide, but I will also know who I genuinely am as a person. The amazing thing about the Mountain is that it allows you the time to look inside yourself and see who you truly are when separated from all of the pressures down below. This amazing quality sets Sewanee apart from all other schools. I am reminded of how special a place it is when I listen to the song "Mayberry" by Rascal Flatts:

"Sometimes I can hear this old earth shouting/Through the trees as the wind blows./That's when I climb up here on this mountain/To look through God's window./Now I can't fly/But I got two feet that get me high up here./Above the noise and city streets/My worries disappear."

With such amazing support, resources, and opportunities available at Sewanee, I know that I could go nowhere but up (literally and figuratively). I cannot wait for the challenges that I will face in the next four years of my life, which will allow me to grow both mentally and spiritually and will prepare me for whatever God has planned in my future.

Catriona Morrison attends the University of the South (Sewanee).

106

TAKING INTROSPECTION TO A NEW LEVEL

It is no coincidence that the first page of the application of St. John's College (MD & NM) is devoted to its essay questions. Applicants are asked to write up to four essays that total five to ten typed, double-spaced pages. St. John's is devoted to the study of the great books—think Plato or Euclid—and it wants students who are dedicated readers, writers, and thinkers. St. John's students take introspection seriously—hence the following essay by author Andrew Perry. It is longer than most essays and deeply self-revealing. It might not be a particularly good essay for someone applying to a business or engineering program, but for St. John's, it is perfect.

Essay by Andrew Perry

Explain in detail why you wish to attend St. John's College; please evaluate the strengths and weaknesses of your formal education to date.

I settled on St. John's a few months after I had finished applying to, visiting, being accepted by, and finally deciding not to attend three colleges. I had finished my senior year of high school by correspondence and a few classes taken credit-by-exam, so in truth my senior year was a year off. I wasn't enamored of the prospect of spending another year away from school and away from activity, but I couldn't in good conscience throw myself into a college I didn't care about. What had bothered me about the schools I had applied to was that all of them seemed to be opportunities to flounder, to waste time in a pre-adult, post-child no-man's land. And who could blame a teenager for floundering when faced with so many diverse choices, with very little experience to guide him. That isn't to say that I am a glutton for responsibility, the point is that there are less expensive ways of avoiding it. I decided not to go without a clear reason why I was going.

Another stumbling block was the lack of structure in so many programs. Take a few classes. Declare a major. Take more classes. Change your mind. Why should a person go to college, voluntarily to choose to continue their education? There may be as many answers as there are people who've asked the question. In my opinion, the answer is in order to come out on the other side a human being, with a more capable mind. Usually I shy away from these kinds of analyses because they tend to sound trite or over-idealized. It might be a handicap to stay away from those kinds of questions—at this rate, I may never be able to articulate why I do one thing rather than another. I prefer to keep those thoughts intuitive; I have the most luck that way. If it isn't right, I'll know it, though perhaps not why.

I can't know St. John's until I try it. My visit gave me an idea of what to expect, and I was fairly well sold when, in my tutor interview, Mr. Cook described the program as "education for the soul." It seems to me that there are many ways to educate a soul; as I write this, I am staying in a hostel in Oregon, and while the different travelers come and go, it occurs to me that one could grow a great deal just by moving from place to place. I, on the other hand, am more likely to hunker down in the first appealing coffeehouse, where I wrote these essays out on paper.

I can't say whether or not I'm an old child or a young adult, whether I'll be fulfilled or miserable, disillusioned or illusioned still in Santa Fe [the location of St. John's]. I have now spent too much time in inactivity, I have found a program that seems worthwhile, one that I think I won't be able to trick, one that I won't be able to cheat or sidestep. Maybe Plato will prove as useful as my car when it sat inert and heavy on jack stands in the driveway for a month, I can't say. What I can say is that I am interested, a rare phenomenon with higher education, and think that four years of reading and writing could prove to be worth the portion of my irresponsible youth.

It occurs to me that one could grow a great deal by moving from place to place.

As for high school and all that came before it, I can't rightly complain. I had it better than most; I took tiny classes in the same building from the time I was five until I was seventeen. The evaluation of my education is another area I'm hesitant to stay in for any length of time. Look at the numbers, but understand that I never thought I fully deserved any of them. This is not false modesty, I was lucky, I flew by the seat of my pants, I picked things up easily, and the only struggles I had were the deadlines that I'd let myself get ever more perilously close to, especially in my last years there.

I could have worked harder, I had the ability to accomplish more, but I didn't have the desire. My evaluation of my education is this, I learned a lot, but I could have learned much more. And now, I want to make up some of that lost ground.

St. John's seems like a place I could test myself in, maybe grow a little more, and dust off some of the disused parts of my mind. I sincerely wish I was more certain, but who is to say whether or not I'd just prefer to float around some more, do something else in a year or a day. For the time being, and time being basically free right now, St. John's still seems like a good choice.

Andrew Perry attends St. John's College.

107

A MASTERPIECE IN
SEVENTY-EIGHT WORDS

Is it a coincidence that the shortest essay in this book just may be the best one? Think about it. Yale's admissions officers liked this essay so much that they mentioned it to the guidance counselor of author David Roosth. Says David, "My best advice for future students is to investigate the college very intensely and write about the little esoteric things that most would overlook. The best way to find those little idiosyncrasies is to ask the students who are on campus."

"Why Yale" by David Roosth

Upon a recent Yale visit, I conversed with a Yale senior in the admissions office about his experiences. He had only two complaints about the university: there were too many student protesters, and the university sands the roads instead of salting them in the winter. I love that Yale is a place where the students are motivated to change the world, and the faculty encourages them to act. Sanding saves the environment. What annoyed this Yale student impresses me.

> **What annoyed this Yale student impresses me.**

David Roosth attends Yale University.

108

FROM BOSNIA, COMING TO PENN

One of the secrets to answering the "why us?" question is to remember that you are making a match. Too many students write about the wonders of First Choice U. and forget the need to highlight corresponding aspects in themselves. Author Nadan Sehic makes a creative analogy between his family's immigrant experience and his first visit to Penn. He then goes on to describe why the Penn campus appeals to him and in the process mentions the name of a particular program (the Huntsman Program in International Studies and Business) and the fact that Penn offers a secluded campus in the middle of a major city.

Essay by Nadan Sehic

Describe the courses of study and the unique characteristics of the University of Pennsylvania that most interest you. Why do these interests make you a good match for Penn?

Visiting the University of Pennsylvania during the early fall of my senior year, I was very much like my father and mother venturing to the United States for their very first time. My parents, who were initially on the pursuit of furthering their education in 1987, never thought that an erupting Bosnian civil war would make their temporary stay a permanent one. I, a senior looking for prospective colleges, never thought that a mere campus tour and information session would make Penn a perfect match for the next four years of my life. While my two-hour drive down to Philadelphia can never compare to my parents' twelve-hour flight to the U.S.A., both excursions quickly evolved from a simple informative experience to an encounter opening the gates to opportunity and possibility.

As I took the tour of Penn, examining the various buildings, dorms, and classrooms, I noticed that Penn's environment and surroundings were idyllic for the student who wanted the perceived impossible, a college campus situated in a bustling city. Nestled in University City of West Philadelphia, Penn displays the atmosphere of a market where students can mingle and barter ideas with a diverse community of residents and scholars. The easy yet discernible transition from a campus livelihood to that of a vast metropolitan center mimics the programmed separation of the four undergraduate schools and inherent freedom to bridge various disciplines with one another. An applicant with a combination of interests, I marvel at the possibility of participating in a joint or dual degree program whether it be the Huntsman Program in International Studies and Business or a constructed program of my own.

Besides the collegiate yet urban environment, the structured yet flexible academics, what makes Penn such a great match for me is the very reason my parents thought

> **An erupting Bosnian civil war would make their temporary stay a permanent one.**

the United States a great place to raise a family. Wherever I end up going, I know that I will uphold the familiar immigrant tradition of working hard, remaining active in the community, and seizing every latent opportunity. The only remaining question waiting to be answered is which university will provide an intellectually and socially stimulating setting. Fortunately for me, I know of at least one answer: the University of Penn.

Nadan Sehic attends the University of Pennsylvania.

109

GOING GA-GA OVER GW

Author Samantha Strauss's essay about why she wants to attend George Washington University contains no startling revelations, but it doesn't need to. An ordinary applicant would talk about wanting to study political science; Samantha knows she wants political communications, a more specialized major that few schools aside from GW offer. Her reference to "the SAC" (Student Activities Center) shows that she knows her way around GW lingo. Samantha ends with a flourish, cataloguing all her contacts with GW and making a smooth reference to the university's advertising slogan.

Essay by Samantha Strauss

Tell us in approximately five hundred words what motivated you to apply to GW and describe what contacts you have had with us. We have told you about the dynamic GW classroom, campus, and city experience; now tell us how you will make use of these resources in meeting your educational goals.

What motivated me to apply to GW is quite simple: it is the best school to study political communications, its location is amazing, and the people/campus fit me perfectly. Because of the long list of majors and class choices, I will have the opportunity to explore all of my interests ranging from political communications to the use of technology in the media to psychology. GW will enable me to reach my undergraduate educational goal of being a part of a rigorous, vibrant academic community, which will then prepare me to succeed in any field of interest I may choose in the future.

I am applying to GW as a political communications major. Where better to study that major than GW? From my experience working with California senators Dianne Feinstein and Barbara Boxer, I learned that the major issues are resolved in Washington and that if I want to be part of that process, then I need to be positioned in the center of the government at the school that will teach me the skills I need to succeed. GW is the perfect match.

Washington, D.C., has everything I want. With its beautiful landscaping in an urban setting and with three major colleges within fifteen minutes of each other, I am provided with the college life that I'm looking forward to. Additionally, with all the museums and archives, I can find information that will allow me to do high quality research. Also, being located in the center of the political atmosphere helps me move forward in my interest of politics and how to make changes in the world.

Then, there are the people. Every single person that I have talked with who has attended or is attending GW has taken the time to answer every one of my questions. All answers have been insightful, informative, and have driven me to understand that GW is the school for me. I already feel like a part of the GW community even though I am still in the application phase.

> **I already feel like a part of the GW community even though I am still in the application phase.**

Finally, the campus. It feels right to me, it is the perfect size, the dorms are unbelievable, the SAC has everything I need, and overall it felt like a good home away from home.

From my visit to the Foggy Bottom campus, to visiting chat rooms and phone conversations with current students, and the information sessions with college representatives, when I imagine where I see myself going to college, GW comes to mind. GW is more than a college for me; it's a once-in-a-lifetime experience that I truly don't want to miss. Just as GW's slogan is "Something Happens Here," I want to be a part of the "something."

Samantha Strauss attends George Washington University.

The Search for an Opening Line

I f there is one part of the essay that applicants sweat over—and rightfully so—it is the opening. For a full discussion of how to begin your essay, turn to page 23.

The pages that follow reproduce the first seventy-five words, more or less, of each essay in this book, from Essay 1 through Essay 109. Browse the excerpts and see which ones pique your interest. Notice that many of them are straightforward—proof that it is not necessary to dream up a catchy opening in order to write an excellent essay.

But many of the openings do have flair. Check out the techniques that are our authors have used and see if any of them might work for you. We're not suggesting that you lift particular topics or phrases, but rather than you pay attention to the literary devices our authors use. We do the same thing in our writing. For instance, at the beginning of chapter 3, we open with a flight of fancy that seems bizarre to the reader—until a voice wakes the narrator and reveals that the scene has been a dream. Did we invent that technique? Hardly. We could have lifted it from dozens of other books, and those authors in turn would have gotten the idea from books they had read.

The most tried and true way to open is with an anecdote. Below are many examples of anecdotal beginnings; particularly good ones include those from Essays 16, 28, 42, 48, 53, 82, and 87. Likewise, there are more than a few zingers from writers who can turn a catchy phrase; notable examples include the openings to Essays 10, 59, 70, 71, 74, 76, and 98.

But these are just a few of many highlights. Take a look and see what resonates with you.

1

"I speak Spanish to God, Italian to women, French to men, and German to my horse."
—Charles V

I don't speak German. Horseless, and with two cats that understand only Russian, I never had the need. Besides, languages don't fall into neat categories for me as they did for Charles. But they do have a place in my life, and recently I have come to better understand just how important a place it is.

2

Now I was at the front of the classroom, using what little artistic coordination I had to draw a great big figure on the board: yes, those had to be eyes, an L-shaped nose, wrinkled eyebrows, a gaping "O" for a mouth. I added little stress lines on either corner of the cheeks, just to show how intent my hastily composed figure was on examining this *"Sylvan historian, who canst thus express a flowery tale more sweetly than our rhyme."*

3

After a pleasant, early morning flight I had finally reached my destination. As I stepped out of the plane and toward the arrival gate I caught a gust of hot, dry, desert air. I knew I was back in astronomy country, where over 80 percent of the nights are clear and the Milky Way's frothy band arches majestically across the black sky abyss.

4

I can say with certainty that there is nothing that has more of a positive effect on my life than Latin. Of course other things have grabbed my interest over the years, like poetry, math, singing, and women, but my true passion is for the Classics.

5

If I could have an entire year to do anything I pleased, I would spend it indulging myself in every book that years of required reading have prevented.

6

The brain: an almost indecipherable (at least to me) mass of neurons. Some extend an infinitesimal distance in the brain while others run through the length of the body. Each neuron is constantly sending and gathering tiny electrochemical signals which travel along a nerve axon, shooting along at incredible speeds towards its destination.

7

AOL Instant Messenger (AIM) is emblematic of my generation. AIM symbolizes many of my generation's positive attributes, but also symbolizes many of our negative ones, too.

8

Through science, humankind is attempting to unravel the mysteries of the universe. Yet when I study scientific truths, I inevitably end up with more questions. Each little piece of knowledge I learn is analogous to a single brushstroke on a grand masterpiece.

9

"E2V2" was my own creation and I would drive it in BattleBotsIQ 2003, a national robotics competition. I felt my body tense for the battle against the spinbot, Chromedome. Before the match, I had reviewed and decided my strategy against spinbots—attack it before it spins up and then keep hitting it.

10

When I was ten years old, I met Vince Lombardi. I saw him at the post office. He was sitting quietly with George Marshall and Humphrey Bogart. Vince cast a triumphant smile in my direction. His excitement was so contagious that I could not help smiling with him.

11

My coach always tells me that there is some reason why we, as debaters, can take four weeks out of our summer vacation, away from our friends and our families, to enclose ourselves in lecture halls and cramped dorm rooms to learn the depths and intricacies of debate. He has never told me what this reason is, but now that I'm beginning my senior year and I have attended three of these camps, I think I finally understand why.

12

I don't watch television. When my friends burst into the senior room, screaming at the top of their lungs about *Real Worlders* MJ and Sarah or the Steven-Kristin-LC love triangle on *Laguna Beach*, the only reason I know what they're talking about is because I hear about it every week.

13

Wedged Clay.
Most people think that clay is clay, that mud is mud. Well as a matter of fact, this is simply not so. Wedged clay is rolled and twisted at a factory to remove air. This clay is much smoother and easier to work with than ordinary clay. It's the best invention since sliced bread for the potter.

14

Every first Thursday of each month I always look around the Van Muren Hall gymnasium looking at the sixty- and seventy-year-old men and wonder what I am doing there with them. They have lived through world-shaping events like World War II, the Korean War, and the Vietnam War yet I sit there and interact with them as if there were no differences at all.

15

Don't you just hate those days where you find the perfect outfit, but don't have the right pair of shoes to complete the look? For me, deciding what shoes to sport depends upon which facet of my personality I wish to reveal or activity I'm about to partake in. Each day I face a dilemma—do I show the flashy, fun side or the conservative, chic side?

16

The rusted ball rests in my hand. My sandals shift in the gravel. My right arm lies loosely at my side, swinging gently. I'm crouched near the ground, concentrating on a little wooden ball ten yards away. I pull my arm back, then swing it forward as my body rises. The heavy ball flies away in a gentle parabola, and scatters pebbles when it lands with a thud…right next to the wooden ball. "*Oui!*" I exclaim as I do a little jig.

17

My mom is already telling me that I will have to clean out my room and throw away most of what fills my desk drawers. I am a very sentimental person and keep large quantities of what friends have given me over the years, so it will be hard for me to decide what to discard. The one thing I will never throw away, though, is my letters.

18

A ball is rolled down the lane. Confidently, I turn around; there is no need to see the result. A perfect strike. I stroll back to the bench, receiving high-fives from not only my teammates, but the opposing team as well. Bowling has been my most satisfying extracurricular activity.

19

Leaning backward in my one-man laser, I hike out hard in an attempt to keep the sailboat from capsizing, the tiller clutched hard in my left hand and the main sheet sliding through my right. These strong thermal winds are exciting yet challenging. I have been waiting for them for some time.

20

It was a thrill to land my dream job this summer as an intern with the Metropolitan Transportation Commission. As long as I can remember, I have been fascinated with every-thing associated with transportation. My commute to high school on the Bay Area Rapid Transit System (BART) and the city bus system puts me on the front lines as a user of public transit.

21

Every Sunday morning until the weather drops below freezing and my parents do not let me use the hose, I wash my car. This may seem like an ordinary job to some, but to me washing a car requires a distinctive technique.

22

Display dagger. Teddy bear. Cheesecake.
I love cheesecake. In fact, a slice of this delicious dessert is on my desk right now, impaled by a pair of chopsticks. These odd juxtapositions of East and West occur frequently at my house; my mother puts peanut butter into her moon cakes, and my dad uses the coffee maker to boil chrysanthemum tea.

23

When I first came to St. Andrew's-Sewanee, I had pretty much led a common life for a child in my area. Athletically, I played baseball, basketball, and soccer. There was peewee football down the mountain in the valley, but on top of our little plateau there never was much inter-est in getting a team together.

24

Glaring floodlights illuminated the brisk autumn night, steam rose from the sweaty players, and screams rang from the abnormally large crowd. With less than ten minutes left to play, the game remained a scoreless draw. I was the only freshman on the field, and I had been run-ning on sheer adrenaline for nearly the whole second half.

25

After deciding it would be fun to play a sport in high school, I joined my school's water polo team as a freshman. Although I had never been particularly athletically inclined, I threw myself into the sport with total energy and enthusiasm, hoping to be a starting player.

26

There I sit, just having eaten a big bucket full of butterflies. They are fluttering about inside my stomach. A warm ball of energy gathers in my chest, and all other problems of the past day, week, and year disappear. All that exists is my moment and I.

27

They say that being a mandolinist is a curse. It is incurred by a genetic defect that dooms one to be at the bottom of the musical totem-pole for life. Once you are in, there is no way out. Together with the accordion, kazoo, and banjo, the mandolin is part of a class of instruments that are the black sheep of the musical world.

28

"Please turn off all cell phones and pagers. Thank you, and enjoy the show." As the echo of my voice subsided, I seized the walkie-talkie that lay resting on the stool and raised it to my mouth. "Justin," I whispered, "kill the lights."

29

"OH MY GOSH! I have a whole new appreciation for the art of dance!"

Who said that? The voice sounds familiar, but those words…they didn't just come out of the mouth of my dad, did they? They did, and wow, how long have I waited to hear something like that from him? Years… fifteen to be exact!

30

Music is my drug of choice. I have become addicted to it—listening, practicing, performing, analyzing, thinking about past gigs and those that I will soon play. The thought of music and the continually playing soundtrack in my head give me a high that other junkies pay hundreds to experience. Like other users, I have deepened my fixation with each new encounter

31

While standing backstage sipping my nth cup of coffee, forty hours awake and counting, I tried to think of what I'd do next. A year's efforts organizing Breakin' Curfew would soon draw to a close with the fall of the curtain; after this last band finished and the packed theater emptied, I'd have to begin again—with nothing.

32

I started playing piano at the ripe old age of ten, but there was an advantage to learning music when I became more mature. Classical music is an acquired taste, and the time to develop that taste enabled me to tolerate the unavoidable lessons on basic notes and rhythms.

33

When I brainstorm the activities I enjoy, a theme becomes apparent. Many of my pursuits give me insight into another way of life and provide fuel for my eager imagination. For example, I seek out films that transport me to an unfamiliar era or region of the world.

34

All six of my elementary school years were spent in the same art room. Miniature tables and chairs sat surrounded by walls covered by prints of paintings and sculptures created by some of the greatest artists of all time. When my young eyes wandered around the room, which was often, I found my attention constantly drawn to a painting of a woman in a red hat.

35

Two works of art have made me shiver. Chartres Cathedral in France and "Dark Star" by the Grateful Dead continue to fascinate me every time I think of them. As art, the two specimens are completely opposite to each other. Chartres is a masterpiece of human ingenuity, architecture, creativity, and order. "Dark Star" is an exercise in improvisation, a constantly evolving work of group invention and lateral thought.

36

Sitting backstage in the cool blue-gelled silence before a show, I sometimes find my mind wandering. It's not that I'm bored or anything, but after all the hectic running around that goes on before a show, it's nice to have a moment to just relax and think, even if it really is only a moment.

37

I tentatively grasped the plastic blue handle of the fattest brush. Its firm but compliant bristles tickled as I pulled them along my palm. I looked around nervously, waiting for my first oil painting class to begin. The intimidating, white primed canvas rested on my easel, boasting its potential. Fresh, plump paint tubes in every color but black sat in a neat line, echoing the rainbow. My water cup was half full. I was ready.

38

Before last year I had always thought of myself as a very shy, uncreative, introspective individual. And I was happy that way. I had found my little niche in the Kinkaid society. I was the jock who excelled in sports and also managed to make pretty good grades as well. But I wasn't an artist.

39

It has been about eighteen years since I was born in New York City, and I have spent roughly the last eight of those years in what I still call a new home, here in Charlotte, North Carolina. My life has followed the clichéd and semi-charmed life of a teenager growing up in a very nice American neighborhood.

40

I have spent the past four summers working as a volunteer and counselor at a summer camp for kids ages four to ten. Each week presents new challenges, opportunities, and surprises and I am often amazed at the wit, intelligence, and confidence that elementary schoolers can display. This year, it was the bright faces of two campers, Alfred and Bill, that provided the most humor, challenge, and surprise to me and the rest of the staff.

41

After climbing a set of dull looking concrete stairs, I entered the kitchen/dining area, a small space complete with a television and curtained windows. Two tables were set for the guests. Down a hallway were two bathrooms, one marked "Men," the other, "Women."

42

My own words were coming back to haunt me as I heard one of my campers yell, "Ewww, Bridger threw up." I froze. I forced myself to turn around and look. I glanced quickly, then immediately looked away. I stopped breathing through my nose so I wouldn't be able to smell it. I was horrified.

43

"Hey, Nickelback, I know that band. You like them?" I ask, leaning over Chipu's shoulder to look at the stickers and pictures she has all over the front matter of her binder.

"Yeah," she looks up at me with her big brown eyes and smiles, clearly as relieved as I am to find something in common. It's my first day tutoring at Webster Middle School.

44

"I am the smartest boy in the world," one of the small boys in the class had said one day. So I asked him, "How do you know that you are the smartest boy in the world?" Then his face began to crinkle and a little angry voice replied: "I just told you! I know, because I am the smartest boy in the world." I could not believe that I was talking to a four-year-old.

45

"I do it for the joy it brings 'cause I'm a joyful girl. 'Cause the world owes us nothing, we owe each other the world."—Ani Difranco ("Joyful Girl")

In the fall of my junior year, my mother announced that she had signed us up for a mission trip to Bolivia for Christmas break. My first thought was, "That's impossible! But I wanted a new computer and some new clothes. How will we ever get all the gifts down there? Our suitcases will be too heavy!" I was careful not to say these selfish things out loud.

46

The summer of 2004 represented a meaningful and eye opening experience for me. I spent the summer as a counselor at an overnight camp, Raquette Lake Girls Camp, where I had attended as a camper from 1998 through 2002.

47

As I am filing all those college applications, the question keeps coming back to me. Who am I? Where do I come from? Where am I heading?

48

I'm tired and a little bit desperate. My clock angrily glares at me through its neon green dial. It's 11:24. The biology exam tomorrow will be murder. I resolutely pass over my textbook, and instead return to the screen where Pandit Jasraj stares back at me.

49

"Lynching was ritualistic public square violence, part of a sordid history of white criminality" (Hakim Hasan). Looking out of the car window onto Crenshaw Boulevard, I do not see an angry mob cloaked in white, dancing on one of the street corners. Nor do I see towering willows ornamented with dangling bodies. As I look out of my window I see young African American boys flaunting diamond earrings that make their earlobes droop; young men and women bumping the latest "Jay-Z" song while bringing their twenty-inch rim-spinning Escalades to a halt at the red light.

50

"Hello 엄마! No. I'm at the movies. 극장! 조금있으면가." Translation: "Mom! No. I'm at the movies. The movies! I'll be home soon." If I'm with my friends, someone will ask: "What was that?" And I answer, "I was speaking in Korean to my mom." This answer is never enough, as I have learned. Only after a few rounds of saying odd phrases for their amusement is everyone's curiosity satisfied.

51

So there's a girl. You've read her application, but do you really know her? You know that she works hard and that she dreams of going to Princeton, but does that count as knowing her? I'll tell you a bit about her. Then, you decide.

52

I stood still, facing the giant bathroom mirror. Whoosh. The bathroom door swung open, and a group of girls came in, chatting and laughing. I stared into the mirror. A blonde, clearly more than a head taller than I, strolled past, reaching for the paper towel dispenser.

53

"May I help you?" the blonde sales associate asked me for the fifth time after watching me like a hawk. Once again, I told her that I would definitely come to her if I needed anything. When I was younger, I naively thought that the clerks were being extremely polite or working hard to earn a commission, but now as a black teenager, I know better.

54

I've been raised in a somewhat sheltered environment, mostly surrounded by wealthy, white kids. Often, I pondered whether or not I was materialistic or blatantly ignorant of my good fortune much like many of my peers. Transferring from a rather small, Catholic school in Rock

Hill, I noticed the different mannerisms—spoiled nature and flaunting of wealth—that a majority of the students possessed and I thought little of it because I was so young and naïve.

55

"Ha ha! Christina is a dirty Mexican!"

Growing up in a small, conservative community, it's easy to be shoved into your own category if you don't look or act like everyone else. My hair and eyes, instead of being blonde and blue like all of my Czech classmates, were chocolate and espresso. My last name had a "z" in it, and my grandmother called me "mija."

56

I had sailed on the *Mayflower*. Fall had settled in its transitional air, slowly parting with the warmth of day. The air of the land was an untouched and virgin as it was to the first pilgrim to set foot on the soil of the New World. My *Mayflower* read "Continental Airlines 011."

57

In the beginning of third grade, I took my first standardized test where I had to fill out my full name, address, my birthday, and to shade in the corresponding ovals. My teacher then said to fill in the oval that represents our ethnicity. One of the choices was "Hispanic/Latino." I paused for a moment. I knew that I was Mexican American; my grandparents emigrated from Mexico to El Paso, Texas, where my mom and her ten brothers and sisters grew up. However, when I came across this question about my ethnicity, I never fully realized what it meant to me.

58

"A time for warm hearts and hot guts." This is the slogan of the annual Hogeye Festival in the Hot Sausage Capital of the World: my hometown of Elgin, Texas. I have lived on Pistol Hill Ranch in Elgin, population c. 5000, for all but the first two of my seventeen years. I have grown up on small-town morals, values, and ways of life. Elgin is a place where parents still teach their children to say "yes, ma'am" and "no, sir."

59

Sometime between waking up at the crack of dawn and fourth period I became a teenage werewolf. No, wait, I mean feminist.

It's as if I didn't know until someone pointed it out to me in English class, but it was more like an "Ooh, dude, I think you just stepped in some feminist," or a "Damn! You smell like feminist," or maybe even an "I think you spilled some feminism on your shirt, and it stains…"

60

As I step up to the pulpit, I feel a familiar sense of calm come over me, the calm I always experience before singing to my congregation. Scanning the audience, I look out at the parents and grandparents, making eye contact with those I recognize and those I do not.

61

I once believed in the power of the majority to make acceptable decisions. Now I realize that that viewpoint was flawed. What I learned about American government came from prescribed classes and from watching C-SPAN. The classes taught me about "the system" and how it should work. C-SPAN showed me various viewpoints, teaching me to see through political rhetoric. The blind worship of democracy is reinforced through every aspect of American life; school, radio, news coverage, and sports programs pay homage to "Democracy."

62

Al Franken's book *Lies and the Lying Liars Who Tell Them* led me to a recent dive into the world of politics that has made me examine my own values and reevaluate how I see the world. My parents are very politically active people. My mom, a social worker, has always been a strong

Democrat. My stepdad is a Lebanese American citizen who sees the world through an immigrant's eyes.

63

I voted on November 2nd. As an eighteen-year-old woman in America, I am legally allowed to exercise my right to vote. Although my heart beat slightly fast, and my hands shook unsteadily at the polling booth, upon arriving home from my first voting experience, I was filled with a sense of accomplishment and relief.

64

Among the constant sea of plaid and enormous initial-embroidered Northface book bags which make up the campus of CSG, a student must find her place of security. She must safeguard herself from examinations, college gossip, and the long night ahead of writing papers and studying which rests cozily in the back of her mind weighing down any hope of an early bed time. I have found my safe haven to be a simple passage-way entitled "Alumnae Hall."

65

It's 256 steps from my front door to my front door; a journey I make every other day that sparks reveries of reminiscing over the days when my parents were one. So close are the two houses that shelter me and yet so far apart are my two parents.

66

On May 30, 2004, I woke up to bloodcurdling screaming that I'd only heard in horror movies. The haziness of the deep sleep from which I emerged was still fading when I realized that the piercing cries were coming from my mother. I rubbed my eyes as she stood over me, frantically sputtering that I needed to get up, that there was a fire.

67

Last year I got to taste life; the lukewarm water of revival flowing down my throat. I got to feel it, in the pumping of my heart, the layers of dry dust encrusted on my hands. I got to smell it; the magnified aroma of my body fused on my clothes. I got to hear it too; the melody of zippers. And I got to see it; the orange mountains and cliffs, and sand that I thought I was used to.

68

I trudged onward at the exhausting pace set by my commander. The stripes of mud on my face mixed with the sweat of the desert, running into my tired eyes. I was not allowed to roll up my pants or long sleeves—the enemy might see my white arms or legs. The M-16 grew heavier as I carried it hour after hour. "*Azar!*" yelled my commander. I ran as fast as I could, counting in Hebrew, "*Esrim v'echad!* Twenty-two! Twenty-three!"

69

On November 1, 2003, halfway through my four-month stay in Leadville, Colorado, the winter's first snow fell from the sky. My peers beamed with excitement; ski season was upon them. I, however, stood staring in awe at the gentle, white flakes floating to the ground. The green and blue world that I was accustomed to faded to shades of grey and white.

70

I won my school's Pickleball tournament in tenth grade. How many National Merit Semi-Finalists can say that?

What? That's not enough to set me apart in the massive pile of applications? Well, maybe I hold the world record for most snow cones eaten in the summer of 2004, or the record for most piggyback rides given as a camp counselor.

71

Do you ever have those dreams where you've arrived at school and suddenly realize you've forgotten to wear pants? Well, for most high school seniors that dream becomes a reality, at least figuratively. We must bare our souls, not to best friends, or family, but to complete strangers who may not even want to hear about it and may even flat out reject us. What twisted institution would ever subject young adults in the formative stages of emotional growth to this experience? Oh, right. College.

72

Contrary to what you may think, buying a bottle of shampoo is a complex and tedious process. First, I chose the five most outwardly appealing bottles, conscious that my seventeen-year-old female mind is being manipulated by blatantly false phrases like "made with real herbs so your hair will stay shiny for up to eight and a half hours."

73

The first thing anyone must know about me is that I love to read. I devour books. If I could, I would eat my favorite books. I would. You laugh, but it's true.

74

I love Perrier water with the depths of my soul. I cannot get enough of the cool, fizzy bubbles rolling on my tongue. The crisp taste is pure bliss for the palate. The bitter aftertaste is the best part of the Perrier experience.

75

Take a moment and look at your hands: their shape, texture, size, and delicacy. These parts of your body are one of the most important creations. They are the scribes of every document; the builders of homes, offices, and shelters; and what comforts many during a frightening experience. But, for me, my hands have yet to display any external similarities to the role they were created to fulfill.

76

Underwear. Say it to a kindergarten class, and they'll giggle endlessly. Write it in a college essay and...well, I guess I'll find out. But specifically I'm talking about long underwear; cozy, toasty, stretchy long underwear. I've never been much of a cold weather person, but give me a pair of long underwear and I'm "good to go."

77

It's odd how a random thought can pop into your head and completely change the way you view something. Well, I realized today that I do not want children. This revelation came to me while walking into the grocery store. An exasperated young mother was trying to comfort her child.

78

...We interrupt our regularly scheduled admissions process for a special report brought to us by a member of the fantastic action-adventure series, *Chicago Survivor: Summer 2001*....

Unbeknownst to the common Angeleno high school student, a strange and wonderful game for the strong of heart is held annually and inconspicuously at the University of Chicago; unbeknownst to the common man, I *am* the Chicago survivor.

79

I identify Laetitia by the tights scented with French perfume in my sock drawer, her ten-pound black boots, which still live in my closet, and her beautiful laugh I hear over the phone every so often. Laetitia lived with us as an exchange student in 1994, the year my youngest sister was born. She was the first and only big sister I have ever had.

80

I grew up in a brick house on Nottingham Drive, a place with old furniture and young faces, with small rooms that never seemed to be empty. I grew up with my pointy nose buried in books, wearing stretch pants and bows and listening to my father's new songs on the guitar.

81

I should not have dressed up. Apparently, no other fifth grader had felt driven to celebrate the first day of school via fancy clothing, and so I stood out not just as a newcomer, but as an awkwardly dressed one. Scratching at grainy black tights with the toe of my sneaker, I paused uncertainly in the doorway of the Writing room.

82

Today's lesson was almost over. Our topic was the alphabet, and my grandmother was intent on expanding my limited knowledge of alpha, lambda, and pi that I had gained from my school science classes. I called her Yaiy, from the Greek word for grandmother. "The Americans, they stole our language," Yaiy would say confidently, "You see this word, psychiatrist? It's is actually 'psychiatros.' You see?"

83

I was never really upset about it. I never resented my parents for it. I didn't ever feel unlucky because of it. My sister had Down Syndrome, and that was that. Sure, I found it a little odd that while most of my friends' big sisters secretly applied lipstick on the walk to school, mine collected worms, which she would make into jewelry. But except for the occasionally painful quarrel (one of which left a bite mark on my right shoulder) my sister and I got along.

84

"I love Winnie the Pooh! Are you related to A. A. Milne?" I can't even count on two hands the number of times I have been asked that question. "No I'm not; our last names are different. Well sort of... Well, there's a story... It's complicated."

85

I remember feeling my stomach do a flip turn as I watched who entered the room. A friend of mine was sitting in front of the Honor Council. At my high school, the Honor Council is an elected group of six students including four faculty advisors, which hears cases of students who have broken the school's honor code: "I pledge on my honor not to lie, cheat, steal, plagiarize, or vandalize."

86

The aim of argument, or of discussion, should not be victory, but progress.
—Joseph Joubert

Much of what we learn, and most of our best thinking, is not because of what is spoon fed to us, but rather as a result of interactions with other people, including active questioning of our surroundings, beliefs, and ideas. Sometimes the best of these opportunities go unexplored. During rehearsal for an American Conservatory Theater production I was in this fall, a fellow cast member offered to tell a joke, which she warned, might offend some people.

87

"So, you want this car or not?" Dr. Matt Petrilla asked again, in his simultaneously pushy yet polite manner.

This smart, stocky man, a medical doctor and the father of a friend, has thrown me into a sudden state of blissful surprise: less than a minute before, he had offered me a free car.

88

The pursuit of being an "original" has widely dictated the actions of my young adult life. From an early age I harbored a zealous fixation for anything different or offbeat. Perhaps I should clarify; you know that clichéd box everyone refers to? Well, I'm not talking simply thinking outside of it. I'm talking looting, plundering, pillaging, strangling, and ultimately killing that box.

89

It was my fifth birthday. Imagine the joy that must pulse through the veins of a hungry homeless person who just happens to find a winning lottery ticket laying in the gutter. The look on that person's face would be much like the one I wore when tearing apart my present to reveal nothing more than a bag of marbles.

90

In my six-year-old mind I see the president, sitting at his plush desk chair in a navy blue suit. He's examining an important document. Or better yet, he's in the middle of a crucial meeting with leaders from all over the world. His secretary enters. She looks worried. "We've received a letter of some importance," she says. His brow furrows as she hands him a small envelope addressed in sparkly pink pen. "Anne Erickson, age six, Oakland, California," he muses, examining the careful writing.

91

"You know that time in your life when you realize the house you live in isn't really your home anymore? That idea of home is gone. Maybe that's all family really is. A group of people who miss the same imaginary place." —*Garden State*, Andrew Largeman

My greatest fear is leaving home. Reaching a place where I do not know that there are exactly six minutes and forty-two seconds left until math is over. It is a place where I cannot talk about the Red Sox game with the dean of students or play hangman with my college advisor.

92

When I was four I adored the Ninja Turtles. I owned all the action figures, T-shirts, and straight to video movies that there were to possess of the Ninja Turtles. Every Saturday morning I would wake up with plenty of time for the nine o'clock start of my favorite half-hour of the week. By the tender age of four my parents (and my dog Tovah) had learned not to bother me during that time.

93

One overpowering image appears whenever I remember my middle school years: the Dark Ages in Europe. Was I suffering through isolation, oppression, or misery? Fortunately not, yet I was, as Plato would put it, in the gloom of my cave, bereft of the light of intellectual illumination.

94

I first became aware of the transformative power of music in the winter of 1992 when I attended my first live concert. This was my first weeknight excursion with my father, the culmination of many episodes of desperate begging and pleading. *Dolly Parton*. The sound of her name alone was enough to get my pulse racing, my feet tapping.

95

My junior year abroad in Germany was a very significant experience for me. At the beginning of my sophomore year of high school my family decided to take in a Japanese exchange student. Over the course of the year, Satoru became a part of our family and a dear friend. I had been thinking about going abroad even before we decided to host Sato, but by observing what a great experience his exchange year was for him, I was given the courage to go ahead and apply for a place in the Youth for Understanding year abroad program in Germany.

96

I'm somewhat used to being a part of the minority. I've always been considered the "different" child of the family, the one not quite like the others. My three older brothers and sisters were all quiet, athletic, highly motivated scholars, excelling in subjects like math and science and being awarded MVP of the team. I was different.

97

The upbeat rhythm of merengue music electrified the air. My unaccustomed feet quickly adapted to the practiced steps of my dance partner. As the tempo of the music increased, my partner swept me across the floor in a rush of quick movements that I carried out with little skill, but with all my heart. As the song came to an end, I breathlessly thanked my partner and tried to explain what a fun time I had in my slightly broken Spanish.

98

Sweltering heat, abhorrently close quarters, and short tempers. Sweatshop? No, such were the family vacations of my youth—countless hours in a poorly air-conditioned vehicle, seven traveling companions and a driver whose frustration often bordered on road rage.

99

I had never been outside the continental United States when I decided to travel to Africa. By the time I returned to school from my two-week-long sophomore spring break, I had landed in England, Kenya, Malawi, and South Africa. Maybe more people would have started smaller with, say, a tame vacation venture to Mexico or Hawaii, but since I had always planned on visiting everywhere eventually, I figured, why not?

100

I am most comfortable when I am lost. Deliberately getting lost fuels my drive for discovery. On a trip to Italy the summer after my sophomore year, I discovered the pleasure of using public transportation to get to know the city of Rome.

101

In June of this year, my parents and I took a weeklong trip to London. This trip was one my parents had been planning to take for years but had never had quite enough money before; it was to be our first real family vacation and my first time to go abroad. Such an event would, under normal circumstances, have inspired in us an unbearable level of excitement, but at the time the trip was scheduled, my grandmother was terminally ill with lung cancer and could die at any time.

102

His teeth clenched over my delicate skull, and I felt hot blood drip down my cheeks as his claws slashed at my face. My legs crumbled beneath his heavy weight as both of us came crashing down the rocky hillside. I fought to thrust myself from beneath him, remembering the mangled stuffed animals surrounding his cage.

103

"Have you considered Swarthmore?"
    Swath what? I remember thinking to myself as I sat there in my college counselor's office. We were discussing which colleges I would be visiting over the spring break of my junior year.

104

Rebecca Kastan's Top Ten Reasons Why Vanderbilt Is Her #1 Choice (David Letterman Style):
    10. Weather: I have lived in Columbus, Ohio, my whole life. Although it has been the best place to grow up, I have to admit that weather is not our forté. Weather can have an effect on people's mood and outlook. I checked out what the Nashville Chamber of Commerce says about weather, and it sure sounds good to me!

105

As we drove up the steep mountain road with rain streaming across the windows of our Hertz Rent-A-Car, my dad assured me that we weren't completely wasting our time: "Just keep an open mind," he said, "at least we can use what they tell us when we're in Nashville tomorrow." I was not amused.

106

I settled on St. John's a few months after I had finished applying to, visiting, being accepted by, and finally deciding not to attend three colleges. I had finished my senior year of high school by correspondence and a few classes taken credit-by-exam, so in truth my senior year was a year off. I wasn't enamored of the prospect of spending another year away from school and away from activity, but I couldn't in good conscience throw myself into a college I didn't care about. What had bothered me about the schools I had applied to was that all of them seemed to be opportunities to flounder, to waste time in a pre-adult, post-child no-man's land.

107

Upon a recent Yale visit, I conversed with a Yale senior in the admissions office about his experiences. He had only two complaints about the university: there were too many student protesters, and the university sands the roads instead of salting them in the winter. I love that Yale is a place where the students are motivated to change the world, and the faculty encourages them to act. Sanding saves the environment. What annoyed this Yale student impresses me.

108

Visiting the University of Pennsylvania during the early fall of my senior year, I was very much like my father and mother venturing to the United States for their very first time. My parents, who were initially on the pursuit of furthering their education in 1987, never thought that an erupting Bosnian civil war would make their temporary stay a permanent one.

109

What motivated me to apply to GW is quite simple: it is the best school to study political communications, its location is amazing, and the people/campus fit me perfectly. Because of the long list of majors and class choices, I will have the opportunity to explore all of my interests ranging from political communications to the use of technology in the media to psychology.

Acknowledgments

W e wish to thank all those who assisted in the preparation of this book. Without the exceptional work of our 109 student contributors, there would be no book, and we wish them all the best in their college years and beyond. We are also grateful to the high school counselors from across the nation who connected us with our student authors. Many of these counselors give us ongoing support through our Advisory Group, and we benefit immeasurably from having them on our team.

Lexi Eagles, formerly of American Hebrew Academy and now at Greensboro Day School, good naturedly took on the challenge of editing the entire book. Guy and Jean Hammond also provided valuable editing assistance. Julie Fiske Hogan, production coordinator of the Fiske Guide to Colleges, has been an important source of support.

We are deeply grateful to Michelle Schoob for her skillful editing and willingness to put in the long hours necessary to make this book a reality. We are also indebted to Todd Stocke, Peter Lynch, Katie Olsen, Heather Moore, Christina Payton, and Dominique Raccah for their dedication to the Fiske guides.

We appreciate the efforts of all, but responsibility for the final product is ours alone.

College Counselors Advisory Group

Marilyn Albarelli, Moravian Academy (PA)

Scott Anderson, St. George's Independent School (TN)

Christine Asmussen, St. Andrew's Sewanee School (TN)

Bruce Bailey, Lakeside School (WA)

Samuel Barnett, SchoolFutures (VA)

Amy E. Belstra, Cherry Creek H.S. (CO)

Greg Birk, Kinkaid School (TX)

Susan T. Bisson, Advocates for Human Potential (MA)

Robin Boren, Dakota Ridge H.S. (CO)

Clarice Boring, Cody H.S. (WY)

John B. Boshoven, Community High School & Jewish Academy of Metro Detroit (MI)

Mimi Bradley, St. Andrew's Episcopal School (MS)

Nancy Bryan, Pace Academy (GA)

Claire Cafaro, Clear Directions (NJ)

Nancy Caine, St. Augustine H.S. (CA)

Mary Calhoun, St. Cecilia Academy (TN)

Jane M. Catanzaro, College Advising Services (CT)

Mary Chapman, St. Catherine's School (VA)

Anthony L. Clay, Durham Academy (NC)

Kathy Cleaver, Durham Academy (NC)

Jimmie Lee Cogburn, Independent Counselor (GA)

Teresa A. Corrigan, Chapel Hill-Chauncy Hall School (MA)

Alison Cotten, Cypress Falls H.S. (TX)

Alice Cotti, Polytechnic School (CA)

Rod Cox, St. Johns Country Day School (FL)

Kim Crockard, Crockard College Counseling (AL)

Carroll K. Davis, North Central H.S. (IN)

Mary Jo Dawson, Academy of the Sacred Heart (MI)

Christy Dillon, Crystal Springs Uplands School (CA)

Tara A. Dowling, Saint Stephen's Episcopal School (FL)

Lexi Eagles, Greensboro Day School (NC)

Dan Feldhaus, Iolani School (HI)

Ralph S. Figueroa, Albuquerque Academy (NM)

Emily E. FitzHugh, The Gunnery (CT)

Larry Fletcher, Salesianum School (DE)

Nancy Fomby, Episcopal School of Dallas (TX)

Daniel Franklin, Franklin Guidance (CO)

Laura Johnson Frey, Vermont Academy (VT)

Phyllis Gill, Providence Day School (NC)

Freida Gottsegen, Independent Counselor (GA)

Molly Gotwals, Suffield Academy (CT)

Kathleen Barnes Grant, The Catlin Gabel School (OR)

Madelyn Gray, John Burroughs School (MO)

Amy Grieger, Northfield Mount Hermon School (MA)

Mimi Grossman, St. Mary's Episcopal School (TN)

Elizabeth Hall, Education Consulting Services (TX)

Andrea L. Hays, Hathaway Brown School (OH)

Rob Herald, Cairo American College (Egypt)

Darnell Heywood, Columbus School for Girls (OH)

Bruce Hunter, Rowland Hall St. Mark's School (UT)

Deanna L. Hunter, Shawnee Mission East H.S. (KS)

John Keyes, The Catlin Gabel School (OR)

Linda King, College Connections (NY)

Sharon Koenings, Brookfield Academy (WI)

Joan Jacobson, Shawnee Mission South H.S. (KS)

Diane Johnson, Lawrence Public Schools (NY)

Gerimae Kleinman, Shaker Heights H.S. (OH)

Laurie Leftwich, Brother Martin High School (LA)

MaryJane London, Los Angeles Center for Enriched Studies (CA)

Martha Lyman, Deerfield Academy (MA)

Brad MacGowan, Newton North H.S. (MA)

Robert S. MacLellan, Jr., The Pingry School (NJ)

Margaret M. Man, La Pietra Hawaii School for Girls (HI)

Susan Marrs, The Seven Hills School (OH)

Karen A. Mason, Wyoming Seminary (PA)

Lisa Micele, University of Illinois Laboratory H.S. (IL)

Corky Miller-Strong, Culver Academies (IL)

Janet Miranda, Prestonwood Christian Academy (TX)

Richard Morey, Dwight-Englewood School (NJ)

Daniel Murphy, The Urban School of San Francisco (CA)

Judith Nash, Highland High School (ID)

Arlene L. Prince, University Preparatory Academy (WA)

Deborah Robinson, Mandarin H.S. (FL)

Julie Rollins, Episcopal H.S. (TX)

William C. Rowe, Thomas Jefferson School (MO)

Bruce Scher, Chicagoland Jewish High School (IL)

David Schindel, Sandia Preparatory School (NM)

Kathy Z. Schmidt, St. Mary's Hall (TX)

Barbara Simmons, Bellarmine College Preparatory (CA)

Joe Stehno, Bishop Brady H.S. (NH)

Bruce Stempien, Weston H.S. (CT)

Paul M. Stoneham, The Key School (MD)

Audrey Threlkeld, Forest Ridge School of the Sacred Heart (WA)

Ted de Villafranca, Peddie School (NJ)

Scott White, Montclair H.S. (NJ)

Linda Zimring, Los Angeles Unified School District (CA)

About the Authors

I n 1980, when he was education editor of the *New York Times*, Edward B. Fiske sensed that college-bound students and their families needed better information on which to base their educational choices. Thus was born *Fiske Guide to Colleges*. A graduate of Wesleyan University, Fiske did graduate work at Columbia University and assorted other bastions of higher learning. He left the *Times* in 1991 to pursue a variety of educational and journalistic interests, including a book on school reform, *Smart Schools, Smart Kids*. When not visiting colleges, he can be found playing tennis, sailing, or doing research on the educational problems of Third World countries for UNESCO and other international organizations. Ted lives in Durham, North Carolina, near the campus of Duke University, where his wife is a member of the faculty. They are coauthors of *When Schools Compete: A Cautionary Tale* and *Elusive Equality: Education Reform in Post-Apartheid South Africa*.

Since entering Yale in the early 1980s, Bruce G. Hammond has devoted much of his time to counseling for college. At Yale, Bruce was editor-in-chief of *The Insider's Guide to the Colleges*. He subsequently served as managing editor of *Fiske Guide to Colleges*. He is also the author of *Discounts and Deals at the Nation's 360 Best Colleges*. He has been quoted in numerous national publications, including the *New York Times*, the *Wall Street Journal*, *USA Today*, the *Washington Post*, *U.S.News&World Report*, *Business Week*, *Money Magazine*, and *Good Housekeeping*. Bruce lives in Albuquerque, New Mexico, with his wife and stepsons and is director of college counseling at Sandia Preparatory School.